THE PLURA
TH

English political pluralism is a challenging school of political thought, neglected in recent years but now enjoying a revival of interest. It is particularly relevant today because it offers a critique of centralized sovereign state power. The leading theorists of the pluralist state were G. D. H. Cole, J. N. Figgis and H. J. Laski, and this volume brings together their most important ideas, making accessible a crucial body of work on radical political theory. It includes their major writings, mostly out of print and difficult to obtain, and here gathered together in an anthology for the first time.

Current in the first two decades of this century, English political pluralism offered a convincing critique of state sovereignty and proposed a decentralized and federated form of authority – *pluralism* – in which the affairs of society would be conducted by self-governing and independent associations. Paul Hirst's comprehensive intro-duction situates English political pluralism historically and gives a critical account of its main theoretical themes and the debate surrounding them.

The book will be of great interest to those who see radical reform as vital for the future health of democracy, to students of political theory and the history of political thought, and also to students of jurisprudence and legal theory interested in the pluralist debate as it affects the concept of legal sovereignty.

THE PLURALIST THEORY OF THE STATE

*Selected Writings of G. D. H. Cole,
J. N. Figgis, and H. J. Laski.*

EDITED BY PAUL Q. HIRST

London and New York

First published in hardback 1989
Paperback edition first published 1993
by Routledge
11 New Fetter Lane, London EC4P 4EE

Simultaneously published in the USA and Canada
by Routledge
29 West 35th Street, New York, NY 10001

Typeset in Baskerville by LaserScript Ltd, Mitcham, Surrey
Printed and bound in Great Britain by
Biddles Ltd, Guildford and King's Lynn

British Library Cataloguing in Publication Data
A catalogue record for this book is available from the British Library.

Library of Congress Cataloging in Publication Data
has been applied for.

ISBN 0–415–03371–3 (pbk)

ACKNOWLEDGEMENTS

I am grateful to the Cole and Laski estates for permission to use copyright material.

I wish to thank Phil Jones, Kelvin Knight, D. Nicholls, and Jonathan Zeitlin for help and advice in preparing this volume.

CONTENTS

INTRODUCTION

The purpose of this book is to put a neglected but important body of work back on the current agenda of political theory. English political pluralism – represented here by selections from the work of its three major exponents: G.D.H. Cole, John Neville Figgis, and Harold J. Laski – offers a vital and missing contribution to the very active contemporary debates on the problems of democracy and the forms and directions of further democratization of both state and society. Political theory has once again become a politically consequential discipline and one directly concerned with the institutions of state as an object of theoretical reflection. These debates on democracy and the problems of modern government have interrupted the long period of torpor in political theory.[1]

Since 1945 the majority current in political theory has taken liberal democracy and representative government as its point of departure. The experience of Fascism and Stalinism discredited a variety of alternatives to and critical views of representative democracy. Thus Anglo-American liberal individualism has dominated, with considerable challenge in the 1960s and 1970s from the sub-text of its Marxist critique. Both excluded consideration of specific constitutional and political issues in relentless forms of abstraction. For the liberal individualists this takes the form of the analytic exploration of concepts like obligation, rights, liberty, equality, etc., in virtual isolation from politics – the vitality and success of representative democracy being taken for granted. For the Marxists constructive engagement with specific forms of democratic government and constitutions as ongoing entities was impossible; they were merely

1

objects of critique. Such 'bourgeois' concerns are of no value because the ultimate aim of Marxism is to smash the state and abolish government as such, and in the intervening period to rely on post-bourgeois forms of popular democracy.[2]

English political pluralism shared with the classical political theory of the seventeenth century to the nineteenth century a primary concern with political institutions, but it offered a critique of the institutions founded on and justified by classical political theory. Its main objects of attack were the theory of unlimited state sovereignty developed by Bodin and Hobbes, and refined by John Austin;[3] the theory of popular sovereignty vested in a representative national government inaugurated by the French Revolution, and in substance little more than a democratization of the claims of royal absolutism; and the theory of representative democracy as embodying the 'will of the people'. Central to pluralism were the belief in the vitality and the legitimacy of self-governing associations as means of organizing social life and the belief that political representation must respect the principle of function, recognizing associations like trade unions, churches, and voluntary bodies. In the pluralist scheme it is such associations that perform the basic tasks of social life. Pluralism is strongly anti-statist in its basic principles. Respect for the autonomy of associations freely formed of citizens and the principle of functional representation both involve a limitation and not an enhancement of the scope of state power. It is thus quite unlike other schemes of functional representation, such as Mussolini's corporativism, which compulsorily mobilize social interests to provide legitimacy for an unreformed centralized sovereign state power. The pluralists differed on the extent to which functional representation was to supplement or to replace bodies elected by citizens organized in representative territorial constituencies. But all the pluralists sought to replace a centralized state which claimed a plenitude of sovereign power, and which must if it followed the logic of its own claims regard all associations as its own creations existing by concessionary licence or as mortal threats to its own existence, with a state in which power and administrative capacity were diffused to autonomous functional and territorial bodies; to self-governing associations and to local authorities.

English political pluralism labours under a difficulty in that it

2

shares the word with a different, influential, and contemporary conceptual scheme. 'Pluralism' is a familiar term in modern social science. Its main contemporary meaning refers to a body of modern American political theory which defines democracy as a form of stable and institutionalized political competition.[4] In this competitive process a plurality of organized interests strive to control government through taking part in electoral contests and/or strive to influence the policies a government adopts, and in either case each of the competing interests has some reasonable chance of success in the contest for office or influence. Inspired by de Tocqueville and developed by modern American thinkers, the most rigorous of whom is Robert A. Dahl, pluralism in this sense places great emphasis on secondary associations which are independent of government.[5] It is the existence of such associations which is the social foundation of democracy and the state control and direction of such associations is a key element in the pluralist concept of 'totalitarianism'.

This current of American pluralism has avoided the abstract conceptualism of much Anglo-Saxon political theorizing. American pluralism considers associations as part of a process of political competition and tends to treat the state and government as intermediary networks through which competing interests strive to influence policy and through which the objectives of the dominant organized interests on any particular issue are carried out. It accords little autonomous role to state institutions and it is not especially concerned with theorizing the institutional forms of political authority. Thus, despite its emphasis on the role of secondary associations, it is very different in substance from English political pluralism.

Pluralism in this latter sense is less a doctrine of political competition than a critique of state structure and of the basis of the authority of the state. The English pluralists challenged the theory of unlimited state sovereignty and of a unitary centralized state embodying such sovereign power in a hierarchy of authority. A 'pluralist' in the American sense could still claim, and with good reason, that the process of political competition in such a sovereign state, if it is effective, made that state democratic. In that case the limits to formal state authority would be mainly the norms and conventions of the political process subscribed to by political actors and publics alike.

English and American pluralism have rather different concepts, objects of analysis, and political emphases, but their schemes by no means lack points of contact nor are they incompatible in principle. In a unitary state with a centralized administration which can effectively claim unlimited sovereign power the restraints on such power *are* indeed normative and conventional. When such normative restraints break down then pluralist political competition becomes the struggle by antagonistic interests for control of unlimited state power to use on their own behalf. The development of antagonistic pluralism in the American sense is facilitated by the type of state which is the object of English pluralist criticism.[6] In a democratic state with a legislature that claims unlimited sovereign power a narrow majority enables the victors to determine how others shall live through their access to legislative and administrative power. Elective despotism is wielded in the service of a fraction of society. De Tocqueville and Mill warned of the threat of the tyranny of the majority, but they could not fully comprehend the pernicious nature of antagonistic pluralism under a modern party system in which the political 'majority' may be dependent on the support of no more than a minority fraction of society. Dahl is clear about this danger but he tends to emphasize in explaining it the breakdown of consensual norms and of the whole political culture, thereby tending to ignore the effect of political *institutions* in making such antagonistic political pluralism possible.

Figgis was clear about the tyrannical tendencies of such an elective despotism. The phrase 'elective despotism' is now commonplace. It was first used by Macaulay and resurrected by Lord Hailsham in the late 1970s when he feared that a left Labour government might gain and abuse a narrow parliamentary majority.[7] But if Westminster is a spectacular example of centralized, unlimited, and omnicompetent sovereign power, it is merely one of a species. The very concept of a national assembly representing the people's sovereign power contained a real threat to autonomous associations; for the independent life of such associations challenges the principle of sovereignty and if their actions clash with state policy they must be broken if that principle is to be preserved. Long before the experience of Hitler's and Stalin's tyrannies, Figgis perceived the threat implied in the monopoly of social power which the claim to state sovereignty seeks to realize. We should not forget that the Nazi terror began with a constitutionally appointed government using the emergency powers of the constitution. Figgis saw this threat in the milder phenomena of Bismarck's *Kulturkampf* against the Catholic church and the anti-clerical politics of Emile Combes at the turn of the century in the Third Republic in France. He understood how centralized state authority claiming unlimited sovereign power could seek to destroy an association which, for its own function, enjoyed the voluntary support and loyalty of large numbers of people. Figgis did not restrict this lesson to the primary object of his own concerns, religious associations, but recognized the threat posed to trade unions too.

Twenty years ago the ideas of Cole, Figgis, and Laski were a dead letter. In 1968 conventional politicians could recognize no danger in a stable two-party system in which both parties were moderate and obeyed the unwritten rules of behaviour in government that allowed the system of political competition to work. A centralized state and legislative sovereignty in the hands of one party simply allowed efficient modernization; particularistic authorities and constitutional limits on legislative and state power were simply brakes on efficient government. The student radicals opposed to conventional politics, on the other hand, sought a participatory democracy without elaborate structures, formal rules, or codified degrees of authority. Political pluralism would be no more than arcane nonsense to them. Moreover, Cole and Laski had entered that fatal period for reputations when once influential figures recently dead have no claim on public attention. Laski died in 1950 and Cole in 1959. Moreover, they had long before abandoned an active advocacy of political pluralism.

Today things look rather different. Mrs Thatcher's government has shown both the dangers of antagonistic pluralism and the defects of the British 'constitution'. Silly people are wont to compare Mrs Thatcher's actions and attitudes with Fascism and even exceedingly intelligent people have claimed her aim is a 'post-democratic bourgeois society'.[8] On the contrary, Mrs Thatcher constantly insists that hers is a democratically elected government and that it has a 'mandate' for change derived from three successive general election victories. Mrs Thatcher needs 'democracy' in its unreformed and increasingly unsatisfactory British form. It provides an essentially plebiscitarian legitimation for her legislative actions against independent associations in civil society. She is using the great authority given by democratic elections for what are often highly unpopular and divisive policies, but she is not alone in this. Many elected governments in other countries have acted in a similar manner.

The relevant point of comparison for Mrs Thatcher is with a democratic politician like Emile Combes rather than with dictators like Mussolini or Hitler. The object of her most draconian measures has been the trade unions rather than the Catholic church, but both are associations freely formed of citizens, with a life and loyalty of their own. Mrs Thatcher has set out to use her majority, a form of *minority* rule with 43 per cent of the popular vote, to dictate by constitutionally unchallengeable state authority and unlimited legislative sovereignty how others shall live. She has further centralized an already highly centralist governmental system and she has treated civil servants as if they are indeed 'servants' of the state, that is, no more than agents of sovereign power who enjoy the duties of unlimited loyalty and obedience but no political rights specific to their position.

Each of these features of modern Conservative government was identified by the English pluralists as obnoxious long before either big government or prime ministerial primacy in the modern sense existed. The pluralists sought a state that was a partnership between authority and associations freely formed of citizens. They sought a system of representation that would be complex and complete enough, paying due regard to function, so that no mere mathematical majority could prevail over the complex web of interests in society. Figgis in particular sought a form of legislative power that could not abolish or override the distinct autonomous bodies and dimensions of authority within its domain but which would concentrate on regulating the interaction of independent associations and on supervising the functionally and territorially specific and autonomous authorities.

Modern critics identify well enough the political dangers and deficiencies of the Conservative government's utilization of the despotic tendencies built into the British constitution. They are, however, either less than radical in the remedies that they propose ('radical' in the sense of going to the root of the problem – which is centralized and hierarchical sovereign state power) or, while seeking extensive social and political changes leading to the radical pluralization and decentralization of authority, lack a coherent theoretical rationale to tie such changes together. A good example of the former case is *The Noble Lie* by Ian Harden and Norman Lewis (1987) and of the latter case, *The People's Kingdom* by Richard Holme (1987).

The widely canvassed measures of political reform such as proportional representation, a Bill of Rights, and a Freedom of Information Act, while desirable changes in themselves, do not fully touch the issue of centralized sovereign state power in a situation where there is no consensus as to how it shall be used. Such measures are restraints on state action rather than a change in state organization such that the state's capacities for action are altered in a way that lessens the need for restraint.

David Marquand's excellent book *The Unprincipled Society* (1988) demonstrates clearly the baleful political inheritance under which modern Britain suffers, and yet which most of our elected politicians regard as the best possible model of parliamentary democracy – the 'Mother of Parliaments'. That inheritance is threefold: the doctrine of unlimited parliamentary sovereignty; the appropriation by the executive of the prerogative powers of the monarch; and the fiction that civil servants are merely executors of their political masters' will and that therefore ministers alone are accountable to Parliament for their actions. He shows how the 'Westminster Model' of government has served in Britain as an obstacle to the evolution of a modern 'developmental state'. Marquand powerfully argues the need to build a consensus for political and economic change through the dialogue of the major organized interests, but he stops well short of conceiving the institutions appropriate to such a dialogue. Such institutions imply the explicit representation of interests and groups according to function and the elaboration of policy by bargaining rather than its promulgation as legislation by a single party with undisputable control of the means of government. Successful 'developmental states' like Sweden have evolved social equivalents of what the English pluralists sought in constitutional terms through forms of corporatist representation outside their parliaments and through accepting the need to make policy through the extensive consultation of organized interests. That route is not currently open to the UK and in the long run constitutional change is needed if we are to have a 'developmental' and yet democratic state.

The Westminster Model is an extreme case of centralized sovereign power in the democratic world, but the relevance of the English pluralist critique does not stop twelve miles from Britain's shores. The most successful and explicitly corporatist developmental states are nearly all small areas like Austria and Sweden.[9] It is difficult to see how such formal or quasi-formal arrangements can simply be transferred to the level of the large national state, let alone the European Community. The Community is faced with both the need for greater economic integration and the need to evolve developmental capacities which ensure that growth and prosperity are relatively evenly shared. No one imagines that a centralized European super-state can do this and preserve accountability, nor can such integration be left to informal or quasi-formal arrangements between national governments' ministers and major organized interests being generalized to the Community as a whole. The Community needs an explicit system of political organization and accountability, but not one founded on the model of national sovereignty writ large. A complex confederal structure of plural authority and a complex multi-layered scheme of representation in which territorial units and social functions are represented in the central community parliamentary bodies are a possible answer. English pluralism provides both a justification and a model for such plural authority and multi-channel representation.

Pluralism is thus of contemporary relevance, it addresses contemporary debates on the nature and future of democratic government, and it adds an important missing ingredient to these debates. But we should not imagine that the Westminster Model has prevailed without challenge until today. It would not be exaggerating to say that English political pluralism set the agenda for political theory in the first two decades of this century in Britain. In 1915 Ernest Barker could feel confident he represented the conventional wisdom of advanced opinion when he claimed that 'the state has generally been discredited in England'.[10] This would appear to be an extraordinary statement, but it reflects the widespread influence of anti-statist opinion in English intellectual circles at this time. Foremost in that challenge to state centralism and growing collectivism were the pluralists. Pluralism was less a tightly integrated intellectual 'school' that a current of opinion. The pluralists differed radically in emphasis and often in basic propositions. Pluralism was also an international movement, with a very strong current of pluralist legal and constitutional theorizing in Europe, notably from the Dutchman Hugo Krabbe and the French theorist Léon Duguit.[11] In Britain, however, pluralism was more than a current in legal theory. It was a political idea which significantly influenced movements such as Guild Socialism, and the Guild idea was popularized among the intelligentsia by periodicals like *The New Age*.

In the early 1920s pluralism in Britain reached its apogee. Its theoretical work was widely reviewed and critically discussed in Europe and the United States.[12] In 1920 even the Fabian collectivists Sidney and Beatrice Webb sought to counter Guild Socialist political success and pluralist intellectual success by incorporating elements of pluralism and functional representation into their *Constitution for a Socialist Commonwealth of Great Britain* (1920). Pluralism's decline was then rapid and dramatic, as was that of Guild Socialism as a political movement. By the late 1920s pluralism's influence had declined to university teaching, to critical asides, and to footnotes in other people's books, and the leading pluralists were either already dead, in the case of Figgis (in 1919), or had abandoned pluralist propositions more or less explicitly, like Cole and Laski.

Who were the pluralists? Such a diverse current of opinion is difficult to unravel, particularly as it ended so dramatically and ceased to have any direct influence. The principle of selection of the three authors offered here is both that they were very influential at the time of pluralism's popularity and that their work is of lasting quality and relevant to contemporary debates. Some possible candidates for inclusion in a 'pluralist anthology' are relatively easy to exclude. Ernest Barker, for example, was influenced by and interested in pluralism, but wrote no major pluralist work and later became decidedly critical. A.D. Lindsay was likewise an early sympathizer but not a major figure.[13] Bertrand Russell actively embraced pluralism during the First World War, before moving on through a long journey of changing causes and ideas.[14]

Others are less easy to exclude. Writers like Hilaire Belloc, author of *The Servile State* (1913), and A.R. Orage, editor of *The New Age*, as anti-collectivists shared some of the pluralist's pre-conceptions. *The New Age* gave a strong impetus to Guild Socialist and functional democratic thinking. It first published S.G. Hobson's articles expounding an industrial democracy based on national guilds, later collected as *National Guilds: An Inquiry into the Wage System and the Way Out* (1914), and it also published the essays of the Spanish philosopher Ramiro de Maeztu in which he expounded a theory of functional democracy.[15] On the criterion of contemporary influence they should certainly be in, but in the end their work is less comprehensive and coherent than that of Cole or Laski.

The only person who meets both criteria and is not included here is Frederick William Maitland, the great Cambridge legal historian. Maitland is important because he was responsible for the English reception of Otto von Gierke's theory of associations and his defence of corporate personality, a central stimulus in English pluralism, and because he was the major formative influence on Figgis in matters non-theological. I have excluded Maitland from this collection with great reluctance for two main reasons. First, while his introduction to Gierke's *Political Theories of the Middle Age* (1900) is invaluable, it is primarily historical, being concerned to demonstrate among other things the modernity of the theory of state sovereignty. It is also currently in print in an inexpensive edition (Gierke, 1988). Second, his contributions to legal history are informed by pluralism and the concept of corporate personality are difficult reading for the non-specialist in legal history and the pluralism is implicit rather than theoretically developed (see Maitland, 1911). Maitland's most explicit and accessible piece is a lecture, 'Moral personality and legal personality', which is already reprinted as an appendix to the best modern book-length introduction to English pluralism, David Nicholls's *The Pluralist State* (1975).

Each of the major pluralist writers I have included here, Cole, Figgis, and Laski, presents special problems of selection and treatment. To begin with Figgis, Maitland's disciple and a formative influence on the young Cole and Laski. Figgis (1866 – 1919) was an Anglican priest. He was active in church politics – a political radical and an Anglo-Catholic theological conservative. Figgis's views on church government and the relationship of church and state, intimately connected with his pluralism, remained influential in Anglican circles long after the demise of pluralism as a political theory. Such prominent Anglicans as

William Temple were advocates of his views on the church as a political society.[16] Figgis's *oeuvre* is complicated. It includes a number of exclusively theological works such as *The Fellowship of the Mystery* (1915). Figgis saw the Anglican church as an association voluntarily entered and dependent on a loyalty stemming from a common love of and search for Christ, not as a state-licensed and state-enforced compulsory association. As a state church the Anglican communion was a relic of the days of compulsory religious obedience and its tie to the state was a brake on the development of the church as a religious community. Figgis's religious concerns are not, therefore, irrelevant to his pluralism. His lectures *Churches in the Modern State* (1913) are his most explicitly political, most articulately pluralist, and most contemporarily relevant work. *Churches in the Modern State* explores problems of church government and the relationships of church and state. These are set in the context of a pluralist account of the rise of the modern doctrine of state sovereignty and offer a blistering critique of its implications for religious liberty and the autonomy of religious associations. I have chosen the second lecture, 'The Great Leviathan', which deals with the rise of the modern theory of state sovereignty and its consequences.

Figgis also wrote three major books on the history of political thought: *The Divine Right of Kings* (1914), *Political Aspects of St Augustine's 'City of God'* (1921), and *Studies of Political Thought from Gerson to Grotius* (1916). All are still valuable and the last is, in my opinion, the best introduction to early modern political thought in existence. These books suffer from their own virtues when considered for inclusion in the present collection: they are resolutely historical and the pluralist perspective, deployed to show the historicity and modernity of the doctrine of state sovereignty, is not over-forced to draw lessons of contemporary relevance. Finally, Figgis wrote a spirited and sensitive critique of Nietzsche, *The Will to Freedom* (1917), challenging his view of Christianity as a life-denying religion expressing the *ressentiment* of the uncreative and envious herd. In this work, Figgis anticipates the disastrous consequences of a doctrine that denies full dignity to all people being adopted by those in political power.

G.D.H. Cole (1889-1959) was a prolific author who wrote some dozens of books and countless pamphlets and articles on many subjects, from poetry and detective stories to social history and socialist planning, in the course of a long and varied career. Cole began his intellectual life as a political philosopher, and his political life in the Fabian Research Department and as a prominent Guild Socialist. Choosing from Cole's work in the period he was influenced by pluralism presents its own difficulties. Cole changed his mind rapidly and radically, virtually with every book he wrote. There is in consequence no representative 'Cole' for his Guild Socialist and pluralist period. *The World of Labour* (1913), *Labour in the Commonwealth* (1918), *Self-Government in Industry* (1917), and *Guild Socialism Re-Stated* (1920a) are all largely concerned with how the trade unions can fully develop their function by aiding the organization of industry by labour in a true industrial democracy, and the last is concerned with the detailed working out of the arrangements for a guild-based organization of national production. They are more or less influenced by pluralist ideas but do not fully develop the theoretical basis of pluralism. *The Social Theory* (1920b) is an exception. It explores the social- theoretic basis for a doctrine of democracy based upon function rather than the fiction of the representation of individual wills. It is pluralist in that it denies the need or legitimacy for a concentrated state power claiming sovereignty over society, and it seeks the merging of state into society, of administration into functional-democratic self-organization, and of imperative authority into co-ordination by the active co-operation of self-governing bodies. A large part of *The Social Theory* is included here, Chapters II and III and V–VIII. The essentials of the political theory of representation and the critique of the state are retained here. Chapters I and IV and IX–XIV have been excluded. Chapters I and IV are primarily concerned with definitions. Chapter XI deals with the economic structure of society, Chapter X with regionalism and local government, Chapter XI with churches, XII with liberty, Chapter XIII with the authority of institutions, and Chapter XIV is the conclusion. While some of these chapters contain relevant material, they are secondary to the main arguments about association, pluralism, and the paramountcy of function, and can often be deduced from the latter. Chapters II and III set out Cole's conception of the nature of communal life and social organization, arguing that associations are central to society, and they are included here for that reason, since they form the theoretic underpinning of his pluralism.

H.J. Laski (1893 – 1950) was equally prolific and he later turned completely from pluralism to a combination of a simplified Marxism and a radical commitment to democracy. Laski's intellectual career began as a legal and political theorist. Laski was strongly influenced by Figgis when in England, and through him Gierke and Maitland. Later, when in America at Harvard (1916 – 1920), he was subject to a wide variety of influences, notably the critical tempering of his very idealistic pluralism by the measured criticism of Oliver Wendell Holmes. Laski also became very strongly influenced by the work of Léon Duguit.[17]

Laski regarded sovereignty as a legal fiction, and was primarily concerned with the legitimacy of the claims made upon the citizen by the state. Viewing political obligation as a *moral* problem, Laski could see no moral superiority in the claims of the state to regulate conduct and enforce obedience. In the matter of obligation the state was not superior to associations, like trade unions, even if it did possess a *de facto* monopoly of the means of violence and a great power of compulsion. Laski's pluralism 'denies, ultimately, the sovereignty of anything save right conduct'.[18] This extreme pluralism stemmed from Laski's own struggles with the legitimacy of authority and was not a defect shared by some other pluralists like Figgis, as we shall see. It also enabled Laski to treat state power in a remarkably objective and matter-of-fact way. This was something that drew him to and that he drew from Duguit, and which later made it easy for him to view the state in quasi-Marxist terms.

Laski's early works, like *Studies in the Problem of Sovereignty* (1917) and *Authority in the Modern State* (1919), are essayistic; their pluralism is often implicit in the text, and they are often written in a prolix style. His monumental *A Grammar of Politics* (1925) and its many subsequent editions mark a critical distancing from pluralism, a distancing that grew into a break by the late 1920s. *A Grammar of Politics* is a complex and transitional text, even if many of its formulations, e.g., on the issues of sovereignty and the federative nature of social life, are sharper than his early works. The principal reason for excluding any material from *A Grammar of Politics* here is that it is still in print in an inexpensive edition.[19] The most effective and accessible pluralist works of Laski are the essays collected in two collections, *The Foundations of Sovereignty and Other Essays* (1921) and *Studies in Law and Politics* (1932). The most important of these essays is 'The problem of administrative areas'. This rather curiously titled text is about the defects of the 'Westminster Model' of parliamentary sovereignty and about how elements of functional democracy and the pluralist autonomy of subordinate authorities may evolve in the British System. Laski regards all society, and political authority along with it, as necessarily federative in principle. Absolute sovereignty is therefore a dream and delusion of certain power-holders. 'The problem of administrative areas' explores the problem of how to recognize that federative reality in appropriate political structures, including discussions of the role of local government and both the self-government and the wider political representation of industry. Laski was over-optimistic about the capacities of trade unions to seek political power and to exercise administrative responsibilities. He was also over-optimistic about the scope of the Whitley Councils and the prospects for genuine industrial democracy. But if mistaken about the trends in current politics, Laski's essay is clear about the *need* for such changes and the defects of both the Westminster Model and the existing pattern of Labour–management relations. Laski was no fool, however, for, in fact, the period immediately after 1918 offered political possibilities that were not subsequently realized: of government support for social reconstruction, and of moves by unions like those of the miners and railwaymen to take an active role in running their industries if they were to be nationalized.

'The personality of associations' is a valuable and effectively condensed review of the debate concerning corporate personality: a central concern of pluralism, which I shall cover in greater detail below. 'The pluralistic state' is a short summary of the quintessential concerns of pluralism. All these three essays are from the 1921 collection. From the 1932 collection I have included 'Law and the state' which explores in an accessible form the relationship between pluralism and jurisprudence.

Essays from the 1921 collection not included here for reason of limited space but of direct relevance to pluralism are 'The theory of popular sovereignty' and 'The foundations of sovereignty' (a piece I would have included here did it not overlap so closely with Figgis's lecture II from *Churches*). From the 1932 collection, 'The state in the new social order' is interesting because it is transitional between Laski the pluralist and Laski the semi-Marxist Labour Party radical. It is necessary to caution the reader about the texts included here and their relation to the originals. I have made extensive cuts in several of the texts, most notably *The Social Theory* and 'The problem of administrative areas'. These cuts are essential to eliminate repetition and redundancy, and to exclude discussion of issues relevant at the time of writing but now no more than an obstacle to the argument. These cuts are clearly indicated. I have also reduced the original authors' notes and references to contemporary literature to those inescapable in terms of sense or where the authors cited are still of relevance. I have occasionally interpolated explanatory editorial notes.

A word of caution about the style and structure of the pluralists' arguments. In devising this book a clear choice presented itself between selecting original texts and offering instead a modern exposition of the pluralists' main themes. In some ways a thorough summary would be more comprehensive and coherent than the texts offered here. The pluralists were, however, *not* a comprehensive and coherent academic school, and it is important to preserve the open-ended and provisional, indeed 'pluralist', character of their discourse. Moreover, their writings have real virtues which summary exposition obliterates. Figgis and Cole in particular did not write for academic audiences or for some ideal reader in posterity. They wrote for popular and political effect. Figgis wrote well and eloquently, but for the intelligent common readers who still existed then. Cole often wrote in a hurry and, even in *The Social Theory*, with Board School educated trade unionists and political activists in mind. In consequence they do not argue as an analytic philosopher might wish or in a way that a Marxist-schooled sociologist might recognize as theory. But there is a strong set of arguments and important concepts there. Provided one persists in seeking them through the somewhat paradoxical 'difficulties' of plain English and easygoing exposition.

Perry Anderson claimed that in the twentieth century the English lacked a native tradition of high social theory.[20] One might say that he didn't look very hard for one or that he expected such theory to look like the work of Max Weber or Theodor Adorno.

But he has a point. A great deal of the most powerful social and political theory in Britain has been studiously neglected by both the academy and political circles. Cole, Figgis, and the pluralists are one clear example, while R.G. Collingwood is another and a shocking one. One of the reasons for that neglect, by the academy at least, is that these authors do not conform to the current models of intellectual rigour and theoretic depth which are a precondition for reception as a 'great thinker'; that is, to write in approved Continental models for some contemporary academics, or to use Anglo-Saxon analytical methods for others.

Having introduced English political pluralism in general terms it is necessary to offer some more substantive comment on a number of the pluralists' major themes and the issues relating to the pluralist current of opinion in early-twentieth-century Britain. These are:

1. Corporate personality and associationalism;
2. Pluralism and the critique of sovereignty;
3. The principle of function and the critique of representative democracy;
4. Pluralism and Guild Socialism

CORPORATE PERSONALITY AND ASSOCIATIONALISM

Pluralism is both an anti-statist, anti-collectivist doctrine and also one strongly opposed to the extreme individualism of free-market liberalism and the narrow definition of human purposes and goods implied in classical utilitarianism. As such it cut across the major currents of opinion in the late-nineteenth-and early-twentieth-century political debate. A.V. Dicey in *Law and Public Opinion in England in the Nineteenth Century* (1905) saw collectivism as a current of opinion and policy that developed inexorably as the latter part of the century progressed. The Liberal governments of 1906 and 1910 marked in many critics' eyes a decisive shift to collectivism, particularly with the enactment of Lloyd George's social insurance legislation in 1911.

The pluralists were different in that they did not reject collectivism in the terms of Spencerian anti-statist individualism. They rejected collectivism not because it offered public action to meet social needs, but because in meeting such needs collectivism enhanced the power of the state as a compulsory organization and thereby diminished the wellsprings of true collective action through the freely associated activities of citizens. The pluralists owed a good deal to the constructive side of English Idealism, represented by T.H. Green and F.H. Bradley. They regarded Bernard Bosanquet, however, with considerable dismay as an Hegelian state-idolater.[21] From Green and Bradley they took the view that persons enjoy freedom and the ability to pursue the good because they are social. The egoistic wants of isolated social atoms necessarily diminish human aims and lead to a sand-heap of several and private purposes and not to a society. But the pluralists claimed that there is no single entity 'society' nor a single common good. Persons develop through contributing to associations in order to fulfil definite purposes. Society is composed of associations freely formed of citizens. It is as a plurality of lesser societies that it exists in any sense as a whole. Figgis conceived the public power as a society of societies, as an association of associations, charged with the task of making the continued existence and mutual interaction of such associations possible through setting rules for their conduct.

Figgis never denied the need for a public power to make and enforce law, as Cole and Laski sometimes seem to do. His point was that the state as at present constituted did not and could not confine itself to that role. In claiming an unlimited plenitude of power it converted legal sovereignty into a doctrine that could only strike at the root of the freedom and the organic self-development of associations. The modern state adopted the concessionist view of secondary associations: they are creations of state law and licenced to act only in the forms prescribed by law. Ultimately, for the concessionist, only the state and the individual are real entities. The state, because it embodies in democratic doctrine the sovereign will of the whole people, is necessarily superior to all more partial associations. Associations and corporate bodies are thus legal constructs for particular purposes and enjoy no other legitimacy than that conferred by their state-sanctioned articles of association.

Through Maitland, Figgis found the intellectual means to challenge the legal positivist and concessionist conceptions of associations, that is, the historical work and the *Genossenschaft* theory of Otto von Gierke.[22] Gierke's views are complex and Maitland and Figgis each adapted them to their own purposes, subjecting them to a definite 'reading'. In particular Gierke did not reject the theory of state sovereignty and was a patriot for the new German empire.[23] What Gierke offered was twofold: first, a history of political thought before the advent of the modern theory of the state, showing the possibility of thinking about politics in terms other than those of Machiavelli and Hobbes; and second, a view of associations as corporate personalities, as real bodies with a life of their own which were not mere legal 'fictions'.

The 'fiction' theory of the corporation was no mere jurisprudential concept but an active doctrine of legal interpretation. The view of corporate personality as no more than a convenient legal fiction and the concessionist theory of corporation as no more than state legal constructs both had real and damaging effects. Associations were viewed by the courts as bound to the powers outlined in their articles of association, and thus denied the capacity to decide for themselves how to develop. In the absence of unanimity in deciding on any change an aggrieved member could insist on the original articles and terms as a matter of strict contract.

Figgis was much exercised by the Free Church of Scotland case.[24] In 1900 the Free Church merged with the United Presbyterian Church on a majority vote of 643 votes to 27. The dissenters members took the case to law and claimed that the union of the two churches was an *ultra vires* act of the majority and was, therefore, null and void. The House of Lords finally decided for the dissenters and awarded all the property of the church to them. This decision involved the courts, in the course of deciding whether the action of the majority was or was not within the powers of the church's constitution, in determining the meaning of Calvinist theology and the appropriate doctrines of religious government. Thus, the courts were determining in effect what the church should believe in if it wanted to keep its original corporate existence and property. This was an irony which Figgis did not fail to point out, citing Mr [later Lord] Haldane lecturing the judges on these theological matters as part of a legal argument.[25]

Figgis saw clearly that 'unless groups are allowed free development the self-development of individuals will be hindered' (1913: 12). An association is just such a means of self-development.

It is a body through which people seek common purposes, including the pursuit of religious or industrial freedom in the case of churches or trade unions. It is not just an aggregation of property for private benefits, to which individuals 'subscribe' without any commitment beyond the satisfaction of their given individual interests. Great associations like churches or trade unions are not just clubs, they demand commitment and loyalty from their members, and thus they have some of the same attributes as 'public' agencies.

Figgis was primarily concerned with such 'public' associations but both he and Laski were also interested in the consequences of the fiction theory in judgments under company law. This is shown clearly in Laski's 'The personality of associations', included in this collection. Laski cites numerous cases of the *ultra vires* rule being applied in respect of commercial companies with decidedly inconsistent results. This issue has now died away. For example, Megalith plc, a multi-industry, multi-national group of companies, could hardly be challenged under the rule if its business is anything and everything. The issue of *ultra vires* now largely appears in legal disputes between the central state and local authorities. But the general issue of the powers of associations remains firmly alive. The complaint that 'trade unions are outside the law' is no longer much heard, mainly because they are so much inside the law that even minor details of their internal voting and balloting procedures are now legally prescribed. The Conservatives' industrial relations legislation denies the trade unions any autonomy in procedures for action and self-government. Whatever the faults of the unions, this is an unjustifiable intervention in the affairs of free associations. Figgis would turn in his grave. We should be shocked too that this assertion of unlimited state sovereignty should have been greeted with such complacency. The unions may have been both unpopular and too powerful in the later 1970s. They were also undoubtedly short-sighted, conservative, and complacent about their own internal procedures and hostile to genuine democratization. However, their internal reform by state *fiat* is both tyrannical and counter-productive. This is because union activists bitterly resent much of the new legislation and, as soon as a political opportunity presents itself, they will throw off as much of it as they can.

Company law is an area where the state's action has been by contrast largely permissive. The Companies Act of 1862 envisaged, as part of its scheme of regulation for the protection of investors, companies as self-governing republics of their own shareholders. This is now a complete fiction and was largely obsolete before the nineteenth century was out. Companies are typically run by a senior managerial oligarchy which is self-renewing if things are going well and with the support of major corporate institutional shareholders. Managements face almost no threat from democratic accountability. Their actions are governed less by shareholders' meetings than by the dual fears of the company's quotation on the Stock Exchange and of takeover bids by rival management cliques in other companies. As far as its employees and the general public are concerned the company is largely unaccountable. For the former the company is an hierarchical authority in whose decisions they have no say and for the latter the company is under no special legal obligation to consult interested parties or pay due regard to community interests. As long as they do not break contracts or commit torts, companies do not have to answer for their actions to employees or to the communities in which they operate. They have to comply with state law, but it places them under no special obligation to answer to anyone with an interest in the company other than a proprietal one. Companies cannot be treated as self-governing associations freely formed of citizens in the pluralist sense, but rather as analogous to centralized sovereign states and, therefore, to be changed and reformed.[26]

It is interesting to note how the issues of industrial democracy and of the accountability of the company to employees and to the community are now on the agenda of mainstream political theory. They are no longer confined to the radical fringes of the advocates of 'workers' control'. Noberto Bobbio, for example, regards big business as one of the 'great blocks of descending and hierarchical power in every complex society' and until this hierarchical power is changed 'the democratic transformation of society cannot be complete' (1987: 57). The acid test of how democratic a country is, is no longer *who* can vote but *where* they can vote. Again, Dahl in *A Preface to Economic Democracy* (1985) argues that until the ownership of property is democratized through the widespread adoption of self-governing co-operatives as alternatives to corporations then the lack of *economic* autonomy of individuals and the concentration of economic power in the hands of corporations will undermine political democracy. The English pluralists would probably have heartily approved.

It is often asserted that the pluralists were committed to a set of romantic metaphysical illusions in their assertion of the real personality of groups. The young Laski did indeed metaphysicalize a good deal and received sharp criticism from the American philosopher Morris Cohen for it.[23] Cohen asserted that the unity of a group is simply the relation between its members. That is a distinct relation to be sure but not a new entity over and above the elements so connected. Laski later introduced substantial elements of American pragmatism into this thought; so pluralism is clearly not dependent on a particular metaphysical view of groups.[28] But, as it happens, Cohen was mistaken. The issue is less that of the nature of the group as an entity in a metaphysical sense, than of how it is regarded by other actors which have power over it. If it takes two oxen to make a plough team, as in the example that Cohen uses to make his point, then certainly he is right that there are still only two oxen in the team and not a new collective animal. But of course it *does* take those two oxen (together with a plough, a yoke, and a ploughman) to do the work of ploughing. It will not help to do the work of ploughing if certain people insist on pulling them apart because of certain anti-metaphysical beliefs that they hold. If the group is a necessary relation then it will not help group life to insist on the primacy and reality only of the elements related.

Figgis is concerned to assert the unity and organic life of groups: a life based on the active co-operation of the people involved in them. He is less interested in a metaphysics of group personality than in the way that the state, law, and other social actors give recognition to groups. In contesting the fiction theory, Figgis saw the association as a living entity only in the sense that it should be left to decide its own internal affairs and to change by its own agreed procedures. This did not lead Figgis to deny the role and value of the legal regulation and recognition of groups, but rather to question the doctrine governing the current form of that regulation. The pluralistic state, as the necessary public power in a society of free associations, has the principal task of both facilitating the formation and activity of groups through its

21

legislation and ensuring through regulation their fair and peaceful interaction.

As David Nicholls says, the pluralists 'saw that *all* legal personality (including that of the individual) is "artificial"', and that 'it is created by being recognised in legal practice' (1975: 70). The issue between concessionism and realism is not that of a metaphysics of corporate personality but is about *how* the law constructs corporate persons and what capacities it recognizes for them in doing so. For the pluralists, law is not a pure *voluntas*, a positive sovereign will; rather, law must also embody reason attuned to the needs of society.[29] The functions that associations serve and their need for autonomy in performing them are not created by the law. That is so even if associations are necessarily defined in a particular institutional form with certain capacities by the law and could not effectively exist otherwise.

Certainly the actual content of the pluralist defence of the 'real personality of groups' does not require any supposition of a 'group mind'. To Figgis, Christian and libertarian, the very idea would have been repellent. Groups do not have 'minds' but they are collectivities with decision procedures. The outcomes of those procedures are not reducible to the wills of the individuals who take part in them. That would be to regard individuals as if they existed only in isolation. Groups imply the institutionalization of new types of activity, and with them new issues, interests, and constraints that did not and would not exist but for the group. The existence of groups creates issues *sui generis*, requiring special decision procedures, and not entities *sui generis*. Methodological individualism may be a good solvent of cloudy metaphysics, but the resulting acid is too strong altogether and it dissolves along with that metaphysics most of the phenomena of group life.

PLURALISM AND THE CRITIQUE OF SOVEREIGNTY

To a casual reader much of the pluralist argument against sovereignty seems like an over-energetic debate with a pale phantom. Surely it is no more than an argument about the history of political thought? Does it really matter today? That the Middle Ages had no developed concept of sovereignty and a more pluralistic political structure is irrelevant since we are unlikely to re-create the social conditions which sustained them – the days of neo-Medievalist 'hey nonny no' and attempts to resuscitate the Guilds are long past. Bodin, Hobbes, and Austin are also long obsolete and their conceptions of the sovereign state are now primitive caricatures.

This simply isn't the case. At the time of the referendum on Britain's entry into the EEC in 1975, left and right, in the respective shapes of Michael Foot and Enoch Powell, both argued for a 'no' vote because to enter Europe would involve the surrender of the sovereignty of Parliament. Parliamentary sovereignty and its legitimation by electoral victory is the basis for Mrs Thatcher's abolition of local authorities like the Greater London Council, the direction of the policy of other surviving local authorities to the last detail, and the legal prescription of how free associations like trade unions should conduct their internal affairs. If sovereignty is a ghost, then it has recently been given a lot of blood to drink.

Pointing to the interdependence of states in the modern world or to the internal complexity of advanced industrial states simply cannot dispose of the issue of sovereignty. Of course it is true that the state's power cannot be unlimited. All power is necessarily limited simply by the very means of its exercise. It is also true that no state is so homogeneous that a single sovereign will could prevail within it without a complex process of mediation that dilutes and even destroys that will. But the pluralists never imagined that sovereignty was a description of state power. Sovereignty is not and never has been a state of affairs, the pluralists were clear about that. Sovereignty is, of course, enmeshed with the history of political thought and with political argument today because it is less a fact than a doctrine. But it is a politically highly consequential doctrine if political actors continue to subscribe to it and if it is not replaced by other doctrines that enable different political consequences to predominate.

Sovereignty is a doctrine that allows political actors to advance claims and to utilize these claims to further their political objectives. The central claim is that some agency enjoys of right a plenitude of power, that it may make any rule or policy within a given territory and put it into effect. Typically the agency now cited as the sovereign power is the Parliament or national assembly of a centralized state and its members enjoy that power because they represent the people. In the classic conception of sovereignty, legal and political power are fused in a single agency; legislation and administration give effect to the 'will' of that agency. This view of sovereignty, the basis for the pluralist critique, is contrary to that held by the defenders of the doctrine of state sovereignty. On the one hand, many legal theorists regard it as no more than a necessary device to assert the primacy of legal over other rules;[30] and, on the other, the active defenders of the political sovereignty of the state see it less as doctrine or claim then as fact. For Tony Benn the people *are* sovereign, and give their plenitude of power to Parliament.

Why are such claims to sovereign power effective? Ultimately because they are widely believed and because the state possesses an effective monopoly of the means of violence. The pluralists saw in the early-modern conception of sovereign state power something entirely new. Maitland and Figgis, for example, were not ignorant of the doctrines claiming for the Roman Emperor a plenitude of power and to be the sole source of law. Is not the essence of sovereignty to be found in the *Lex Regia*?[31] Yes and no. Hobbes was new because he stated an unlimited plenitude of power for a state with a monopoly of the means of violence and a society whose members were equally citizens–subjects, subordinated to the sovereign power in an equal way. Between the state and the individual citizens stands nothing that is not a creature of or licensed by the sovereign: no ancient and privileged provinces, no private armies, no differences of status like slavery or serfdom, no self-governing communities with their own unalterable customary laws, etc. The entire structure of particular authority, privilege, and status distinctions common to both the Roman Empire and Medieval states in both doctrine and practice is swept away. The monopoly of the means of violence, the levelling of the citizen body, and the claim to unlimited sovereign power go together in a new synthesis.

Hobbes, Like Machiavelli, was an unpopular, indeed scandalous political thinker precisely because he let the cat out of the bag. No state in 1651 corresponded to the *Leviathan* and no state does today. But it mapped out the aims of royal absolutism in the seventeenth and eighteenth centuries and those of the successor revolutionary-democratic absolutisms of the French Revolution and the nineteenth century.[32] Sovereign power is a project and one that is necessarily tyrannical in creating a monopoly of power, unless it is restrained by political and social forces and circumstances quite outside the doctrine. Figgis perceived that the combination of an all-powerful state and a mass of individual citizens created the space for political tyranny. Individuals can only further their own personalities and objectives through association, and if autonomous associations are regarded with suspicion and are objects of state suppression then genuine freedom is at an end.

Sovereignty was a problem for the pluralists for three connected reasons.

1. It necessarily undermined autonomous associations, as Rousseau said:

> But when factions arise, and partial associations are formed at the expense of the great association, the will of each of these associations becomes general in relation to its members, while it remains particular in relation to the state. . . .It is therefore essential, if the general will is to be able to express itself, that there would be no partial society within the state.
>
> (Rousseau 1762: 23)[33]

All political agents may not exploit the doctrine in this way but its tyrannical potential against the complex web of functional associations is always there.

2. The doctrine of sovereignty treats the state as if it were a single agent, with a single will – like an absolute monarch – whereas it is a complex amalgam of agencies and persons with different objectives and means of decision. The notion of a single legitimate 'will' is central to the doctrine of sovereignty. That will issues in commands to all subordinate agents that they are both obligated and compelled to obey. But there is no such 'will' in society. Society is also a complex amalgam of agencies, persons, and objectives. Sovereignty supposes a subjective view of political authority; will becomes command and, on the model of an individual, 'decides' something shall be done and issues orders to others to make it so.

3. A society in which all individuals are equally citizen–subjects, in which there is nothing between them and state power, and in which they are obliged to obey the commands of that power would

by tyrannical to the point of intolerability were that power not subjected to some legitimation. Hobbes at least offers the bleak honesty of a *pactem subjectionis* made in mortal fear of civil war. Later legitimations seek to square this state power, its will to command, with a popular sovereignty, a will of the people that this power be so. Rousseau has it neatly: the people in obeying the laws of the sovereign legislature are obeying their own commands. Popular sovereignty is legitimate as expressed in state power because it embodies the general will. But this is to suppose that the state expresses a coherent 'will of the people', as if there could be such an entity. Once Rousseau's conception of people-as-sovereign, giving direct assent to legislation, is dispensed with as impossible in any society above a few thousands then the notion of sovereignty as the will of the people becomes absurd. The people 'donate' their sovereign power to their representatives, but a will cannot be donated. The 'will' becomes the decision of a body of representatives not the 'people'. Once the complexities of electoral systems and political parties are introduced, then a party representing a minority of the electorate itself directed by a small leadership stratum comes to claim the legitimacy of the 'will of the people'.

Once the fact of plural interests and objectives is recognized, the very idea of a sovereign 'will' becomes absurd. At best it is the annexation of the claim to sovereign power by a fraction of society. Sovereign state power is compatible with democracy only on the assumption the people are homogeneous, have one interest, and will one thing. This assumption is inherently implausible and can only lead to projects to make it plausible, by annihilating sources of difference and other interests by means of state power. Once this is recognized, then some form of pluralism, either the American form which mitigates sovereignty through the consensual norms of a democratic political culture or the English one which seeks to change state doctrine and institutions, becomes absolutely necessary. A democratically legitimated sovereign 'will' cannot be made compatible with the rights of either individuals or associations. Where these rights clash with a political decision, they will be swept aside, subject as they are to a plenitude of legislative power.

A representative democratic system which embodies an unlimited sovereign legislature like the British must threaten both the legitimacy of democracy and the rule of law if the normative restraints on the type of action initiated through the state by the ruling majority party break down. These political conventions are not part of the doctrine of sovereignty; they are restraints on it which come from the wider political culture but by which a party which rejects them is in no sense bound. As Franz Neumann pointed out in *The Rule of Law* (1986), the doctrines of the unlimited sovereignty of Parliament and of the rule of law are in direct conflict, and they have only been held in tension by political culture and by political outcomes which ensured that Parliament did not enact legislation that undermined the rule of law in a substantive sense. The pluralists saw this long before Mrs Thatcher's government forced it upon the attention of the more liberally minded in Britain. They understood the tyrannical potential in the doctrine of state sovereignty which no amount of 'fair weather' politics could conceal. We should remember that the last years of Liberal England were closer to the fundamentally contested politics of today and that the image of a continuous history of political stability and tranquillity in England is a myth.[34]

What sort of political doctrine and what form of state did the pluralists envisage as a replacement for the doctrine of sovereignty and the centralized state with a monopoly of legislative power? As one might expect, the pluralists were largely in agreement in their critique of the ruling doctrine of sovereignty. Figgis and Duguit, Laski and Cole advance with variations the same arguments, Cole drawing on Figgis, Laski on Duguit and Figgis. But they did not agree on what should replace the object of criticism. This should hardly surprise us, for if pluralism had not given birth to a variety of alternative conceptions and institutional arguments rather than one dogmatic and monist counter-proposal to sovereignty it would have betrayed its own assumptions. Figgis does not envisage the abolition of a public power, the main function of which is to make laws for associations to thrive and co-exist. Duguit does not imagine that the state is other than a coercive and administrative power, but for him the state is subject to a juridical principle (*une règle de droit*). State action is governed by law. The law which is above the administrative apparatuses of the state and which can judge and review their actions is not superior because of a natural law but because of certain objective necessities of carrying on the affairs of state that are recognized in the law. Law has social utility

27

in prescribing for the state the demand to meet certain needs which arise from society as a solidaristic body. For his conception of social solidarity and the complex intermeshing of interests in a division of labour, Duguit is dependent on the sociology of his colleague at Bordeaux, Emile Durkheim.[35] The state is an organ of social co-ordination and, under modern industrial and social conditions, it is necessarily a collection of public service agencies unified in a legally codified form. The judicial principle governing its actions is that of the demands of carrying on a service and Duguit illustrates this in *Law and the Modern State* (1913) by the growth of French administrative law and the growth of legal review of the state's administrative action.

Figgis and Duguit in their different ways give a place both to legal regulation and to a public power. In the work of Cole and Laski this is often less clear. Laski's work before 'The problem of administrative areas' and *The Grammar of Politics* often appears to see the state as merely one association among many, and one whose claims to loyalty and legitimacy are no higher than those of other associations as far as the conscience of the citizen is concerned. The authority of the state is thus dependent on consent in more than the formal sense of representative-democratic legitimation. The citizens' consent cannot simply be presumed from a political device like elections. A citizen may find it necessary to give greater loyalty to another association if the state's policy is contrary to conscience.

In 'The problem of administrative areas' and *The Grammar of Politics* Laski was to give greater emphasis to the necessarily federative structure of society and, therefore, to the plural structures of authority and obligation that arise from it. We shall discuss this further when we consider the functional principle of representation in greater detail below. Cole, like Laski, carried his anti-statist impulses further than Figgis. Cole's pluralism is inextricably tied in with his Guild Socialist conception of a society based on self-governing associations of producers, and in that society what central power there is arises from the co-ordinative co-operation of associations and the *ad hoc* adjudications of his court of functional equity. We shall cover this in greater detail in the sections of functional representation and Guild Socialism below.

Cole and Laski in their more unguarded moments are sometimes open targets for the anti-pluralist critics. Critics, like K.C.

Hsiao in *Political Pluralism* (1927), often concentrate on what they see as the inherent contradiction involved in the denial of legal sovereignty. How can one have more than one set of laws? If law is to be primary in regulating conduct and at least tolerably consistent, then it must have a single source in a legislature that claims to predominate over all others. This is specious, since pluralism never argued against a legal order. To suppose it did is to identify all legal regulation with the full consequences of the doctrine of sovereignty.

Pluralism is not an anti-legal political theory like Marxism, which conceives law either as an instrument of class oppression or a phenomenon associated with commodity production and exchange, and contends that it will wither away like the state in a socialist society. Even Cole does not deny the need for regulation or the need to achieve co-ordination in the organization of social affairs. One may question the effectiveness of his arrangements – a congress representing all the functionally organized bodies in society and a 'democratic Supreme Court of Functional Equity' (1920b: 137) – but the aim is a co-ordinated pluralist system in which agencies know what they can and cannot do and in which they can appeal in cases of clashing functions to the decisions of the court. In fact, the *ad hoc* decision-making of Cole's court would undoubtedly hinder co-ordination, producing inconsistencies and anomalies that require further *ad hoc* adjudication to sort them out, and so on *ad infinitum.* To recognize this defect in Cole's argument is to accept the need for formally codified law and settled judicial procedures, not to wallow in the excesses of the doctrine of sovereignty.

Figgis's conception of the pluralist state as the association of associations defines a state which is both a public power, able to ensure public peace, and a legal order, which sustains that peace through the rule of law. In Figgis's view the more of the work of society done by associations freely formed of citizens the better. The pluralist state will be a minimal state but one whose primary task is to create the conditions for associations, and through them individual citizens, to be free to pursue their purposes. A pluralist legal order, in defining the rights of associations, would pay due regard to their autonomy and their right to develop as determined by their own internal decision procedures. It would also police the conduct of associations to ensure their stable and equitable interaction. It would set rules of conduct with regard to other associations and individual citizens, whether they be members or not, and provide means of pursuing relief for those who had suffered harms.

Figgis's state will, indeed must, claim primacy in making rules. But it will do so only within its own constitutional limits and in terms of its own social objectives. A pluralist claim to legal primacy, with the aim of securing a pluralist political and social order, will be quite unlike the classic doctrine of sovereignty. Hsiao and others like him are logic chopping in confusing the two. The constitution of a pluralist state would seek to ensure that there is no agency that can claim a plenitude of power, that associations are consulted in the process of law making, and that the objective is to promote the autonomous action of freely associated citizens. Figgis never wrote a model 'Constitution for a Pluralist Commonwealth'; he was too concerned to *defend* the free life of associations against the claims of sovereign power. The fact that he did not do so, however, does not mean that he had no coherent constitutional doctrine in his work.

THE PRINCIPLE OF FUNCTION AND THE CRITIQUE OF REPRESENTATIVE DEMOCRACY

In a paper read to the Aristotelian Society in 1915, 'Conflicting social obligations', Cole first explicitly expressed the principle of function as the basis for a comprehensive criticism of the theory of state sovereignty and its legitimation in representative democracy. This principle was largely implicit in the early Guild Socialist writings of authors like A.J. Penty and S.G. Hobson. Cole had been preceded in his functionalist democratic arguments by the essays of Ramiro de Maeztu collected in *Authority, Liberty and Function* (1916); de Maeztu later became a Fascist in Spain.

Cole argued that only society as a whole could contain that plenitude of powers and that omnicompetence of purposes implied in the concept 'sovereignty'. The error of political theorists like Rousseau was to vest in a specific political body, the state, what could in fact only be contained in the whole of society itself. Cole challenged three doctrines that submerged this complex whole into an undifferentiated part:

With Society, the complex of organized associations, rests the final more or less determinate sovereignty. We cannot carry sovereignty lower without handing it over to a body of which the function is partial rather than general. We must, therefore, reject the three theories of state sovereignty, Theocracy and Syndicalism, the theories of political, religious and industrial dominance. All these mistake the part for the whole: our difficulty seems to be making the whole out of their parts.

(Cole 1915: 157)

That latter task is addressed in *The Social Theory* (1920b). The basis of the functional theory of democracy is a theory of social organization. For Cole, 'society' is not an entity, a totality, but a grouping made up of specific associations and institutions performing definite purposes and interacting one with another. Associations are formed by persons coming together to fulfil definite purposes that they cannot accomplish as isolated individuals. Cole is the relentless opponent of any narrowly reductive and utilitarian individualism, but the whole ethical and analytic basis of his social theory is an exalted conception of the individual. Associations are necessarily specific to certain purposes, but '[e]very individual is in his nature universal; his actions and courses of action, his purposes and desires, are specific because he makes them so; but he himself is not and cannot be made specific, and therefore cannot be expressed in terms of function' (1920b: 49–50).

It follows from this exalted conception that individuals as such cannot be represented – they are potentially infinite in their purposes and wills while any scheme of representation, whatever its own claims, is necessarily finite. Certain necessary social functions require a form of association which is inclusive of all individuals. 'By a *political* organisation I mean an association of which the main purpose is to deal with those personal relationships which arise directly out of the fact that men live together in communities, and which require, and are susceptible to, social organisation' (1920b: 67). This function is essentially regulative and concerned with the most general interactions of all social agents. But other functions do not require to be performed by a single and inclusive body such as the state. The economic and co-ordinative functions are complex and differentiated tasks, affecting different agents in different ways, and should be organized by and at the level of the agents they affect. The inclusive political association is thus far from omnicompetent. It need not be the only inclusive association in society. It is, moreover, not necessarily superior to those other inclusive associations outside of the sphere of its own function. Thus alongside the inclusive political association there may be an association representing certain general interests of all consumers.

It is on the basis of this doctrine of function and this conception of the individual that Cole challenges the concept of 'representation'. Representative democracy is commonly justified on the ground that it gives expression to the will of the people, and that in choosing certain persons to 'represent' them the people consent to and give a mandate for the decisions those persons assembled together may take. The legislative assembly is sovereign because it expresses the constitutive power of the people which is embodied in their elected representatives. But this political body claims for itself a plenitude of rule-making power and must, therefore, claim to represent the people in each and every possible respect: thus, whatever their representatives decide to legislate is formally to be derived from the will of the people.

An omnicompetent legislature must claim to represent the whole of its electorate's personalities and every aspect of their interests. If it does not, then representative legitimation is less than complete. If the legislature can pass any act concerning any aspect of life it must claim to 'represent' people in their fullness. But no 'representative' can actually represent other individuals; their actual wills are diverse. It is absurd to suppose that a political body can encompass each and every purpose of each constituent. It is equally absurd that the complexity of all of social life can be represented in a *political* 'general will'. Hence this doctrine of representation is absurd when applied to an omnicompetent sovereign body. It is less effective as legitimation, however, if the doctrine of the representation of will is dropped, for then elective democracy is simply the choice of personnel and *not* of the legislative and governmental acts they perform. Democratic legitimacy then rests on the narrower ground that the governing personnel offer themselves up to veto when they seek re-election and that their acts are only thus subject to review.

Functional representation at first sight appears to get over such problems and contradictions. The representatives on the governing body of an association or those representing its interests on some co-ordinative external body can approximate to the actual wills and expressed interests of its membership because the purpose of the association is specific and the position of the membership on issues is determinable. The representatives on the governing bodies of functional associations are answerable to continuous and organized social constituencies, that is their members engaged in the activity in question, whereas the national electorate is constituted as an active body only every few years. The ordinary members of associations have as individuals as many votes as they have involvements in distinct associations. The representatives they elect are not mere delegates and fulfil a leadership function (although they should be subject to recall). Democracy thus becomes a co-ordinated system of functional representation.

Cole tended to slip into the view of functional democracy as 'true representation' (1920b: 119n.). Yet in terms of his critique there can be no such thing. It is true that functional representatives are likely to be concerned with fewer constituents and a more specific range of issues than the members of a parliament, but the problems of 'representing' wills remains if the number of persons to be represented is greater than a single agent and if the issue in question is more than a single discrete decision with a yes/no answer where the members' views can be canvassed and reported.

Functional representation cannot, therefore, be 'true representation', but simply a less defective and less generalized form of representation which still suffers from the same defects as all other members of the class when presented with the problem of expressing the actual wills of the represented. In fact Cole recognizes this, citing Rousseau as the source for the proposition that '[a]ll action through representatives. . . involves to a certain extent the substitution of the wills of the representatives for those of the represented' (1762: 120). At points Cole comes close to accepting the logic of Michels' *Political Parties* (1911), which would vitiate the democratic logic of any scheme of functional democracy.

Or would it? A series of functionally specific associations in which organization indeed leads to oligarchy would be less of a disaster than one inclusive and omnicompetent body in which the same substitution of the wills of the representative for those of the represented must necessarily occur. A plurality of specific oligarchies touches individuals less; since the purposes of associations are specific, and since they are not inclusive, members may withdraw from them, which they cannot do with the state. Thus overweening associational cliques face a real check. If Cole had kept to the critique of representation and not tried to eat his cake and have it by talking of the 'true' representativeness of functional democracy his position would have been more coherent and yet not less substantial.

The logic of function is the logic of plural association. One body cannot include all purposes and all individuals. Once we ignore the issue of the true representation of actual wills then it is likely that specific functional associations will indeed be more accountable to their members, but only if those members choose to involve themselves actively in their affairs. If they do not, then presumably cliques will run things and the members will tolerate this state of affairs because the very specific purpose of the organization leads them to respond on a 'limited liability' basis.

It might be argued that Cole's criticisms of representativeness follow from sticking too closely to the problematic of Rousseau. Yet Cole's choice of Rousseau is sound. Although it must be said that Rousseau sets the stakes impossibly high:

> The problem is to find a form of association which will defend and protect with the whole common force the person and goods of each associate, and in which each, while united himself with all, may still obey himself alone, and remain as free as before.
>
> (Rousseau 1762: 12)

But then the justificatory pay-off of any doctrine of representation that even approaches Rousseau's is correspondingly high, if it were to work. The concept of a represented popular will is the one way to square a sovereign legislative power with a strong doctrine of the rights of the governed. Democratic theory gropes toward Rousseau's problem whenever it is set a hard task of legitimatory practice. The French Constitution of 1791 is a good example; in this the national assembly embodies the sovereign power and will of the people, and simultaneously recognizes the inherent and inalienable 'rights of man and the citizen'.

Other conceptions of representative government which make less play with representing the will of the people involve fewer contradictions but also involve a weaker legitimation of the procedure. For example, the view of democracy as a decision procedure for selecting governing personnel and, thereby, offering some constraint on their actions if they subsequently wish to be re-elected is defensible but offers only a minimal justification. It is little more than a claim of 'what else?' It is a doctrine of the lesser evil, which relies on wholly unaccountable political power as its foil to make the minimal chance to reject rulers seem a real gain. It has worked to a considerable degree in the twentieth century, but largely because nakedly dictatorial power without real electoral challenge has existed aplenty. Cole was thus right to emphasize the doctrine of the representation of the will of the governed, because only such a doctrine can make the decisions of government appear to arise from the represented rather than their representatives.

In Britain, moreover, constitutional doctrine has been well hidden. Politicians have talked a language of democracy, mandates, the will of the people, etc., to the people, while constitutional lawyers talk another language entirely. British parliamentary government pre-dates modern representative democracy and the classic constitutional doctrine of the unlimited sovereignty of the King in parliament is entirely pre-democratic. Parliament is not sovereign because it is elected by the people but because it claims for itself a constitutive power. It can by a simple legislative act change its own procedures for elections or suspend elections altogether and indefinitely. This is indeed contestable constitutional law; although the idea of 'law' when confronted with such a boundless power seems absurd in all but the formal sense that laws are what Parliament enacts. It is, of course, lousy democratic legitimation, and even so formidable a constitutional lawyer as Dicey was driven to try and square the circle by positing a correspondence between the sovereign acts of Parliament, unconstrained and inimitable, and the wishes expressed by the people in elections. Here we have the coincidence of unconstrained political will and an electorally expressed will.

While this avoids the problems of wills being 'represented', the notion of coincidence presents him with even greater problems. In the end it rests on nothing more than providential beliefs about British political life.[36]

Laksi's defence of the principle of function is somewhat different from that of Cole. Laski conceived the real relations of authority in modern complex societies as federative and this 'federalism' as based on the interaction of social interests. Merely territorial units of representation and government tend to deny this complex pluralism adequate expression. Laski does not argue 'that representation by function is more real than representation by area' (1921: 69). Territorial units have a place. Rather, he argues, that 'the political opinions of men are largely determined by their industrial situation' (ibid.). Laski is not in favour, in 'The problem of administrative areas', of adding functional representation to that of territorial constituencies, nor of suppressing the latter. The answer is to give to major industrial interests full self-management:

> The real way, surely, in which to organize the interests of producers is by making out a delineation of industry and confiding the care of its problems to those most concerned with them. Anyone can see that the railways are as real as Lancashire; and exactly as the specifically local problems of Lancashire are dealt with by it, so could the specifically functional problems of the railways be dealt with by a governing body of its own.
>
> (Laski 1921: 70)

Ultimately such devolved functional self-managements would come to see the need to federate to solve common problems. Such an economic federation would carry on its business much like the self-governing Dominions before 1931: decentralized and outside Parliament's active control, but still under the formal scope of its legislative power.[37] Laski insists that democracy is incomplete despite the fact that the worker has the vote. For workers are limited in *where* they can vote: they can influence the complexion of the national government but lack even influence over the affairs of their place of work. As he says, 'It must be understood that there is a politics of industry not less real than the politics of the House of Commons' (1921: 84).

Laski's argument for functional decentralization is also as much an argument against state socialism or workers' power as it is a criticism of the *de facto* control of parliament by the capitalist class. Where political power is able to subordinate the other areas of society and in the interest of a particular group then liberty is threatened. Whether the control of state power be at the service of religious dogma or economic interest, and whether that interest be that of the capitalists or the workers, the result is to 'tread the path of despotism' (1921: 86). Laski thus does not favour a 'workers' state' or a system in which industrial councils enjoy *political* power, that is, power beyond their own sphere. A territorial system of representation is a check to the dangers of unconstrained industrial power. Laski would have no truck with syndicalism nor with conceptions of Soviet democracy.

Laski explicitly defends a pluralism both of social interests and of political institutions:

> The real truth is that the members of a state are powerless against an efficient centralization wielded in the interest of any social fragment, however large. It prevents that balance of associations which is the safeguard of liberty. . . . That is why the secret of liberty is in the division of power. But that political system in which a division of power is most securely maintained is a federal system.
>
> (Laski 1921: 86–7)

Laski's defence of the principle of function is thus closely tied to the view that function is one of the core elements of a *de facto* federalism, and that as such it helps to secure liberty by devolving power to the levels where it is best exercised. Laski's functionalism is based on actual political relations rather than formal constitutional law. A formally federal constitution is no guarantee of a federative system of authority. An explicitly federal political system may be capable of a strong centralizing tendency, whereas a centralized state may coexist with extensive devolution of power to functional self-government. It was Laski's hope that the latter could occur in Britain by a process of political evolution, and that the formal legal status of Parliament could be left untouched while a real and irreversible shift in power relationships took place outside it.

That shift did not occur and Laski's point is questionable in that the British central state has been so jealous in defending its claims to sovereign omnicompetence that it is difficult to see devolutionary political change happening without formal constitutional change.

One great advantage of the pluralist critique of representative democracy is that it undermines the classic critical response to attempts to extend the corporate representation of organized social interests: the claim that it undermines the sovereignty and authority of elected assemblies.[38] This seems to be a suitably 'democratic' criticism, until one remembers that democracy and representative democracy are not identical and that there is more than one possible scheme of representation. Arguments like those of Cole and Laski deny to the representation of individual electors through territorial constituencies any special privilege. Moreover, if the railways *are* as real as Lancashire, then there is every reason to seek the representation of that interest as directly as possible in any council where its affairs are debated and affected. The purpose of such corporatist representation is not to make laws but to secure the co-ordination of social activity and the compliance, based on consultation and bargaining, of organized social interests in an agreement for future action. The state is not thereby diminished but enhanced, not in its role as a 'sovereign' power, but as a social leader, orchestrating the affairs of society. The sociologist Emile Durkheim defined this form of democratic state best in his *Lectures on Civic Morals*. Democracy does not consist in representative assemblies *per se* but in the close and continuous communication between state and society. Durkheim envisaged such communication and co-ordination as best effected through the corporative representation of functional associations, professional guilds. In many ways, therefore, Durkheim is close to pluralism and, as we have seen, influenced Duguit. Democracy in this broader sense, which the pluralists in substance share with Durkheim, requires functional-corporate representation rather than being negated by it.[39]

Britain's Conservative government has set its face like flint against such a conception of the state's role and such a process of generating public policy from the co-ordinated agreement of organized social interests. Mrs Thatcher has done everything possible to maximize the distance between state and society, to act *on* society with the concentrated power of a hierarchical and centralized state. Necessarily, therefore, she has to emphasize 'sovereignty', a plenitude of exclusively directed power. To render this tolerable she must also of necessity place an intolerable burden on the democratic legitimation of electoral victories. Pluralism's conception of functional democracy provides a *principle* to justify corporatist arrangements, rather than merely pragmatic arguments of economic necessity (as with Wilson's 'Social Contract') or the economic success of those nations which practice such arrangements.

PLURALISM AND GUILD SOCIALISM

This is not the place to retell the history of Guild Socialism in great detail.[40] Of our three writers only Cole was an active Guild Socialist – although absolutely central to the movement. Guild Socialism, moreover, did not require doctrinal purity as a condition of membership and not all Guild Socialists were pluralists. For example, S.G. Hobson in *National Guilds and the State* (1920), despite his commitment to industrial democracy, seems to leave the territorial and sovereign state in place, but he is extremely vague on the matter.

Of greater interest is the parallel and rapid decline of the political movement and the theoretical idea. Guild Socialism's demise can be simply explained. As a political movement it eschewed parliamentary action and yet in practice relied absolutely on a friendly attitude or, failing that, favorable policies on the part of the state. It eschewed the Labour Party and yet depended on support for its programme from major unions. For a while unions like the Miners, Railwaymen, and, to a lesser extent, the Engineers were at least partly sympathetic in the immediate post-war period. Management, organized labour, and the state were exploring new solutions under the threat of the Bolshevik Revolution and syndicalist labour unrest in Britain – as the example of the National Industrial Conference of 1919, for which Cole helped organize the union side, indicates. The Whitley Report of 1917 promised a measure of co–determination in industry. The nationalization of the mines and railways was contemplated. The Housing Act of 1919 provided central government finance for house building and in the form of regular advances of working capital which enabled the Building Guilds, the most successful of Guild Socialist practical ventures, to get started.

Once the post-war fear of a revolutionary crisis passed then management and the state returned to distinctly 'business-as-usual' attitudes and refused to contemplate any active policy of co-determination with organized labour. The Guild Socialists were the major losers, because without state support for co-determination they had no political space within which to push their ideas and little political credibility. With a change in the system of house-building finance in 1921 the Building Guilds collapsed for want of working capital.

Guild Socialism failed to convert the Fabian Society, let alone the Labour Party. In order to survive as a political programme it required, contrary to its own beliefs, the electoral victory of a sympathetic government. The conservative trade unionists, who saw their function as obtaining a better deal for wage labour and not an abolition of the wages system, would have none of it, and they set the agenda of the Labour Party. The Liberals when running scared of Bolshevism offered more openings in fact, but Liberalism was about to undergo a fatal and rapid decline as a party. Guild Socialism was finally rent apart when its left wing joined the newly formed Communist Party and worked to wreck the Guild Socialist movement from within.

Pluralism as a political theory expired because it lacked any credibility when there was no major political force or social interest pushing for changes in the constitution and the structure of power. State power and state sovereignty were decisively asserted over organized labour in the General Strike of 1926. The Labour Party had no serious plans for political reform. Cole and Laski both moved on to involvement in ideas and projects where they could have influence. The state which had seemed discredited before the First World War, unable to cope with labour, syndicalist, suffragette, and Irish unrest, was massively strengthened during the First World War. National ownership, planning, and the efficiency of state-run services gained a tremendous fillip, and became the model for Labour Party socialists. Anti-collectivism and anti-statism were in retreat. The Great Crash of 1929 prompted demands from the left for more not less state action.

Indeed, the statist current was massively reinforced by the experience of state economic control during the Second World

War and the 1945 Labour Government. The Labour party, already set in a statist mould and rejecting all serious reform of the major political institutions, identified state provision with best practice. A large part of it still does. It has fallen to Mrs Thatcher and the Conservatives to try to 'discredit' the state in matters of economic welfare and distribution. Yet the Conservatives have a resolutely anti-pluralist conception of state power and Mrs Thatcher is the stoutest defender of the unlimited sovereignty of Parliament. If pluralism has returned to the political agenda it is because of the political excesses of an anti-collectivist and self-confessed advocate of 'rolling back the state'. This is an irony the pluralists might well have appreciated.

NOTES

1. This revival of radical democratic thinking about government is both international and so prolific that one can do little more than list some of the more interesting contributions: Bobbio (1987), (1988), Bowles and Gintis (1986), Burnheim (1985), Dahl (1985), Held (1987), Keane (1988), Rustin (1985), and Walzer (1983).

2. This may appear to be a caricature, but it is the strict logic of Marxism as political theory, and even Marxists who see that modern forms of democracy and law are complex, have real benefits, and that these benefits may need defending, like Bob Fine (1984), still end up treating them as way stations to a more real future in which the state will vanish. For the anti-political logic of Marxist political theory, its disastrous mixture of cynicism about current politics and utopianism, see Polan (1984).

3. Jean Bodin (c. 1530-96) – Les Six Livres de la République (1583): for a modern abridged translation, see Bodin (1955); Thomas Hobbes (1588-1679) – Leviathan (1651); John Austin (1790-1859) – The Province of Jurisprudence Determined (1832).

4. There is, of course, a third current of thinking in social science termed 'pluralist' – the concept of 'plural society', originated by J.S. Furnivall and critically developed by L. Kuper and M.G. Smith, in which in a colonial or post-colonial situation social groups live side by side but have a distinct communal existence, and in which they mix through and are linked only by the market. For a brief account see Nicholls (1975: 119-23) and for a major statement of the position see M.G. Smith (1974: chapter 7).

5. For the clearest example of the theoretical spelling out of pluralism see Dahl (1956), and for a defence of Dahl's theory of political competition against Marxist criticism see Hirst (1987a).

6. Antagonistic pluralism is a condition in which fundamentally opposed political forces compete through formally democratic institutions to

41

pursue their own specific interests by means of state power. In its most extreme form each of the political forces is willing to dismantle the democratic apparatus once it has propelled them into power. Late Weimar is the classic case of antagonistic pluralism and the Communists and Nazis the main players. The threat of antagonistic pluralism is accurately defined in modern pluralist analysis – see Dahl (1982) – but was first diagnosed by the conservative legal theorist Carl Schmitt. For a brief discussion of the term and Schmitt's analysis see Hirst (1986: 13-14 and chapter 4).

7. See Lord Hailsham (1978).

8. The phrase is Eric Hobsbawm's in *Marxism Today* (April 1988: 14).

9. For an exceptionally enlightening view of how such corporate co-determination of economic policy though inter-interest bargaining in states like Austria and Sweden has worked see Katzenstein (1985).

10. 'The discredited state', *The Political Quarterly* 5 (February 1915): 101 – this is *not* the same journal as the later and better-known *Political Quarterly*; it is reprinted in Barker (1930). See also Barker (1918).

11. Krabbe's work is extensively, if critically discussed in Hsiao (1927); see also and English translation of Krabbe's *The Modern Idea of the State* (1922). Duguit is discussed below and references are given in the notes for further reading at the end of this section; see also Coker (1921).

12. For samples of the contemporary reception of pluralism see: Coker (1921), Elliott (1928), Ellis (1920), Follet (1918), Korff (1923), Renner (1921), Sabine (1923), and Schmitt (1930). Other critical receptions of pluralism are mentioned in the text and in suggestions for further reading, most notably McIlwain (1939) and Hsiao (1927).

13. See the reference to Barker in Note 10 above – his critical views on pluralism and its limitations are to be found in his textbook *Principles of Social and Political Theory* (1951) written long after the intellectual demise of pluralism. For an example of Lindsay's work in the heyday of pluralism, see 'The state in recent political theory' *Political Quarterly* 1 (February 1914): 128-45; the remarks about this journal in Note 10 above apply here too.

14. For an example of Russell's view of the state in this period see his contribution to the symposium 'The nature of the state in view of its external relations', *Proceedings of the Aristotelian Society* NS, XVI (1915): 301-10. The other papers by C. Delisle Burns and G.D.H. Cole are of interest. See also Russell's *Principles of Social Reconstruction* (1916).

15. For studies of Orage and *The New Age* see Mairet (1936), Martin (1967), Matthews (1979), and Selver (1959). For Hobson see his autobiography *Pilgrim to the Left; National Guilds. . .* (1914) does not have Hobson's name on the title page and he accused Orage of plagiarizing his work; see also Hobson (1920) and (1936). For de Maeztu see his *Authority, Liberty and Function* (1916).

16. For Figgis's influence on Temple and church politics see Nicholls (1975: 109-10), and for a study of Temple's Christian Socialism see Dorrien (1986).

17. For Figgis's influence on Laski see Laski's letter to Bertrand Russell (Russell *Autobiography*: 342), and Nicholls says: 'Barker tells us that it was Figgis, and through Figgis Maitland and Gierke, who were the chief influences on Laski in his New College days' (1975: 45). For Barker's own memoirs see *Age and Youth* (1953). For Holmes's influence on Laski see *Holmes-Laski Letters* (1953). Laski's and Cole's careers proceeded on parallel lines, but there seems to have been no love lost between them, see M. Cole (1971: 201-3).

18. H.J. Laski 'The pluralist state' in *The Foundations of Sovereignty*. . . (1921: 244), cited by Nicholls (1975: 46).

19. See H.J. Laski *A Grammar of Politics* fifth edition (1967 and still in print).

20. In his 'The components of the national culture', *New Left Review* 50, 1968.

21. Cole (1920b: 93) says: 'For an awful example [of metaphysical theory of the state] see the writings of Dr Bernard Bosanquet'. For Green, see his *Lectures on the Principles of Political Obligation* (1882) and for an outstanding critical study Richter (1964). F.H. Bradley's most influential work on social and political thought is his *Ethical Studies* (1876); see Wollheim (1959: chapter 6) for a critical discussion of his ethical theory. Ernest Barker's *Political Thought in England from Herbert Spencer to the Present Day* (1915a) is an invaluable guide to political thought in this period and the context from which the pluralists emerged.

22. For Gierke's work see *Political Theories of the Middle Age* (1900), *Natural Law and the Theory of Society* (1934), and *The Development of Political Theory* (1939), a work on the influence of Johannes Althusius.

23. See Lewis (1935) for a valuable monograph on Gierke which makes his non-pluralism clear; see also S. Mogi (1932).

24. See *Churches in the Modern State* (1913: 18-22). Lord Macnaghten in a dissenting judgment in the Free Church of Scotland Appeals case said:

> Was the Church. . . so bound and tied by the tenets prevailing at the time of the Disruption, that departure from these tenets in any matter of substance would be a violation of that profession or testimony which may be called the unwritten charter of her foundation, and so necessarily involve a breach of trust in the administration of funds committed for no other purpose but the support of the Free Church. . . ? Was the Free Church by the very condition of her existence forced to cling to her Subordinate Standards with so desperate a grip that she had lost hold and touch of the Supreme standard of her faith? Was she from birth incapable of all growth and development? Was she. . . a dead branch and not a living Church?
>
> Orr, Report of Free Church of Scotland case
> p.573, S.C.1f. 1083 (1903)

This passage is cited by Laski in 'The personality of associations' (1921: 160), but is omitted in the text printed below.

25. Figgis developed the irony of the Law Lords simultaneously sticking to the terms of the original trust and in fact delving into theology to determine what powers the Church had:

> Tacitly, if not explicitly [the Lords] denied any real and inherent power of development; and further, so far from refusing to consider theological questions, they listened to a long argument of Mr. (now Lord) Haldane designed to show that from the higher Hegelian standpoint Calvinism and Arminianism were really the same thing. This the Lords were forced to do in order to judge whether or no the new Act contravened the trust. Thus on the one hand the judgement denies to a Free Church the power of defining and developing in its own doctrine, and on the other, while disclaiming interference in theological matters, it practically exercises it under the plea of considering the question of whether or no the trust had been violated.

> (Figgis 1913: 21-2)

26. See Hadden (1977) for an account of company law from a radical perspective, which discusses the issue of legal obligation to employees and the community and how best to incorporate it in company law. See also Hirst (1979) for a critique of the Marxist account of the joint-stock company and a challenge to Marxist indifference to company law reform; chapter 5, especially pp. 127-44.

27. Zylstra discusses Cohen's critique (1970: 35-7); the essay of Cohen that embodies the views which persuaded Laski is 'Communal ghosts and other perils in social philosophy' (1919).

20. Laski had the greatest respect for William James's A Pluralistic Universe (1909). Carl Schmitt, in an essay sharply critical of pluralism (1930), noted this influence and claimed that pragmatist (anti-)metaphysics were the 'political theology' of pluralism. 'Political theology' for Schmitt is the correspondence between theological and metaphysical world views and a definite conception of the state, see Schmitt (1985). Schmitt's (1930) critique of pluralism is the most insightful and challenging, in large measure because pluralism is in direct contradiction to his own view of politics and the state. For Schmitt the definitive feature of the political is the opposition of friend and enemy: politics is a struggle, and is only stabilized in the force of a decisive decision which constitutes the sovereign power. The very ideal of plural loyalties within the state threatens to create that *bellum omnium contra omnes* which stabilized sovereign power must use its power of decision to prevent. For this see Schmitt's The Concept of the Political (1976) and Hirst (1987b).

29. This is clear from Laski's 'Law and the state' below; it is also interesting to note that Laski was the supervisor of Franz Neumann's

Ph.D. thesis in 1936 when Neumann was a refugee from Nazi persecution. Neumann's thesis, now at last published as *The Rule of Law* (1986), conceives law as a complex interweaving of *voluntas*, the positive political will and power to make rules, and *ratio*, the requirement that the regulative activities of law strive to embody social utility.

30. This view is strongly pressed by C.H. McIlwain in his paper 'Sovereignty' *Economica* November 1926, and reprinted in McIlwain (1939).

31. The *Lex Regia* – the claimed basis of third-century jurists for the Emperor's right to be sole legislator. That it is a fictional legitimation of a *de facto* power is clear from Buckland (1921: 16). The point often made against Figgis, that the Middle Ages did indeed know and expound the concept of 'sovereignty', depends on reading into the claims of Pope and Emperor to a power of universal dominion stretching back to Rome a modern concept of *state* sovereignty. This is not implied, since the modern concept of the state is lacking. Figgis is too good an historian to make this error; it results from absolutist jurisconsults seeking previous legitimations for the claims of absolutism, not from Figgis's misreading of the departure involved in absolutism. See *From Gerson to Grotius* (1916: 7-9).

32. For an analysis of Bodin and Hobbes and their relationship to absolutism see Kosselleck (1988). It is mutual fear of civil war and unchecked religious tensions that leads both of them to support absolutist sovereign power.

33. Rousseau advocates a policy of *divisio et impera*, which strengthens the state by minimizing the power of associations if they cannot be dispensed with: 'But if there are partial societies, it is best to have as many as possible and to prevent them from being unequal' *Social Contract* (1762: 23).

34. See George Dangerfield's classic *The Strange Death of Liberal England* (1962).

35. See Hayward (1960) for the relationship between Durkheim and Duguit.

36. Dicey says:

All that it is here necessary to insist upon is that the essential property of representative government is to produce coincidence between the wishes of the sovereign and the wishes of the subjects; to make, in short, the two limitations on the exercise of sovereignty absolutely coincident. This, which is true in its measure of all real representative government, applies with special truth to the English House of Commons.

(Dicey 1920: 81).

I am grateful to Anthony Carty's (unpublished) 'A postmodernist critique of parliamentary sovereignty', *Critical Legal Conference* (1988), for this point.

37. That was the position of the self-governing Dominions before they were granted full legislative autonomy by the Statute of Westminster 1931 – Laski's essay dates from 1921.
38. See S. Brittan (1983).
39. For discussions of Durkheim's political ideas see Hayward (1960), Hearn (1985), and Richter (1964).
40. For those interested in its history see the suggestions for further reading. Glass (1966) and Matthews (1979) have useful bibliographies which cite most of the relevant literature; works either not cited there or to which attention must be drawn are Pierson (1979), Pribicevic (1959), and Black (1984). Two Ph.D. theses are of particular value on Guild Socialism: Keith Hotten *The Labour Party and the Enterprise*, chapter 4, pp. 186-264, University of London, 1988, and H. Irving *Romanticism and British Socialism: Art and Work in Socialist Thought (1889-1920)*, University of Sydney, 1986. Major Guild Socialist texts – other than those of Cole and Hobson cited in further reading, in Note 15 above, and in the main text – are: 'The Storrington Document' (1914), a brief manifesto, in Briggs and Saville (eds) (1971); G.D.H. Cole and W. Mellor *The Meaning of Industrial Democracy* (1919); G.D.H. Cole 'Guild Socialism', *Fabian Tract* 192 (1920); M.B. Reckitt and C.E. Bechofer *The Meaning of National Guilds* (1920).

SUGGESTIONS FOR FURTHER READING

A comprehensive bibliography of pluralist texts and commentaries on them is unnecessary as full bibliographies of pluralism are to be found in Hsiao (1927), Magid (1941), and Nicholls (1975). Zylstra (1970) contains a full bibliography on Laski, Wright (1979) on Cole.

David Nicholls's *The Pluralist State* is the best overall book on English pluralism and also the best introduction to the ideas of J.N. Figgis. K.C. Hsiao's *Political Pluralism* (1927) is a thorough early survey that covers both English and continental sources, but is highly and often irritatingly critical. Bernard Zylstra's *From Pluralism to Collectivism* (1970) is the best book on this aspect of Laski's work and is definitely superior to H.A. Deane's *The Political Ideas of Harold J. Laski* (1955). A.W. Wright's *G.D.H. Cole and Socialist Democracy* (1979) is excellent on pluralism and for Cole's continuing commitment to industrial democracy and is much superior to L.P. Carpenter's *G.D.H. Cole: An Intellectual Biography* (1973). Margaret Cole's *The Life of G.D.H. Cole* (1971) is consistently valuable for Cole's Guild Socialist period and beyond, if the reader is interested.

For Gierke's thought see J.D.Lewis's *The Genossenschaft Theory of Otto Von Gierke* (1935). For Duguit, apart from Laski's Introduction to Duguit's *Law in the Modern State* (1921) and Duguit's survey of 'The law and the state' *Harvard Law Review* (1917, 31 (1): 1-185), see 'Solidarist Syndicalism: Durkheim and Duguit' by J.E.S. Hayward, *Sociological Review* 8 (1), July 1960: 14-36 and 8 (2), December 1960: 185-202. For

Guild Socialism proper there is a vast literature. By far the best source is the contemporary blow by blow account of the American academic Niles Carpenter, *Guild Socialism* (1922). S.T. Glass's *The Responsible Society: The Ideas of Guild Socialism* (1966) is a short and useful modern introduction. Frank Matthews's 'The ladder of becoming. . . ', in David E. Martin and David Rubenstein (eds) *Ideology and the Labour Movement* (1979), is good for the origins of Guild Socialism and the ideas of A.J. Penty and the influence of A.R.Orage.

Part One

THE SOCIAL THEORY

G.D.H. Cole

Chapter One

SOME NAMES AND THEIR MEANING

Every developed *community* may be regarded as giving rise to an organized *society*, within which there exists a vast complex of social *customs, institutions,* and *associations,* through which the *members* or citizens express themselves and secure in part the fulfilment of the various *purposes* which some or all of them have in common. There are in this sentence at least seven words upon the clear definition of which success in our subsequent inquiry largely depends.

Community is the broadest and most inclusive of the words which we have to define. By a 'community' I mean a complex of social life, a complex including a number of human beings living together under conditions of social relationship, bound together by a common, however constantly changing, stock of conventions, customs, and traditions, and conscious to some extent of common social objects and interests. It will be seen at once that this is a very wide and elastic form of definition, under which a wide variety of social groups might be included. It is, indeed, of the essence of community that its definition should be this elastic; for 'community' is essentially a subjective term, and the reality of it consists in the consciousness of it among its members. Thus a family is, or may be, a community, and any group which is, in a certain degree, self–contained and self–subsistent is or may be a community. A medieval university, a monastic brotherhood, a co-operative colony – these and many more may possess those elements of social comprehensiveness which give a right to the title of community.

But, if the word is wide and inclusive enough in one aspect, it is essentially limited in another. In order to be a community, a group

'Some names and their meaning' first appeared as Chapter Two of G.D.H. Cole (1920) *The Social Theory.*

must exist for the good life and not merely for the furtherance of some specific and partial purpose. Thus, a cricket club, or a trade union, or a political party is not a community, because it is not a self–contained group of complete human beings, but an association formed for the furtherance of a particular interest common to a number of persons who have other interests outside it. A community is thus essentially a social unit or group to which human beings belong, as distinguished from an association with which they are only connected.

Yet, despite this wholeness and universality which are of the nature of community, it is not the case that a man can belong to one community only. A community is an inclusive circle of social life; but round many narrow circles of family may be drawn the wider circle of the city, and round many circles of city the yet wider circle of the province or the nation, while round all the circles of nation is drawn the yet wider and more cosmopolitan circle of world civilization itself. No one of these wider circles necessarily absorbs the narrower circles within it: they may maintain themselves as real and inclusive centres of social life within the wider communities beyond them. A man is not less a member of his family or a citizen of his city for being an Englishman or a cosmopolitan. Membership of two communities may lead, for the individual, to a real conflict of loyalties; but the reality of the conflict only serves to measure the reality of the communal obligation involved.

Our definition does not, of course, enable us to say exactly and in every instance what is a community and what is not. Being a community is a matter of degree, and all communities, being actual, are also necessarily imperfect and incomplete. There may often arise, not merely a dispute, but an actual doubt in the minds of the persons concerned to what community they belong, as for instance in a border country which hardly knows with which of the peoples it lies between its community of tradition, interest, and feeling is the stronger. Again, a province or a town may be merely an administrative area, with no common life or feeling of its own, or it may be a real and inclusive centre of social life. Moreover, it may pass by insensible stages from one condition to the other, as when a depopulated strip of countryside becomes first a formless urban district and then gradually assumes the form and feeling of a town or city, changes and developments in administrative organization usually, but not necessarily, accompanying the change in feeling. There are groups which obviously deserve the name of communities, and groups which obviously do not deserve it; but there are also countless groups of which it is difficult to say, at any particular moment, whether they deserve the name or not.

It is plain, then, that our thing, 'a community', does not necessarily involve any particular form of social organization, or indeed any social organization at all. It is not an institution or a formal association, but a centre of feeling, a group felt by its members to be a real and operative unity. In any community larger than the family, however, this feeling of unity, with its accompanying need for common action, almost necessarily involves conscious and formal organization. The feeling of unity makes it easy for the members of a community to associate themselves together for the various purposes which they have in common, and, where the community is free from external hindrances, such association surely arises and is devoted to the execution of these common purposes. Where a community is not free, and an external power hinders or attempts to prevent organization, association still asserts itself, but instead of directing itself to the fulfilment of the various social needs of the group, almost every association is diverted to subserve the task of emancipating the community from external hindrances. This, for instance, is the position in Ireland at the present time.

We are concerned in this study with community as a whole, and with communities of every kind; but our chief interest is necessarily with those larger and more complex communities which have the largest social content and the most diversified social organization. It is, indeed, in relation to these that the principal difficulties arise. The simple fact of community is easy enough to appreciate; but in a large and highly developed social group, internal organization, and cross–currents of organization which, assignable to wider communities, overleap the frontiers of the smaller groups and communities within them, often loom so large that the fact of community itself tends to disappear from sight. The desire to counter this tendency is, as we shall see later, one of the principal causes of the facile, but fatal, identification of community with 'state', which is so often made by social theorists.

'Every developed community', we began by declaring, 'may be regarded as giving rise to an organized *society*'. In the small community of the family this distinction does not today, or usually, arise. But for larger communities the distinction is of vital importance. In every such community there is a part of the common life which is definitely and formally organized, regulated by laws and directed by associations formed for social purposes. I mean to use the term *society* to denote the complex of organized associations and institutions within the community.

I am conscious in this use of giving the word 'society' a more definite meaning than those with which it is customarily employed. Indeed, the meaning here assigned to it is to a certain extent artificial, but by no means entirely so. We do in fact constantly speak of society when we wish to denote neither the whole complex of community nor any particular association or institution, but the sum total of organized social structure which is the resultant of the various associations and institutions within a community. . . .

'Society', then, is not a complete circle of social life, or a social group of human beings, but a resultant of the interaction and complementary character of the various functional associations and institutions. Its concern is solely with the organized co-operation of human beings, and its development consists not directly in the feeling of community among individuals, but in the better coherence and more harmonious relationship of the various functional bodies within the community.

We have seen that a developed community, larger than the family, can hardly exist without institutions and associations; that is, without society. Society, on the other hand, may exist, if imperfectly, yet in a developed form, without real community, or with only a very slender basis of community. The union of Ireland and Great Britain under a single Parliament, and with a large system of associations and institutions extending to both, is an instance of a society with but the shadow of a basis of community. In such a case, as we shall see, the more artificial an association or institution is, or the greater the element of coercion it includes, the more it is inclined to persist, whereas the more voluntary and spontaneous forms of organization find it hard to live under such conditions. The growth of a purely Irish Labour Movement, with a tendency to break away from the British Movement, is an example of this difficulty.

Society, as a complex of organizations, cannot stand for, or express, all human life within a community, or the whole life of any single human being. Indeed, it is probably true that what is best and most human in men and women escapes almost entirely from the net of society, because it is incapable of being organized. Society is concerned mainly with rights and duties, with deliberate purposes and interests. While the community is essentially a centre of feeling, society is a centre, or rather a group of centres, of deliberation and planning, concerned far more with means than with ends. It is, of course, true that an association or an institution can arouse in us and make us attach to it sentiments of loyalty as well as calculated adherences; but at least the better part of our feelings of love and devotion are put forth in purely personal relationships, or in the narrow but intense community of the family. It is essential that associations and institutions, and even that society itself, should be able to appeal to our sentiments of loyalty and devotion, but it would be wrong to desire that these sentiments should be absorbed in them. As long as human life remains, most of the best things in it will remain outside the bounds and scope of organization, and it will be the chief function of society so to organize these parts of human life which respond to organization as to afford the fullest opportunity for the development of those human experiences and relationships to which organization is the cold touch of death.

Society, like community, is a matter of degree. It depends not only on the volume and extent of associative and institutional life in the community, but still more on the coherence and co–operative working of the various associations and institutions. Where associative and institutional life is vigorous, but there exist distinct castes and classes, each with its own network of organizations, not co–operating but conflicting and hostile, then society exists indeed, but only in a very low degree. The highest development of society consists not only in the general diffusion of associations and institutions over every organizable tract of social life, but also in the harmonious co-operation of all the various bodies, each fulfilling its proper function within society, in harmony and agreement with the others. . . .

We have so far spoken of *associations* and *institutions* uncritically, without any attempt to examine their nature, or to define the sense in which the terms are used. To do this is our next task. We have seen that every developed community includes a network of associations and institutions of the most various kinds, and we have now to explain their character. . . .

By an *association* I mean any group of persons pursuing a common purpose or system or aggregation of purposes by a course of co–operative action extending beyond a single act, and, for this purpose, agreeing together upon certain methods of procedure, and laying down, in however rudimentary a form, rules for common action. At least two things are fundamentally necessary to any association – a common purpose or purposes and, to a certain extent, rules of common action.

The primary condition of all association is a common purpose; for the object of all associations being the attainment of some end, there can be no association unless the attainment of that end is the purpose of the members. The 'end', 'object', or 'interest', or, as I prefer to call it, the 'purpose', is the *raison d'être* of every association. But, while this is a fundamental point, it is important that it should not be pushed too far. The presence of a common purpose does not imply that it must be fully and consciously apprehended by all or, even in the case of already established associations, a majority of the members. . . .

Second, it must be borne in mind that very many associations have, not a single, clearly definable purpose, but a number of purposes more or less intimately related one to another. In these cases, while, except in the circumstances contemplated above, each member is as a rule conscious of at least one of the purposes of the association, it does not follow that each member is conscious of, or shares in the desire to forward, each of the purposes in view. This may occur either because a member does not fully appreciate the interrelation of the various purposes, and therefore fails to appreciate the significance of some of them, or because he does really differ from his fellows as to some of the purposes contemplated by the association, while agreeing with him about the rest, and feeling the association to be worth while for their sake alone. For example, when a trade union or an employers' association combines political and industrial activities, there will be some who, agreeing with the principal objects of the association and therefore desiring to remain members, will dissent from some of its purposes and methods. The Osborne Judgment controversy some years ago, and the recent controversy about the use of 'direct action' for political purposes, alike served to force this issue to the front in the case of trade unions. . . .

Third, we must remember that associations are sustained by human beings, and are therefore capable of constant development. Changing circumstances, or a changing appreciation of the same circumstances, may impel the members of an association to widen or to narrow its objects, or to vary them from time to time. All associations possess a considerable elasticity in this respect, the degree of their elasticity varying largely with the amount of coherence they possess – which in turn depends mainly upon the intensity of the communal feeling which inspires them. But there is for every association a limit of elasticity, and, strained beyond this point by the inclusion of new purposes, the association will break, and a new one have to be created to fulfil the new purposes. The atrophy of the original purposes causes associations to decay. They may renew themselves by assuming new purposes; but, if the change is too big or too violent, they break. Decay or breakage is the fate of every association in the end; and as, from one cause or the other, associations disappear, men create new ones to take their place.

So much for the common purposes which are the moving and sustaining principle of all associations. But, as we saw, there is a secondary characteristic which is essential. Every association must, in some degree, prescribe common rules of action for its members. These rules may be very few and very rudimentary, and they commonly deal with the conduct of the members only in relation to the purposes of the association, though they often include written or unwritten moral rules of conduct designed to preserve the reputation of the association. . . . These rules generally include both general rules designed to cover particular cases as they arise, and particular directions issued by the governing body of the association for guidance in particular cases directly. . . .

Our definition of the word 'association' is clearly very wide indeed. It excludes momentary groups formed, without definite organization, to carry out some single immediate object; but it includes all organized groups possessed of a purpose entailing a course of action. It draws no distinction between groups whose purpose is in some sense political or social or communal, and groups whose purpose is purely sociable or recreational. It covers a football club or a dining club fully as much as a church, a trade union, or a political party.

Of course, it makes a great difference in the importance of an association, not only how far it is representative of those concerned in its purpose, but also how important its purpose is. But it is impossible to draw a theoretical line of distinction between associations which are 'social' and associations which are only sociable. For some practical purposes, as for representation upon public bodies, it is no doubt essential to draw such a distinction; but it is necessary to recognize that, however drawn, it cannot be more than empirical. *All* associations are, in their various manners and degrees, parts of society.

We can now turn to the word which, in the early part of this chapter, was so often used in close conjunction with the word 'association'. What is an *institution*, and in what sense is the word used in this book? I find the thing for which the word stands difficult to define at all, and impossible to define in any but a largely negative manner. It is not, though it may manifest itself in or through, a group or association, nor has it, strictly speaking, any members. It does, of course, being a social thing, appear in, and operate through, human beings and associations; but it depends for its institutional status, not upon a particular group of persons who are its members, frame its rules, and seek to effect through it a common purpose, but upon a general acceptance and recognition by the members of the community, backed by a sustaining force of custom or tradition, with or without the sanction of law. It is easily recognizable in some of its principal instances – marriage, monogamy, monarchy, peerage, caste, capitalism, and many others belonging to different ages and civilizations. . . .

It is important to notice that, in the sense in which we are using the word, army, navy, church, and state are not 'institutions', but associations in which institutions may be held to be embodied or expressed. Thus the church is an association in which the institution of religion is more or less perfectly embodied, the state an association more or less perfectly embodying the institution of political government, army and navy associations expressive of the institution of natural force, and so on.

Now, an idea is not an 'institution' merely because it is widely or generally held or accepted. It is an 'institution' only if, in addition to being so accepted, it is embodied in some external form of social structure or communal custom, either in an association or in some actual form of social behaviour.

We may, then, provisionally define an 'institution' as a recognized custom or form of social tradition or idea, manifested in and through human beings either in their personal conduct and relationships or through organized groups or associations. Thus, the institution of monarchy is manifested in a king and the social recognition accorded to him, the institution of peerage in the various peers and their status, the institution of marriage in the various married persons and their social recognition. In the second group of cases, the position appears to be rather different for there we first encounter a form of association and then recognize that its social status is due largely to the fact that it embodies an institution. In these cases, we have to study the association directly as an association, and then to study it further in its character as the embodiment of an institution.

An institution is, in fact, an idea which is manifested concretely in some aspect of social conduct, and which forms a part of the underlying assumptions of communal life. This does not make it permanent, or immune from decay or dissolution, though. . . it does give to it an additional strength and power of survival. It can, however, change or decay. A monarchical society may become a republic, if it finds that the monarchical institution has outlived its use. The guild system was in the Middle Ages the embodiment of an institution, but the modern [livery] companies which have descended from the guilds have sunk down to the level of unimportant associations and have lost all claim to institutional status.

But, although institutions and their embodiments change, decay, and die, it is characteristic of them to possess a greater degree of permanence than belongs to most associations. This relative permanence has both its good and its bad side. It helps to assure to an association or custom, which successfully embodies an idea found to be vital to the community, a greater stability than its members or its familiarity alone could assure to it, by giving it a communal sanction and status; but it also tends to cause the survival of associations and customs which have acquired an institutional character long after they have ceased to be useful. Our estimate of the advantages and disadvantages of institutions will depend mainly upon our temperament. The temperamental conservative (in no party sense) sees in institutions the bulwark of society: the temperamental innovator sees in them the greatest barrier to progress. . . .

Chapter Two

THE PRINCIPLE OF FUNCTION

Although our last chapter was concerned primarily with definitions, a number of important conclusions have emerged from it. We have learnt to regard community as a complex of individuals, associations, institutions, and customs in varied and multiform relationships; we have learnt to regard society as a complex of associations and institutions expressing, not the whole of the communal life, but that part of it which is organized; and we have learnt to see in associations bodies created by the wills of individuals for the expression and fulfilment of purposes which they have in common. We have, in fact, already penetrated the essential and underlying structure of social life.

There is, however, at least one point of ultimate principle in relation to which our vision is still fundamentally incomplete. Our method has forced us so far to look at each form of social structure in something like isolation from the others. . . . But we have not . . . as yet made clear the structural principle which makes the complexities of social life into something at least approaching a coherent whole. The underlying principle of community, indeed, is neither more nor less than community itself – the sense of unity and social brotherhood which permeates a mass of men and women and makes them, in a real sense, one. But we have not seen what is the underlying principle of *social organization,* a principle which must be distinct from the principle of community, however dependent upon it. This principle is the principle of *function.* . . .

We have seen that men make, and enter into, associations for the purpose of satisfying common wants, that is, in terms of action, for the execution of common purposes. Every such purpose or

'The Principle of function' first appeared as Chapter Three of G.D.H. Cole (1920) *The Social Theory.*

group of purposes is the basis of the *function* of the association which has been called into being for its fulfilment. Again, every institution in society has an object which has determined the main lines of its growth. The fulfilment of this object is, then, the necessary basis of the function of the institution. Of course, either an association or an institution may be itself complex and have a variety of related purposes or objects, and therefore perhaps a variety of related functions. But as the purpose or object behind an association or institution must be specific and in some degree intelligible in order to have the power to call the association or institution into being, so the functions of all associations and institutions, however they may change and develop, are, in the last resort, also specific.

This is the reason why the functional principle is finally applicable to associations and institutions, but not to individuals. Every individual is in his nature universal: his actions and courses of action, his purposes and desires, are specific because he makes them so; but he himself is not, and cannot be, made specific, and therefore cannot be expressed in terms of function. This essential difference makes once more manifest the falsity of the parallel that is often drawn between individuals and associations. An association is not, and cannot be, in any real sense, a 'person', because it is specific and functional, and not universal. The individual becomes 'functional', or rather 'multi-functional', only by limiting himself; the association is functional and limited by its very nature.

But function is not so much the final cause of each separate association, as the principle underlying the unity and coherence of associations. We have seen that the value and full development of society depends not only on the wide prevalence and diffusion of association in the commonwealth, but also on the successful co-operation and coherence of the various associations. The possibility of this coherence depends upon the fulfilment by each association of its social function. In so far as the various associations fulfil their respective social purposes, and in so far as these purposes are themselves complementary and necessary for social well-being, the welter of associations in the community is converted into a coherent society. In so far as the associations work irrespective of their function in a social whole, or set before themselves purposes which are mutually contradictory and

61

irreconcilable with the good of the whole, the development out of the welter of associations of a coherent society is thwarted and retarded.

It will be observed that a new consideration has been introduced into the argument in the course of the preceding paragraph. In treating function as the characteristic, not of an isolated association, but of an association as a factor in a coherent social whole, or at least a social whole capable of coherence, we have introduced a consideration of value which compels us to scrutinize the purpose of each particular association in the light of its communal value in and for the whole. . . .

The members of an association can only come together and work together in the association if they have, to a certain extent, a common object or purpose. . . . Such a purpose may be one that is socially desirable, or it may be one that hardly affects any person outside the association for either good or ill, or it may be definitely anti-social. The mere fact that the association seeks only the 'interest' of its own members (as, if the word 'interest' is understood in a wide enough sense, every association, like every individual, must do) is not enough to make it anti–social, or to prevent it from being socially desirable. It is for the good of the community that each group within it should keep itself amused, instructed, developed; for these goods of individuals are, so far, clear additions to the common stock of happiness, which can only be the happiness of individuals. An association becomes anti-social not in seeking the good of its own members, but in seeking their good in ways which detract from the good of others. Such detraction only occurs either when one association's objects come into conflict with those of another, so that both cannot be fully satisfied, or when an association aims at an object which conflicts with the personal objects of some individual, whether a member of the association or not. Wherever such a conflict occurs, coherence is impaired, and the complementary working of associations and individuals is made less perfect. The existence of conflict shows that something is wrong; but it does not, of course, show on which side the wrong lies, or how it is distributed between the two.

We seem here to be confronted with a difficulty. We cannot accept the objects of each association, just as its members have made them, as making for a coherent society and a development of the sense of community. It is, indeed, manifest that very many associations, in seeking a partial good for their own members, are acting anti-socially and impairing the coherence of society as a whole. We must, therefore, criticize and value associations in accordance with some definite standard.

The term 'function' is in itself, as applied to associations, a reference to such a standard of value; for it places each association in relation, not only to its own members, but to other associations and institutions, that is, to society, and also to individuals – to both the organized and the unorganized parts of social life, that is, to community. If our first question in relation to any association must be, 'What are the purposes which this association was created and is maintained by its members to subserve?', we must ask that question only in order to be able the better to proceed at once to a second question, 'What is the function which this association can serve in society and in community?'

This does not mean, of course, that it is possible arbitrarily to determine from outside what the function of an association is. The first question is no less essential than, and is essential to, the second. A 'function' can only be based upon a purpose. If men have formed an association for one purpose we cannot properly tell them that its function is to do something quite different which has never entered into their heads. . . .

Social purposes are, thus, the raw material of social functions, and social functions are social purposes selected and placed in coherent relationship. This selection cannot have a purely scientific basis; for it is a matter of ends as well as means, and depends upon individual standards of value and the kind of social life which the individual desires. Thus at this, as at every other fundamental point of social theory, we are driven back upon the individual consciousness and judgement as the basis of all social values. . . .

Each of us has in his mind, whether we rationalize and systematize it or not, some conception of the sort of social life which is ultimately desirable. Our conceptions of the functions of particular associations are inevitably formed in the light of our ultimate conception of social value. . . .

Function, we have seen, emerges clearly when, and only when, an association is regarded, not in isolation, but in relation to other associations and to individuals, that is, to some extent in relation to a system of associations, a society, and a system of associations and individuals, a community. Such a system evidently implies a more or less clear demarcation of spheres as between the various functional associations, in order that each may make its proper contribution to the whole without interfering with the others. It is, however, easy, in search of symmetry, to push this point too far. It is essential that the main lines of demarcation should be laid down, and, in the case of the more vital forms of association, that they should be most carefully and exactly drawn, wherever possible by experience rather than by arbitrary 'constitution-making'; but in the case of the less vital forms of association, which affect the general structure of society only in a small degree either for good or for ill, the same exact delimitation of spheres is unnecessary, and even undesirable as detracting from the freedom and spontaneity of association.

Associations are not mere machines, but are capable of growth and development. We must not, therefore, even in the case of the most vital associations, so exactly define their function and sphere of operation for today as to prevent them from developing the power to exercise their function of tomorrow. If we do, the result will not be in most cases what we expect. The association will develop in spite of prohibition; but in developing it may well break the society which encloses it, or at the least cause vast waste of energy and unnecessary friction. We must remember always that it is of vital importance for a community not to be compelled constantly to make for itself new sets of associations, but rather to develop out of old ones the changed forms which are required for the fulfilment of new functions. It is this vital need of community that makes it so important to preserve as far as possible the freedom of association and the greatest spontaneity of associative action that is consistent with social coherence.

There are, of course, risks attached to this course. If association is left largely free and untrammelled, many associations, instead of fulfilling their function in the social whole, will concern themselves to a considerable extent in fulfilling even the anti-social purposes of their members, or in doing something which, while it is in itself not anti-social but even socially valuable, falls within the function of some other form of association. There arise in this way two main forms of *perversion* of function, leading respectively to *opposition* and to *confusion* in society. . . .

Opposition arises... when an association pursues a purpose which, being a purpose of its own members, is anti-social in that it not only conflicts with the purposes of other associations or individuals, but with the good of the community. Opposition, then, arises from the pursuit of anti-social purposes. Strictly speaking, no anti-social purpose can be a part of the function of the an association, in the sense in which we are using the term 'function'. But, as a function is always a complex thing, the element of 'opposition' may arise in the course of the pursuit of a socially desirable function. Thus, the production of commodities for use and the preservation of order are both socially desirable functions; but either of them may be pursued in anti-social ways which give rise to 'opposition' and perversion of function. If an association producing commodities for use make its main object not the production for use, but the realization of a profit for its members, perversion of function arises. Commodities are still produced 'for use' in a sense; but the function of the association is perverted by the introduction of the profit-making purpose. Similarly, if an association whose function is the preservation of order preserves order in the interest of a single class and deals unequal justice to rich and poor, law and order are still partially preserved; but the function of the association is perverted by its partiality and the foundations of justice are to some extent undermined. ...

Confusion arises when two associations attempt to fulfil the same purpose, and when the purpose is such as requires not a multiplicity of doers, but doing on a co-ordinated plan. Such confusion may be perfectly *bona fide* and even fortuitous. There are functions which lie on the borderline of two or more associations, but which must be fulfilled by only one if confusion is to be avoided. Again, there are many cases in which two or more associations, whose purposes were originally distinct, develop towards the same object, and become wholly or partly identical in function. Such cases are often dealt with by amalgamation; but failing this or an agreed re-allocation of functions, confusion arises. Again, in many cases there is some job which badly needs doing, and two or more groups of men simultaneously conceive the idea of forming an association for the doing of it. Here again amalgamation is often the obvious remedy. ...

It is important to notice that perversion of function in one case, especially where the perversion gives rise to actual opposition, frequently leads to, and even necessitates, perversion of function in other cases. If the appropriate organization is not fulfilling a particular function, it may become necessary or desirable for some other organization, less fitted by its nature for the task, to undertake to fulfil it as best it can. Again, if one association is fulfilling its function in a perverted manner, so as to serve a sectional instead of a general interest, it may be necessary or desirable for some other organization to intervene in order to redress the balance. Current controversies about the use of direct action (i.e., the strike) for political purposes serve to illustrate this point. It is contended by many of the advocates of direct action that the perversion of function on the part of the state makes it necessary for the trade unions to act in the industrial field in order to counteract the effects of this political perversion. . . .

At the same time, it must always be remembered that perversion of functions is always, in itself, a bad thing, whether it is spontaneous perversion or consequential perversion designed to counteract a perversion which has already taken place. It may be necessary in certain cases; but the mere fact of its necessity is a clear indication that all is not well with society. When society is in health, each association fulfills its social function with the minimum of perversion.

Indeed, when counteracting forms of perversion become necessary on any large scale, they serve as a clear indication that the structure of society requires to be overhauled. Perversion, carried to an extreme, and accompanied by its counteracting forms, leads to revolution, followed by a reconstruction of the body social. Such revolution can, of course, be more or less complete, and involve a more or less complete reconstructing and a more or less complete 'sweep' of the old social regime. Often, lesser degrees of perversion and counter-perversion compel a readjustment of social organization without the need for a general evolution in the body social. The first so-called 'revolution' in Russia was rather such a readjustment than a real revolution; but, this proving inadequate, it was followed by the 'November Revolution', which was a real revolution involving a fundamental reconstruction of society. . . .

In this chapter, our object has been merely that of laying bare the functional principle itself, on the basis on which society, as a complex of associations and institutions, must rest if it is to achieve any degree of coherence or to make possible a real and abiding spirit of community. Perversion of function, by destroying the coherence of social organization, not only upsets the balance of society, but stirs up bad blood between the members of the community, and thereby impairs that part of the life of the individual which falls outside the sphere of social organization almost equally with that part which falls within it. Due performance by each association of its social function, on the other hand, not only leads to smooth working and coherence in social organization, but also removes the removable social hindrances to the 'good life' of the individual. In short, function is the key not only to 'social', but also to communal and personal well-being.

Chapter Three

THE STATE AND INCLUSIVE ASSOCIATION

What is the state? And what is its function in society and in the community? These questions appear to us already in a different light from that in which they appear in most books on social theory. They are still vital problems; but they are no longer the centre of the whole problem of community. The state, however important, is and can be for us no more than the greatest and most permanent association or institution in society, and its claim even to any such position will have to be carefully considered.

We must bear in mind throughout our consideration that it is not a question of *the* state, a single unique entity existing alone in a circumambient void, but of 'states' existing in many different communities at different stages of development, and entering into the most varied relationships one with another. When we speak of 'the state', therefore, we are only using a class name to which we can attach our generalizations as predicates. We are ignoring non-essential differences between one state and another, and concentrating on those essential characteristics which states have in common.

This, however, is to give too inclusive and generalized a scope to our treatment of the subject. Although we shall some- times be referring to characteristics common to all states at all times and stages of development, we shall be using in the main for purposes of illustration 'the modern state', that is, the states which exist in our own time and stage of civilization. Taking the nature common to these states as our basis, we shall attempt to arrive, from the study of their common nature, at some conception of their true function in the society of today and tomorrow. . . .

'The state and inclusive association' first appeared as Chapter Five of G.D.H. Cole (1920) *The Social Theory.*

Let us begin with a brief summary and analysis of the principal activities of the modern state, that is, of the states which exist in civilized communities in the world of today. . . . In order to discover the function of the state, it is therefore necessary to adopt a double procedure. We have first to examine, and select from, the actual activities of the state those which are, *prima facie*, essential, and we have then to examine the fundamental nature and constitution of the state with a view to determining which of these essential activities can be regarded as belonging to its function.

It is a commonplace observation that during the last two generations at least the activities of the state have been undergoing constant and rapid multiplication and expansion. Moreover, it is generally recognized that this expansion has been far more extensive in the economic, than in any other sphere. When Locke wrote his [*Two*] *Treatises on Civil Government*, interpreting in them the ideas and social situation of the English Revolution of 1688–9, it was still easy to regard the function of the state as strictly specific and limited, because its actual activities were in the main specific and limited, and were in process of actual contraction. Today, whatever may be the true function of the state, there is an undeniable temptation to conclude, on the basis of its actual activities, that its functions are practically universal and unlimited. Such a conclusion, whether it be right or wrong, at least goes with the grain of present-day society. Yet it may be that Locke was nearer to being right than those social theorists who are ready to conclude, because the state does everything in fact, that its social function is pantopragmatic and universal.

Today, almost every developed state is ceaselessly active in economic affairs. It passes Factory Acts, and other legislation designed to ensure a minimum of protection to the workers engaged in production; it regulates wages and hours; it attempts to provide for and against unemployment; it intervenes, successfully or unsuccessfully, in industrial disputes; it compels employers to provide compensation for accidents, and both employers and workers to contribute to social insurance funds which it administers. On the other hand, it regulates to some extent the commercial operations of financiers and employers, restricts or pretends to restrict trusts and profiteering, uses its consular service and special agents to aid foreign trade, encourages, subsidizes, and assists in industrial research, enacts laws affecting and enters into many formal and informal relationships with capitalist interests and associations. Moreover, more and more it embarks itself upon economic enterprises, conducts a post office or a railway service, and becomes the direct employer of vast numbers of its own citizens, incidentally often imposing political and other disqualifications upon them on the ground that they are state employees.

To all this industrial and commercial activity of the national state must be added the no less complex activities of local authorities acting under the laws enacted by the state-municipal and other local bye-laws regulating industry and commerce, and the extending operations of 'municipal trading'. It will, however, be more convenient to consider the character and activities of local authorities separately at a later stage, although no clear or hard and fast line can be drawn between a state and a local authority in those cases where 'federal', 'Dominion', or even 'regionalist' forms of government exist.

There is a further economic activity of the state which is more and more becoming manifest in our own day. Taxation is, in its origin, merely a method of collecting from individuals that proportion of their incomes which must be diverted from their personal use to meet the necessary expenses of state administration. But, as the activities of the state expand, taxation shows a marked tendency to become also a method of redistributing incomes within the community. This new tendency emerges already in systems of graduated taxation; but it becomes the leading principle in those proposals, nowhere yet carried far into effect, which aim at its definite and deliberate use as a means to at least comparative equality of income.

Apart from taxation for administrative purposes, the present economic activities of the state are largely of recent growth. This is not to say that the state had not previously engaged in economic action on a large scale, as for instance under what is known as the 'mercantile system'. But between the 'mercantile system' and the economic activity of the modern state intervenes in many cases a period of comparative inactivity – *laissez faire* – following upon the changes caused by the Industrial Revolution. In the Middle Ages, when economic activities were largely in the hands of the guilds and in the period of the Industrial Revolution, when they were largely in the hands of competitive capitalists, the state's intervention in economic matters was, comparatively, very restricted indeed.

Extensive as the economic activities of the state are, it will be agreed that they have not yet, in any actual state, reached an essentially central position. This might occur, and would probably occur if the pure collectivists had their way; but, for the present, the central position is still occupied by political and co-ordinating rather than by economic activities, although the latter constantly threaten the position of the two former. Our next inquiry must be into the nature of the *political* activities of the state.

The word 'political' is one round which a high degree of ambiguity has gathered. It has very various associations, with the [*Polis*], or city-state, of the Greeks, with the modern nation-state, with the whole complex of social action, with purely party and parliamentary activities, and so forth. Here I am using the word in a definitive and specific sense. I mean by *political* activities those activities which are concerned with the social regulation of those personal relationships which arise directly out of the fact that men live together in communities, and which are susceptible to direct social organization.

In this, as in many other cases, it is easier and perhaps more illuminating, to illustrate than to define. What, we must ask, are the main types of actual political activity exercised by the state?

Marriage is at once a civil and religious institution. The state regulates the relations between individuals by enacting laws dealing with marriage and its dissolution, the care of children, the conduct arising out of sexual relationships in all their forms. It makes laws for the prevention and punishment of crime, for the care and treatment of lunatics, the feeble-minded, and others who are not in a position to look after themselves. It is vitally concerned with many relationships quite apart from sex, crime, or abnormality, and constantly lays down rules of convenience and convention for the guidance of men in their mutual relationships. If it covers any considerable area or includes any large number of inhabitants, it must recognize or establish local authorities similar to itself but with more limited powers, and make general rules for the guidance of these bodies in their various activities. In fact, it is concerned mainly with personal rights and the means of reconciling them, and with those limitations of personal conduct which are essential to the existence of a co-ordinated system of personal rights.

Where classes exist in the community, the state often exercises further political activity in sustaining, recognizing, and modifying class privileges and class exclusions. It creates, say, a peerage, and from time to time elevates the latest exalted servant of the public, or newspaper proprietor, or *nouveau riche*, to membership of the peerage. It enacts special privileges for one class or another, or passes special legislation discriminating against a class. In the extreme case, its political activity assumes the form of a class dictatorship. This is the bad side of the state's political activity.

Third, the state of today possesses increasingly important activities of *co-ordination*. It is largely concerned in adjusting the relations between association and association, or institution and institution, or institution and association, or between other associations or institutions and itself. It enacts laws regulating the form and scope of associative activity, friendly society law, law affecting banks, companies, partnerships, trade unions, clubs, associations of any and every sort. In some degree, it regulates all religious associations, and, in some countries, the existence of an established church considerably increases the extent of its religious intervention. There is one theory of the state which regards it as primarily a co-ordinating body, devoted not to any specific functions of its own, but to the co-ordinating of the various functional associations within society.

I do not claim that this summary of the activities of states is exhaustive or inclusive, nor do I desire to make it so. It can, with one further development, be made sufficient for our purpose. I have so far dealt almost entirely with the internal activities of 'the state', and ignored its external relations, whether with other states, or with anything wholly or partly outside its geographical boundaries. I have done this because 'international' or external activity cannot be regarded as a particular province of state activity, in the same sense as economic, political, and co-ordinating activities. International action arises in relation to each of these provinces of state activity, and has, besides, special problems of its own. Thus the state takes external economic action in the development of foreign trade, external political action in connection, say, with international provisions regarding crime, marriage, naturalization, and other questions of personal status and convenience which involve a measure of activity transcending state boundaries. In its activity of co-ordination, it is confronted with the problem of international association, from the Roman Catholic Church to the Socialist International.

These forms of external state action may either lead to quarrels and disagreements between states, or they may bind states together and lead towards a sort of super-state, or at least society or league of states bound together for the performance of specific functions or the exercise of specific activities. Hitherto, the external actions of states have been far more fertile in disagreement than in organized co-operation; but it does not follow that this will always be the case. Indeed, a proper understanding and adjustment of the internal functions of the state will be likely to exercise a profound and beneficent action upon its relations with other states, and to set it upon the road of organized international co-operation which other forms of association are more forward in following than the state has been in the past.

A full discussion of the external aspects of state action, however, would be foreign to our present purpose, which is in the main that of disentangling the true functions of the state from the network of its present activities. By what test can we so test these activities as to make the real nature and function of the state stand out from among them, clear and well-defined? The first step in applying our test must be to investigate the state from a different point of view, to regard it in the light, not of its activities, but of its structure and composition. We may then hope, by bringing its activities into relation to its structure, to discover its function in the complex of organized society.

How, then, is the state composed? And what is its structural principle? These are not easy questions to answer, because any attempt to answer them is likely to open at once large controversial questions. Moreover, the structure of different states, or of the same state at different times, appears to be essentially different. What is there in common between the structure of a pure despotism, in which a monarch is supposed to possess absolute and unlimited power, and a state in which all power rests, at any rate in theory, upon the consent and active co-operation of the whole body of the people?

It must be noted that the activities of a 'despotic' and of a 'democratic' state may be identical, while their structural principles seem to be vitally different. But are their structural principles as fundamentally different as they seem? Every despotism which seeks at all to justify its existence seeks to do so on one or another of three principles. Either it claims to be based upon 'divine right and appointment' of the ruler, or it claims to be acting in the interests of the ruled, and therefore in conformity with their real will, or it claims to be based upon the actual consent of the ruled, tacit or expressed. With despotisms which do not seek to justify their existence we are not concerned, since in them it is manifest that social obligation, on which the possibility of a coherent society depends, is not present.

We are left, then, with three possible justifications of despotism, and it must be admitted that all three finally reduce themselves to a common form – the consent, in one form or another, of the ruled. This is clear in the third form of the theory of despotism, which is based on actual consent. In the second form, the consent is not actual, but unless it is real the justification fails. It depends upon the metaphysical conception of the 'real wills', different from the actual will and willing always the good. It claims, in fact, to be the consent of the 'better selves' of the ruled. The first theory, that of divine right, seems at first sight to have nothing to do with human consent; but if God has willed that a man shall be king, it is clear that the 'better selves' of all men have willed this too, and that, if divine right is established, universal consent ought to follow as a matter of course.

Any attempt to justify a despotic state therefore brings us back to the same principle as that on which 'democratic' states are usually justified – the consent of the ruled. It is true that in a despotism this consent cannot, unless the despot is elected, pass beyond acquiescence, whereas in democracy consent may become, and in real democracy must become, active co-operation. Still, a common ground of principle has been established, and the state, whatever its form of power, is seen to rest on the consent of those who are its citizens, subjects, members, or human constituents.

If once the principle of consent is established as the basis of the state, it is impossible to set limits to the operation of the principle. If the members consent to despotism, well and good; but as soon as they desire to assume a more active co-operation in the affairs of state, they have clearly a right to do so. *The fullest democracy in action is only the logical development of the principle of consent, expanded by the application of actual human wills – that is, of the will to self-government. If this is so, we can safely take the 'democratic state' as the developed form of the 'the state', and expect, in laying bare its structure, to lay bare the structure of states in general* [editor's emphasis].

The only obstacle in the way of our immediately adopting this course is the metaphysical doctrine of the real 'will' – a doctrine which we shall again and again encounter as an influence obscuring our attempt to study the character of social organization. If the doctrine of a real will different from anybody's actual will is accepted, all arguments for democracy, that is government by the actual wills of the ruled, go by the board. But so equally do all arguments for everything else; for we are left without means of ascertaining the nature or content of this real will. The content of actual wills we can know up to a point: the content of the real will we cannot know at all. We can only know what we believe to be good, and thereupon, by a quite gratuitous assumption, assume our conception of the good to be the content of everybody's real will. Or, if we are not quite sure ourselves that we know all the good, we can stand back astonished at the magnitude of the state and its works, and say that anything so big must be good. Many idealist social theorists have virtually done this, and made of the doctrine of the real will, in its application to social theory, no more than a colossally fraudulent justification of 'things as they are'.[1]

I shall content myself with leaping rather lightly over this metaphysical obstacle. . . . I shall assume, then, that actual wills are real wills, or at least near enough to reality to be going on with, and I shall therefore assume that the basis of the state's structure is to be found in the actual consent of its members.

But here we encounter our first real difficulty. Who are the *members* of the state, and, indeed, can the state be said to have any members? I am using the word 'members' because it is the most neutral word I can find. We usually speak of 'citizens' or 'subjects'; but one of these words has about it the implication of despotism and the other that of the actual exercise of political rights. I therefore avoid them for the present, because I want to avoid equally for the present both these implications.

The state, as an association, has members, and its members are all the persons ordinarily resident within the area within which the state ordinarily exercises authority. Such persons are members of the state, whether or not they have votes or other political privileges, by virtue merely of their ordinary residence within the state area. For the state is, for the dwellers within its area, a compulsory association, and its compulsory character is revealed in two ways – in its power to compel all persons in its area and in the right of all such persons to membership of it. When we say that the state rests upon consent, we mean that it rests upon the consent of an effective proportion of *all* the dwellers within its area.

Membership of the state is, however, an almost barren theory without recognized political rights – for without such rights a member can only make his voice heard in time of revolution, when the ordinary procedure of the state is in abeyance. What right, we must ask, does membership of the state give to the recognition of actual political rights? The answer is partly implied in what we have said already of consent as the basis of the state. The members of the state have the right to translate a passive consent into an active co-operation by the assumption of political rights. This they habitually do by gradually extending the franchise and other political rights to new sections of the population, as these sections become articulate in advancing their claim. The logical completion of this development is universal suffrage as the expression of a political articulateness generally diffused through all sections of people.

I shall take, then, as the basis of examination of the structure of the state, a state possessing the institution of universal suffrage. What is the structural principle of such a state? Regarded as a whole, it is a compulsory association including all the dwellers within a particular area. Its basis is therefore territorial and inclusive, whereas the basis of a trade union is vocational and selective. The essence of the state is to include all sorts of people, without reference to the sort of people they are, the sort of beliefs they hold, or the sort of work they do.

I do not mean, of course, that there is not usually a very important element of identity of character, way of life, and even occupation, among the members of a particular state. This element of identity is strongest in the city-state, and very strong in the state whose area is the area of a nation. But it is not the essential principle of the state form of grouping. There are states which are not coterminous with nations, and state and nation are essentially different things. A nation may be a community but it cannot be, though it may possess, a state. A nation is not an association; a state is.

The state, then, is an inclusive territorial association, ignoring differences between men and compulsorily taking in everyone who ordinarily dwells within its area. This being its principle, how can we discover its function? The answer will be found by asking and answering a further question.

Why does the state ignore the differences between men and include all sorts and conditions, and what is the sphere of action, or social function, marked out for it by the adoption of this structure? It ignores the differences between men because it is concerned not with their differences, but with their identity, and its function and interest are concerned with men's identity and not with their differences. Objectively stated, this principle takes the following form. The concern of the state, as an association including all sorts and conditions of men, must be with things which concern all sorts and conditions of men, and concern them, broadly speaking, in the same way, that is, in relation to their identity and not to their points of difference.

The state must exist primarily to deal with things which affect all its members more or less equally and in the same way. Let us try to see clearly what are the effects of this principle. It excludes from the primary functions of the state – from its social function *par excellence* – those spheres of social action which affect different members of it in different degrees and in various ways. This does not mean that the state must not concern itself with any such spheres of action, but only that they do not form part of its primary function. We are not concerned as yet so much with limiting the province of the state as with discovering what is its undisputed and peculiar sphere.

Let us look back now to the point from which we set out – to our brief account of the existing activities of the state. Which of these activities clearly fall within the definition we have just given, and may therefore be functions of the state or some structurally similar association? We divided the actual activities of the state into three main divisions – economic, political, and co-ordinative. Let us first look at each of these three divisions in general and as a whole, proceeding to a further analysis of them as we find it to be required.

Economic activities for the most part clearly affect the various members of the community in different degrees and in various ways. For it is here that one of the most easily recognizable and organizable differences between man and man comes into play. Coal mining affects the coal miner in quite a different way from that in which it affects the rest of the people, and so through the whole list of trades and vocations. Of course, coal mining does affect not only the miner, but also everybody else; but the point is that it affects the miner in a different manner and degree.

Here, however, a difficulty at once arises. Each trade or vocation affects those who follow it in a different way and degree from the way and degree in which it affects others; but many vital industries and services do also, from another point of view, affect almost everybody in very much the same way. We must all eat and drink, be clothed, housed and warmed, be tended in sickness and educated in childhood and youth, and our common needs in these and other respects give rise to a common relation, that of consumers or users of the products and services rendered by those who follow the various trades and vocations concerned.

It is upon this fact that the collectivist theory of the state is based. The collectivists, or state socialists, regard the state as an association of consumers, and claim for it supremacy in the economic sphere on the ground that consumption, at least in relation to the vital industries and services, is a matter that concerns everybody equally and in the same way. This, however, is to ignore a difference as vital as the identity on which stress is laid. The most that could be claimed for the state in the economic sphere on account of the identical interest of all the members of the community in consumption is state control of consumption, and not state control of production, in which the interests of different members of the community are vitally different.

The economic sphere thus falls at once into two separable parts – production and consumption, in one of which all interests tend to be identical, while in the other, production, they tend to be different. Consumption is thus marked off as falling, *prima facie*, within the sphere of some inclusive body, whether it be the state or some other body or bodies possessing a similar structure, while production is less clearly outside it. . . .

We saw in our summary of state activities that taxation tends to become, and to be regarded as, not merely a means of raising revenue for public purposes, but a means of redistributing the national income. May not this tendency provide the key to the economic function of an inclusive body? If there is one thing in the economic sphere which affects everybody equally and in the same way it is the question of income, on which the nominal amount of consumption depends. Closely bound up with this is the question of price, which, in its relation to income, determines the real amount of consumption. Income and prices, then, seem to fall clearly within the province of some inclusive body.

Consumption, then, is socially regulated primarily through income and prices, either by the state or some other inclusive body, which by this means acts upon the general level and distribution of consumption, and not directly upon the consumption of any particular commodity. It is, however, clear that, in the case of many staple commodities and vital services, not only the general level of consuming power, but also the consumption and supply of a particular commodity or service, affects everybody more or less equally and in the same way. Of course, there are many other commodities whose consumption affects only a part of the people, or affects different sections in unequal measure. In such cases an inclusive body has no primary function. Having regulated the general distribution of consuming power, it can leave to *ad hoc* bodies the expression of the consumers' point of view in relation to such commodities or services.

But in the case of the vital commodities and services which, broadly speaking, affect everybody equally and in the same way, there is a *prima facie* argument for action by an inclusive body, and it is clear that regulation must be done by such a body acting either alone or in conjunction with the vocational bodies which are specially concerned with supplying these commodities and services. The question of whether the state or some other body or bodies so constituted should assume these functions depends upon the degree to which the combined performance of political functions and of these specialized economic functions can be undertaken with satisfactory results by the same group of elected persons, or whether it is necessary that the same body of electors should choose different persons and representative bodies for the performance of functions so essentially different and calling for such different capacities and acquirements.

The *political* activities of the state give rise to no such complex problems as its economic activities. Here the only question that arises in most cases is whether a particular sphere of personal relationship ought to be regulated or left unregulated. If it is to be regulated at all, it falls clearly according to our principle within the sphere of an inclusive body. For in personal relationship, whether regulation is based on moral principles or on principles of convenience, the regulation clearly affects, or should affect, and would but for class and economic distinctions affect, everyone equally and in the same way. 'Political' activities, then, in the sense which we have given to the phrase, either belong to an inclusive body, or should be left unregulated.

What, then, of activities of *co-ordination*, such as we described earlier in this chapter? Here a far greater difficulty arises. To entrust the state with the function of co-ordination would be to entrust it, in many cases, with the task of arbitrating between itself and some other functional association, say, a church or a trade union. But just as no man ought to be the judge of his own case, so ought no association. Therefore, co-ordination cannot belong to the function of the state; but neither can it belong to that of any other functional association.

We should reach the same conclusion if we ignored the argument against making the state judge in its own cause, and attended only to the nature of co-ordinating activities. For such activities clearly bring in many questions which do not affect everybody equally and in the same way, but affect various groups in essential different ways. Therefore, once more, we must conclude that the function of co-ordination does not belong to the state.

This is a conclusion of far-reaching and fundamental importance; for if the state is not the co-ordinating authority within the community, neither is it, in the sense usually attached to the term, 'sovereign'. But the claim to 'sovereignty' is that on which the most exalted pretensions of the state are based. Almost all modern theories of the state attribute to it not merely a superiority to all other forms of association, but an absolute difference in kind, by virtue of which it is supposed to possess, in theory at least, an unlimited authority over every other association and over every individual in the community.

If the foregoing account of the state is correct, its claim to sovereignty falls utterly to the ground. Indeed, it becomes doubtful whether any body properly to be called a state can establish its claim to survival and allegiance. Some form of inclusive association of which every member of the community is a member is indeed clearly necessary; but it may well be that there will be more than one such inclusive association in the community, and that the functions which in this chapter we have reserved as possible functions of inclusive associations will have to be divided among several such bodies. We cannot, however, so lightly dismiss an almost universally held theoretical position in favour of a unitary form of sovereignty, and, in order to make plain our reasons for denying it, we must now embark on a discussion of the closely related questions of democracy and representation. We can then return to our study of the position of the state and other inclusive associations with a better hope of making the argument perfectly clear.

NOTE

1. For an excellent onslaught upon some such theories, see Hobhouse (1918) *The Metaphysical Theory of the State* [London: Allen & Unwin]. For an awful example of them, see the writings of Dr Bernard Bonsanquet.

Chapter Four

DEMOCRACY AND REPRESENTATION

There is in our own day an almost general prejudice in favour of democracy. Almost everybody is a 'democrat', and the name of democracy is invoked in support of the most diverse social systems and theories. This general acceptance of the name of democracy, even by persons who are obviously not in any real sense 'democrats', is perhaps largely to be explained by the fact that the idea of democracy has become almost inextricably tangled up with the idea of representative government, or rather with a particular theory of representative government based on a totally false theory of representation.

This false theory is that one man can 'represent' another or a number of others, and that his will can be treated as the democratic expression of their wills. Stated in this form, the theory admits of only one answer. No man can represent another man, and no man's will can be treated as a substitute for, or representative of, the wills of others.

This may look, at first sight, like a complete denial of every form of representative government, and an affirmation of the futility of all elections. It is, however, nothing of the sort; it is not an attack upon, or an attempt to destroy the theoretic basis of, representative government, but an attempt to restate the theory of representation in a truer form. In order that it may be fully understood, we must bring it into relation to the doctrine of function expounded in previous chapters. We have seen that, just as every action of an individual aims at some specific object, so men form and enter associations in pursuit of specific objects which can be best pursued in common by or through an organized

'Democracy and representation' first appeared as Chapter Six of G.D.H. Cole (1920) *The Social Theory*

group. Every association, then , has a specific object or objects, and it is in pursuit of some or all of these objects that men consent to be members of the association.

Every association which sets before itself any object that is of more than the most rudimentary simplicity finds itself compelled to assign tasks and duties, and with these powers and a share of authority, to some of its members in order that the common object may be effectively pursued. It elects, perhaps, a secretary, a president, a treasurer, and an executive committee, and empowers these persons to act on behalf of the association in certain definite ways and within certain limits. In the smaller and more localized associations, much of the control of the proceedings of the association may remain in the hands of the general body of the members; but as soon as it becomes too large or too dispersed for a general meeting to transact business, or if the members are too preoccupied with other affairs to make it their constant concern, the detailed regulation of its proceedings passes largely into the hands of a comparatively small number of its members, officers, committee men, delegates, or representatives. In the largest and most complex forms of association, such as the state, the ordinary member is reduced to a mere voter, and all the direction of actual affairs is done by representatives – or misrepresentatives.

At the best, representative government gives rise to many inconveniences, to what Walt Whitman described a 'the never-ending audacity of elected persons', and Rousseau as 'the tendency of all government to deteriorate'. With these inconveniences we shall have to deal at a later stage; but here we are concerned only to make clear the nature of the representative relation as it exists in such associations as we have spoken of.

In the majority of associations, the nature of the relation is clear enough. The elected person – official, committee man, or delegate – makes no pretension of substituting his personality for those of his constituents, or of representing them except in relation to a quite narrow and clearly defined purpose or group of purposes which the association exists to fulfil. There is, then, in these cases, no question of one man taking the place of many; for what the representative professes to represent is not the whole will and personalities of his constituents, but merely so much of them as they have put into the association, and as is concerned with the purposes which the association exists to fulfil.

This is the character of all true representation. It is impossible to represent human beings as selves or centres of consciousness; it is quite possible to represent, though with an inevitable element of distortion which must always be recognized, so much of human beings as they themselves put into associated effort for a specific purpose.

True representation, therefore, like true association, is always specific and functional, and never general and inclusive. What is represented is never man, the individual, but always certain purposes common to groups of individuals. That theory of representative government which is based upon the idea that individuals can be represented as wholes is a false theory, and destructive of personal rights and social well-being.

The fact that a man cannot be represented as a man seems so obvious that it is difficult to understand how many theories of government and democracy have come to be built upon the idea that he can. Each man is a centre of consciousness and reason, a will possessed of the power of self-determination, an ultimate reality. How can one such will be made to stand in place of many? How can one man, being himself, be at the same time a number of other people? It would be a miracle if he could; but it is a risky experiment to base our social system upon a hypothetical miracle.

Functional representation is open to no such objection. It does not lay claim to any miraculous quality: it does not profess to be able to substitute the will of one man for the wills of many. Its adherents recognize the element of distortion which exists in all representation; but to them this distortion is not a problem, but an inevitable fact. It does not annihilate or detract from the will of any individual; it merely provides a basis whereby, when the individual has made up his mind that a certain object is desirable, he can co-operate with his fellows in taking the course of action necessary for its attainment.

Of course I do not intend to convey the idea that there are just so many functions in society, and that to each corresponds exactly to its own functional association and form of representation. The need of society for functional association and representation expands and develops as society becomes larger and more complex. A special form of association and representation, at one time unnecessary, may become necessary as the work of society increases in a particular direction. Moreover, in a very small society, such as the ancient city-state, where the direct participation of the mass of the people in government was possible, functional association was only needed in a very limited degree, and it was often possible for the people to choose directly their functional representatives without any intervening stage of functional association. The principle of representation, however, is the same; the representative represents not persons, but definite and particular purposes common to a number of persons.

Having made plain our conception of the true nature of representation, we can now look more closely at its consequences. In proportion as the purposes for which the representative is chosen lose clarity and definiteness, representation passes into misrepresentation, and the representative character of the acts resulting from association disappears. Thus, misrepresentation is seen at its worst to-day in that professedly omnicompetent 'representative' body – Parliament – and in the Cabinet which is supposed to depend upon it. Parliament professes to represent all the citizens in all things, and therefore as a rule represents none of them in anything. It is chosen to deal with anything that may turn up, quite irrespective of the fact that the different things that do turn up require different types of persons to deal with them. It is therefore peculiarly subject to corrupt, and especially to plutocratic, influences, and does everything badly, because it is not chosen to do any definite thing well. This is not the fault of the actual Members of Parliament; they muddle because they are set the impossible task of being good at everything, and representing everybody in relation to every purpose.

There can be only one escape from the futility of our present methods of parliamentary government; and that is to find an association and method of representation for each function, and a function for each association and body of representatives. In other words, real democracy is to be found, not in a single omnicompetent representative assembly, but in a system of co-ordinated functional representative bodies.

There is another, and a simpler, line of argument which leads straight to the same conclusion as we have already reached. It is obvious that different people are interested in, and good at doing, different things. It is therefore equally obvious that, if I am a sensible person, I shall desire to choose different people to represent my wishes in relation to different things. To ask me to choose one man to represent me in relation to everything is to insult my intelligence, and to offer me every inducement to choose some one so colourless that he is unlikely to do anything at all – because he will at least probably do no great harm, and no great notice will be taken of him. This is how parliamentary elections usually work out at the present time.

But, if I am asked to choose a different person to represent my wishes in relation to each of the main groups of social purposes of which I am conscious, I shall do my best to choose in each case the man who is most fitted to represent my views and to carry them into effect. In short, the one method will inevitably result in government by the incompetent; the other will at least give every chance for competent representatives to be chosen.

Democracy, then, must be conceived in the first place as a co-ordinated system of functional representation. But, as soon as we introduce the word 'democracy', we raise a further question, that of the relation between me and my functional representative after I have chosen him. In fact, we find ourselves in the thick of the old controversy of 'representative versus delegate'.

Does our revised theory of representation throw any light upon this controversy? Or, in other words, is the question whether the elected person, once he has been elected, should follow his own will or should be instructed as far as possible on every issue by those who have chosen him, to be answered in a different way when the theory of representation is different? I think the theory of representation which we adopt must make a considerable difference to our view of the relation of the elected person to his constituents.

In the first place, attempts to make the elected person a mere delegate must always break down, whatever the form of representation. There are many issues on which it is not merely undesirable, but impossible, to tie down a delegate by instructions, because unforeseen situations and complications constantly arise. If for no other reason, pure delegation must break down because the delegate is so often waiting for further instructions that nothing gets done, and the best opportunities for action are continually being missed. On the other hand, pure 'representation' without instructions or counsel from the electors approaches very nearly to false representation, substituting, even within a restricted sphere, the will of one for the wills of many.

Our functional democracy, based on functional associations and representations, provides a way out of this difficulty. It enables us to combine representation with constant counsel from the constituents, and thus makes it possible to abandon the theory of delegation without imperilling democratic control. The chief difficulty of democratic control over the representative in the political sphere today is that, as soon as the voters have exercised their votes, their existence as a group lapses until the time when a new election is required. No body or group remains in being to direct upon the elected person a constant stream of counsel and criticism. Consequently, the elected person must either receive full instructions at the time of election, which produces an intolerable situation as soon as there is any change in the circumstances, or else he must become a pure representative, acting on his own responsibility and consequently expressing only his own will and not those of his constituents. This dilemma exists wherever the body of electors does not remain in being and activity as a body throughout the tenure of office of the elected person.

Functional democracy, in which representatives emanate from functional associations which have a permanent being, meets this difficulty. It is no longer necessary for the group to instruct its representative, because it can continue throughout his time of office to criticize and advise him, and because, I would add, it can at any time recall him if it is not satisfied with the way in which he is doing his job. Recall is, in fact, the final safeguard, while criticism and advice are the normal means of keeping the representation democratic.

In our own day, experience of bad leaders, both in the state and in other forms of association, has bred an almost general distrust of leadership, and a strong desire, especially on the so-called 'left wing', to do away with leaders, and substitute direct control by the 'rank and file' through delegates duly instructed how to act and vote. But there is no reason to take the badness of present-day leaders as a sign that the whole idea of leadership should be given up. Certainly, before we adopt any such drastic expedient, all the circumstances ought to be fully explored. But, at the very beginning of this explanation, the biggest single cause of the collapse of leadership is plainly to be seen. The absence of any true principle of representation in the sphere of the state, the failure, that is, to 'functionalize' the state, and to make the political representative a functional representative, is the main cause of the perversion of political leadership. But the perversion of political leadership is, in its turn, the main cause of the perversion of leadership elsewhere. The trade union leader and many other 'functional' leaders have their eyes fixed upon Parliament, and the thought of Parliament distracts them from their proper work. Moreover, this parliamentary *arrière-pensée* is an important factor in causing the wrong leaders to be selected, and the wrong candidates to offer themselves for selection.

We must preserve leadership without sacrificing democratic control. Leadership is as vital to a democracy as to an aristocracy or a monarchy. And it is as true in a democracy as anywhere else that the good leader must be given a great deal of rope.

In a functional democracy, where the elected person is a representative and not a delegate, and where he acts not as a rule upon instructions, but upon criticism and advice, I believe that the good leader will find ample scope, as soon as the distrust which is born of false democracy has had time to wear off. It is true that he will be liable to summary recall; but who believes that, after the initial mistakes, this power would be too freely exercised? The risks are all the other way: it is of a too long tenure of office by second-rate men that we should be afraid. Functional democracy will give the good leader his first real chance of leading by his merits, with an instructed and active body of constituents behind him. For it must be remembered that not only will the representative be chosen to do a job about which he knows something, but he will be chosen by persons who know something of it too. Truly a revolutionary proposal for a democrat to make!

But some one will object, if I have this respect for leaders why do I insist on the right of recall? I do so, because I have even more respect for human wills and personalities, and because I feel that democracy implies far more than the passive consent of the mass of the people in government. Democracy implies active, and not merely passive, citizenship, and implies for everybody at least the opportunity to be an active citizen, not only of the state, but of every association with which his personality or circumstances cause him to be concerned.

Those who profess to find the bond of society in the passive consent of the mass of the people fall between two stools. If the mass of the people are necessary to the justification of the social order, they are necessary in the active and not in the passive mood. In other words, if we base our social theory upon the attitude of the mass of the people, we are logically driven to insist that this attitude ought to be as explicit and positive as possible.

A well-organized society is one in which not merely is the administration good, but the wills of the members of the community are active, and find expression through the various associations and institutions of which society is made up. It should be the aim of those who strive to direct the course of social organization to promote the fullest participation of everybody in the work of government. This alone is true democracy, and this can only be secured by the fullest development of functional organization. The current theory of representative government is a denial of this principle; for, having chosen his representative, the ordinary man has, according to that theory, nothing left to do except to let other people govern him. Functional organization and representation, on the other hand, imply the constant participation of the ordinary man in the conduct of those parts of the structure of society with which he is directly concerned, and which he has therefore the best chance of understanding. A man may be pardoned for not quite knowing for whom to vote in a parliamentary election, or how to appraise the career of his Member of Parliament, because the Member of Parliament of today is elected not for any clearly defined purpose, but in the void, to deal with anything that may chance to turn up. A functional association, on the other hand, is concerned with doing a definite job, and its officers are also concerned with getting that definite job done. The member is connected with the association because its business is his business, and he is therefore able far more intelligently to initiate and criticize action in relation to it than in relation to an *omnium gatherum* miscalled 'politics'. Functional organization gives everyone the chance of being, in the measure of his competence and interest, an active citizen.

This does not mean that, in a functional democracy, each person will count for one and no person for more than one. That is the cant of false democracy. The essence of functional democracy is that a man should count as many times over as there are functions in which he is interested. To count once is to count about nothing in particular: what men want is to count on the particular issues in which they are interested. Instead of 'One man, one vote', we must say 'One man as many votes as interests, but only one vote in relation to each interest'.

This restatement of a democratic principle still leaves intact the equal voting power of unequal persons voting on a particular issue. That, too, is democracy, not because equalization of votes can make unequal persons equal, but because the right way for the better man to 'pull his weight' is not by casting more votes himself, but influencing others to vote aright. Democracy involves leadership by influence.

Before we end this chapter, we must face a very foolish, but very often urged, objection to the whole idea of functional representation. Functional representation, we are told, is impossible because, in order to make it work, everybody will have to vote so many times over. I fail to see where the objection arises. If a man is not interested enough to vote, and cannot be roused to interest enough to make him vote, on, say, a dozen distinct subjects, he waives his right to vote, and the result is no less democratic than if he voted blindly and without interest. It is true that the result is not so democratic as it would be if everybody voted with interest and knowledge, but it is far more democratic than it would be if everybody voted without interest or knowledge, as they tend to do in parliamentary elections. Many and keen voters are best of all; but few and keen voters are the next best. A vast and uninstructed electorate voting on a general and undefined issue is the worst of all. Yet that is what we call democracy today.

Chapter Five

GOVERNMENT AND LEGISLATION

We have seen that, as soon as any association passes beyond the doing of the most simple and elementary acts, it becomes necessary for it to have representatives – persons endowed with the right, within certain limits, to speak and act in the name of the association, to deliberate on its behalf, and to take the steps necessary for carrying out its decisions. The character and complexity of the representative methods adopted varies both with the size and geographical dispersion of the association, and with the complexity of the functions which it exists to perform. Thus, as long as it is possible for all the members to meet together and discuss each issue of policy as it arises, representatives, where they are required, will be unlikely to acquire any very great power, and will be mainly engaged in doing the routine work necessary to carry out the decisions of the general meeting. This is the position today in those parishes which are governed by a parish meeting, or in a small local trade union or other association.

At this stage, it will be seen, there may be rudimentary officials, permanent or occasional, corresponding to the fully developed executive officers of more advanced forms of association: there may be a committee, permanent or occasional, and also of an executive character. But there is as yet no representative legislative assembly, no body of men selected from the association, and legislating or laying down the main lines of policy in the name of all the members. This is a further development, which arises when it becomes impossible or inconvenient for all the members to meet and deliberate together. It is at this stage that the real problem of government arises, and the association creates for itself a

'Government and legislation' first appeared as Chapter Seven of G.D.H. Cole (1920) *The Social Theory*

representative assembly, entrusted with the task of legislation.

This does not mean that the final decision on questions of policy passes altogether and necessarily away from the whole body of the members. There remain two ways in which the whole of the members may still keep important decisions in their own hands. They may choose to act through delegates rather than representatives, and, although they cannot all meet together, the local members may hold meetings in a number of centres to instruct their delegate, or, in the alternative, to advise their representative, how to vote. Or they may adopt the institution of the referendum, and insist that important issues shall be submitted to a ballot vote of all the members.

Both these expedients, however, are extremely clumsy, when it is attempted to apply them to any but the broadest and simplest issues. For, in either case, every question has to be reduced to a simple Aye or No, and the possibility of adjustments, amendments, and new situations has to be left out of account. The method of referendum or instruction is, I believe, the right method where the broadest and simplest issues are concerned; but it offers no help in dealing with the more complex and detailed issues which are constantly arising in almost every association.

Men are driven, therefore, to the expedient of the representative[1] legislative assembly for getting the ordinary day-to-day work of the more complex associations efficiently accomplished. In the less complex associations, very often no separate legislative assembly is created, but the executive committee acts also as a legislature within the limits which the purposes of the assembly require. The more complex type of association, however, usually creates a separate body for the task of legislation, and calls this body together as required, the executive committee remaining in being to carry out its decisions. In the most complex types of association, such as the state, the legislative assembly, as well as the executive committee, tends to become permanent and to remain in almost continuous session. Even Parliament, however, has only very gradually developed this permanent and continuous character. The early parliaments were occasional bodies.

The purpose of this chapter is to investigate more closely than we have yet done the actual ways of operation of representative bodies and persons, in order to se how the will of the members finds expression through their representatives, and also how it is sometimes perverted and twisted in passing through the representatives' intermediary. One of the most illuminating chapters of Rousseau's *Social Contract* [2] deals with the 'tendency of government to deteriorate'. All action through representatives, he explains, involves to a certain extent the substitution of the wills of the representatives for those of the represented. Moreover, all groups of men, by experience of acting together, tend to develop in some degree a 'common will' of their own. Chosen to express the 'common will' of those whom they represent, they acquire a 'common will' of their own different from that of the represented.

We have given in the last chapter our reasons for supposing that the definite limits and purposes of functional representatives make these dangers far less applicable to it than to so-called 'representation' which is general and not functional. This, however, does not mean that, even with functional representation, the danger altogether disappears. It is, indeed, impossible that it should ever disappear, unless as the result of a miracle which would be also an overwhelming calamity. For the possibility of society is based on the fact that, by acting together, men do as a rule develop an increasing sense of community. This is the very basis of society; but it has inevitably its bad, as well as its good, side. For it means that there is a sense of community among thieves as well as among honest men, and among members of committees and representative assemblies as well as among members of groups and associations. It means, that, however faithfully the members of a committee may try to fulfil their whole duty to their members, an element of committee loyalty will almost inevitably enter into their actions. They will tend to back one another, whether they are right or wrong, and, when one of them is in danger of not being re-elected, the rest will often tend to support him even if they are aware that he is not the best man for the job. They will say one to another: 'After all, we can't let down old Jones.'

It is an easy and a highly popular pastime to gird at this idiosyncrasy of elected persons. But it is useless to abuse men for being clannish: we must rather recognize that the tendency to clannishness is the cement of the social system, and make up our minds to adopt the proper treatment in dealing with it. In the first place, we must always try to make the position of the representative as clear and definite as possible, clearly marking out his powers and functions and sphere of action and responsibility. And second, we must always try to provide as a background for the action of the representative, an active and continuously resourceful organized body of constituents. It is, I believe, the presence of this continuously active constituency that gives to the Soviet system, despite its countervailing disadvantages, its peculiar vitality. In short, it is for the body of the members to counteract the tendency to clannishness and even conspiracy on the part of the elected persons by being clannish and alert in pressing forward their own common wills.

I have so far spoken of the tendency of bodies of elected persons to substitute their own wills for the wills which they are supposed to represent as if it were a single and indivisible phenomenon. There is, however, an important distinction not so much in kind as in degree. There is the involuntary and often quite unconscious perversion or substitution which arises directly out of the fact that the members of the representative body are constantly acting and deliberating together; and there is also the conscious and voluntary perversion which may easily develop out of the unconscious perversion unless it is strongly checked by the presence of an active electorate. Cabinet government is probably the worst instance of such deliberate and conscious perversion, of which the party system is also an awful, but illuminating, example.[3] Any long continuance of this aggravated form of perversion proves that there is something seriously wrong either with the electorate as a whole or with the form of representation. Its constant presence in the political system of almost every country shows either that the peoples of the world are fundamentally corrupt or foolish, or that the generally accepted theory of representative government is radically wrong.

Perversion, by the substitution of the will of the elected person for the wills he has been chosen to represent, is liable to occur in all types of representative body, and in all representative officials. We have therefore been able so far to treat representative institutions together without distinguishing for the most part between the various types. The next stage in our argument requires a more careful and detailed examination of the types of representative institutions with a view to ascertaining their right relationship one to another and to the represented. This brings us at once to a further discussion of the relation between legislative and executive power.

94

Many of the older writers on social science based the greater part of their exposition on the forms of social organization upon the double distinction of legislative and executive power, or upon the triple distinction of legislature, executive, and judiciary. I have endeavoured elsewhere to show that the distinction between legislature and executive provides no adequate basis for classifying the activities of modern societies.[4] It may be possible to distinguish with clearness sufficient for all practical purposes between the work of law-making and the work of seeing to the execution of the laws (leaving aside for the moment the judicial aspect) as long as the social situations to be dealt with remain essentially simple and free from technical complications. But in the communities of today law-making and law-administering inevitably run together. It is impossible to draft a law which will meet all the complexities of the case, and consequently our Parliaments and other legislative bodies are continually passing laws, many of whose clauses virtually delegate the power of legislation to the administrators, by providing that such and such matters may be dealt with by order in council or special order, or that the minister concerned may make orders and regulations dealing with such and such a matter – provisions which effectively blur the already faint line of division between legislation and administration. In some cases, the legislative body attempts to retaliate and to establish a control over administration through parliamentary questions, interpellations, adjournment motions, votes to reduce a salary or a credit, standing committees, select committees, and what not. The honours, however, under the parliamentary system, rest as a rule with the executive, which steadily and successfully encroaches upon the sphere of legislation.

Nor are these phenomena confined to cabinets and political assemblies. They appear also in other forms of association. Trade union executives try to seize the power of legislation out of the hands of delegate meetings; and delegate meetings retaliate by encroaching upon the sphere of administration. Wherever much detailed and complicated business has to be transacted, the line of demarcation between legislature and executive tends to break down.

This breakdown has the most far-reaching consequences for social theory. Great stress used to be laid on the balance of powers between legislature and executive as a safeguard against tyranny and perversion. Whatever value this principle may have had in the past, it has little or none today, except as a minor safeguard within each particular association. Those who seek a balance of power in social organization are therefore compelled to seek for a new principle of division. The old theory was an attempt to divide by *stages* – the law was first enacted by the legislature – and it then passed on to the succeeding stage of being administered by the executive. If this method of division by stages has broken down, there seems to be only one alternative open, if we desire to adhere to the principle of balance in any form. That alternative is to divide by *function*

[In the discussion above]... I have tried to establish the pre-eminence of function as the primary principle of social organization. We have now to see what are the consequences of the acceptance of this principle in the sphere of government. Instead of a division based on the stage which an associative act has reached (the stage of law-making or the stage of administration), it gives us a new principle of division according, not to the stage, but to the *content* and purpose of the act. In other words, the principle of function implies that each functional form of association has and is its own legislature and its own executive.

This may seem either a very startling or a very commonplace proposition according to the manner in which it is interpreted. It is commonplace, if it only means that each association has to frame rules or laws for its own guidance, and to administer the rules or laws which it has made. It is startling, if it means that the laws of other functional associations have the same binding character and social status as the laws of the state.

Nevertheless, it is the startling form of the proposition which more nearly expresses what I mean. It flows as a necessary consequence from the denial of state sovereignty and omnicompetence, and the affirmation of the functional character proper to all the various forms of association, that the state's exclusive claim to the right of legislation goes by the board. It retains, if it continues to exist, its right to legislate within its function; but this right belongs also to other associations in relation to their numbers and within their respective functions.

This does not mean that all forms of functional legislation are equally important, any more than all forms of association are equally important. But it does mean that, in the measure of their importance, all forms of association acquire for their legislative acts a comparable social status. . . .

I must. . . try to meet, at least, provisionally, an objection which is almost certainly present already in the reader's mind. If the power of legislation is divided, he will ask, does not this also imply the division of coercive power? Or, in other words, if one body's exclusive right to legislate is challenged, must not one body's exclusive right to use coercion be challenged also?

I answer unhesitatingly that it must, and that the state's monopoly of coercive power disappears with its loss of sovereignty and of the monopoly of legislation. But, before we deal finally with the huge problem which is here raised, we must make quite certain that we know what we mean by coercion, and distinguish between various forms and uses of coercive power.

NOTES

1. It is necessary to bear in mind, throughout this chapter, the sense attached to the word 'representation'. It is always functional representation alone that is to be regarded as true representation.
2. Rousseau, J.-J. (1762) *Social Contract,* book 3, chapter 10.
3. See *The Party System* by Hilaire Belloc and Cecil Chesterton [1913, London: H. Latimer] and *Democracy and the Organisation of Political Parties* by Robert Michels [1911, reprinted 1962, New York: Free Press].
4. See Cole (1917) *Self-Government in Industry* [London: G. Bell], chapter entitled 'The nature of the state'. The final section of the same chapter deals with the judiciary.

Chapter Six

COERCION AND
CO-ORDINATION

We ended the last chapter with what was virtually an interrogation. What is the nature of coercive power in the community, and how, and in what forms, is it exercised?

Every association, by the mere fact of its existence, is endowed with some coercive power, and actually exercises some such power in the course of pursuing its object. This coercive power is not necessarily recognized by the community, and the courts of law sometimes disallow particular exercises of it by voluntary associations. Nevertheless it exists, and is freely exercised every day. Very many associations claim the right to fine their members for breach of the rules, and nearly all claim the final right of expelling a member who offends against the etiquette or rules of the association, or even who, in the opinion of the members, acts con- trary to the interests of the association. Trade unions and many other kinds of association constantly fine and often expel members, and it is very seldom that their right to do so is challenged by the courts in some particular case. Indeed, often the law of the state, so far from disallowing such associational coercion, backs it up and gives it legal sanction, or at least acquiesces in its decisions. This is especially the case in the 'self-governing' professions, where the benches of the Temple, or the Law Society, or the General Medical Council freely use coercive power with the approval and sanction of the state. Thus, we can find ample instances of coercion by associations other than the state without inviting that great coercionist, spiritual and temporal, the church.

'Coercion and co–ordination' first appeared as Chapter Eight of G.D.H. Cole (1920) *The Social Theory.*

There is, however, a distinction between three kinds of coercion which it is important to recognize at the outset. There is one kind of coercion which only affects a man's purse or property, that is coercion by fine. This is freely employed, not only by the state, but by most important types of association. There is a second kind of coercion which affects a man's freedom of action by limiting directly his range of opportunity and self-expression, as, for instance, by disenfranchising him or forbidding him to work in a particular factory or occupation. The first is employed by the state and also by other forms of association; the second occurs when the members of a trade union refuse to work with a non-unionist, or expel a man from the union and then refuse to work with him, or when an employers' association 'blacklists' a man, and so prevents him from getting a job. 'Sending to Coventry' is a less organized example of this kind of coercion.

The third form of coercion is that which directly affects a man's body, by limiting his right of movement, interning him, imprisoning him, or, in the last resort, hanging him, or shooting him, or cutting off his head. In civilized counties and in modern times these forms of coercion are usually, at least in the case of adults, the monopoly of the state. Civilization, however, is often ready to resort to them without calling in the state in its dealings with what are politely called 'non-adult' races, and also, in a less degree, in the case of children. The persistence of 'lynch law' in some parts of the 'civilized' world is an exception.

How are these forms of coercion related to the functional theory of society which is propounded in this book? Where, in other words, in a functionally organized society, would the power of coercion in its various forms reside?

It is clearly useless to deny all coercive power to any association which we are prepared to recognize at all as legitimate; for whether we recognize the right to coercion or not, the power will remain and will be used. The most that is possible is to limit the forms of coercion which may be used by any particular functional association, and to reserve the right to the more stringent forms of coercion in the hands of that body which is most fit to exercise it. It is futile to endeavour to prevent an association which is allowed to make rules, and must make rules if it is go get its work done at all, from using some means to enforce their observance. Even if an association is deprived of the means of coercing its members directly, it will find indirect means of coercing them by placing obstacles in their way or withholding opportunities from them. Moreover, it is impossible altogether to prevent an association which exists to secure a particular object from coercing to a certain extent persons not its members who refuse to join it and pursue a contrary object or the same object in a different way. Here, again, the range and forms of coercion can be limited, but the possibility of coercion cannot be altogether abolished.

In a functionally organized society, it seems reasonable to suppose that each functional association will employ directly the minor forms of coercion in relation to its own members, acting within strictly limited powers, and without the right to interfere with life or liberty of person. This, however, only drives us back upon a further question. What body in a functionally organized society will define the limits within which coercion may be employed by the various associations, and itself exercise directly the major forms of coercion, if and when they are required?

It is not difficult to recognize that this question brings us back to the very point at which we broke off in our discussion of the state (see chapter 3). We were there confronted with the question of the body which would, in a functional society, exercise the powers of co-ordination at present claimed by the 'sovereign state'. But clearly co-ordination and coercion go hand in hand.

We are now in a position to restate more clearly and fully the reasons which make it impossible to recognize the task of co-ordination as falling within the true function of the state. The claim on the state's behalf is usually based on the assumption that the state, because it represents and includes everybody within its area, is necessarily superior to other associations which only include some of the persons within its area. But in what sense does the state represent and include everybody? If our functional theory of representation is right, it may include everybody, but it does not include the whole of everybody; it may represent some purposes common to everybody, but it does not represent all the purposes common to everybody. This being so, it can no longer lay claim to sovereignty on the ground that it represents and includes everybody; for the sovereign, if there is one, must represent and include, as far as possible, the whole of everybody.

This it is impossible for any single association today and indeed impossible for any complex of associations to do completely. For there are vast tracts of life which are simply not susceptible to social organization, and the purposes which they include are therefore not capable of being represented at all. This is, however, only a statement in other words of a fact which we have already recognized: that, as the state is not co-extensive with organized society, so society is not co-extensive with community.

The principle of co-ordination which we are seeking cannot therefore be a principle co-ordinating all life within a given area, but only that part of life which is social and susceptible to social organization. But it must co-ordinate the whole of that organizable social life. It cannot therefore be found in any one of the various forms of association which we have described; for to each of these forms all the others are external, and no one of them could act as a co-ordinating agency either between the others or between itself and the rest. We are therefore reduced to the conclusion that no one among the many forms of functional association can be the co-ordinating body of which we are in search.

A dim perception of this difficulty has led social theorists into a variety of expedients. Some have maintained, like Rousseau, that sovereignty resides inalienably in the whole body of the people and is incapable of being conferred upon any form of organization at all. But such a view inevitably encounters the difficulty that, although the sovereignty of the people is affirmed, no means can be found of making it actual, and all the important exercises of it pass into the hands of governing bodies which thus become virtually sovereign, even while their sovereignty is being denied.[1]

Where this difficulty is recognized as being insuperable, at least in any large society, the attempt is sometimes made to preserve popular sovereignty by the constant use of the referendum. But a mere 'yes or no' vote, without the possibility of discussion or amendment, reduces popular sovereignty to a farce except on the broadest issues, and once more the real power passes to the government, or to whoever draws up the ballot papers and so decides the form of the question to be submitted. None of these mechanical expedients really gets over the difficulty. The referendum may be the best way of dealing with certain simple issues; but by itself it certainly does not maintain popular sovereignty; nor does the addition of the initiative to it make any substantial difference.

If neither any single functional association nor the people itself can be the normal co-ordinating agency in a functionally organized society, only one possibility remains. The co-ordinating body must be not any single association, but a combination of associations, a federal body in which some or all of the various functional associations are linked together.

In [Cole's original Chapter IV] 'The forms and motives of association', some attempt was made to discriminate between *essential* and *non-essential* forms of association.[2] It was recognized that any such discrimination could be only approximate, because even the essential forms would tend to vary in different times and places. We did, however, succeed in establishing a working principle of discrimination. 'The key to essentiality', we saw, 'is the performance of some function which is vital to the coherent working of society, and without which society would be lopsided or incomplete'. We saw there that, apart from religious association, which we reserved for special treatment, there are at least three forms of association which are to be regarded as generally essential. These are *political* association and the two forms of 'economic' association or rather of association centring round the giving and receiving of services, that is to say, *vocational* and *appetitive* association. We saw also that the essentiality of these forms of association in general does not suffice to establish the essentiality of any particular association belonging to one of these forms, unless two further conditions are satisfied. The motive which binds men together in the association must be a truly 'associative' motive, and the content or function of the particular association, and not merely its form, must be important enough to warrant its being regarded as 'essential' in accordance with the criterion stated above.

I do not propose to push further... [here] the analysis of the essential forms and instances of association. To determine what actual associations are to be regarded as essential at a particular time and for a particular society is a practical question, and is therefore alien to a work dealing with social theory.[3] Here we are concerned only with the general question – with the attempt to discover the principle of co-ordination in a functionally organized society.

This principle has already been made inferentially clear. The co-ordinating agency can only be a combination, not of all associations, but of all essential associations, a joint council or congress of the supreme bodies representing each of the main functions in society. Each functional association will see to the execution of its own function, and for the co-ordination of the activities of the various associations there must be a joint body representative of them.

Here a serious objection will almost certainly be encountered. Is not his, it will be asked, merely a very roundabout way of proposing a change in the method of electing the representatives who form the state? It has often been proposed that the principle of vocational electorates should be partially recognized and incorporated in the constitution side by side with the geographical principle – that, for example, the House of Lords should be replaced by a vocational chamber. It will be suggested that, after all our blare of trumpets, this is what our 'great change' comes to in the end.

This is not so. There are two absolutely vital differences between the theory which I have been putting forward and the proposal to establish a vocational second chamber.[4]

In the first place, the assumption of the 'vocational chamber' theory is that all forms of legislation, no matter what their content, continue to be dealt with by both chambers and initiated in either. Functional organization, on the other hand, is explicitly designed to enable each functional body to deal with those matters which belong to its function, without interference in its normal operations from any outsider. It is only when a question affects more than one form of association, that is, affects men in more than one capacity or function, that it is necessary to appeal beyond the purely functional body to some body on which the various functions are represented. The whole basis of functional organization is designed to enable each functional body to get on with its own job – the job which the members know how to do, and by virtue of their common interest in which they have become associated.

Second, the co-ordinating or 'joint' body which I have in mind is less an administrative or legislative body, though it cannot help partaking in some degree of both these charters, than a court of appeal. It does not in the normal case initiate, it decides. It is not so much a legislature as a constitutional judiciary, or democratic Supreme Court of Functional Equity.

If this is clear, we can return to the question from which we were led into this discussion. Coercion and co-ordination, we said, go hand in hand. If the supreme power of co-ordination rests in the hands of this 'joint' body compounded from the essential functional associations, it seems clear that the supreme power of coercion must rest in the same hands. This involves that the judiciary and the whole paraphernalia of law and police must be under the control of the co-ordinating body.

We saw in the last chapter that the functional organization of society necessarily involves the division of power of legislation, as well as of administration, along functional lines. It does not, however, involve a similar division of the judiciary. This question, it will be remembered, we reserved for further treatment, our reason being that it could not be dealt with until we came to discuss the questions of co-ordination and coercion.

The sole possession of a high degree of coercive power, and especially of coercive power of the third kind, which directly affects a man's body, by any single form of functional association, would clearly upset the social balance at which we are aiming, and place the ultimate social power in the hands of that form of association. On the other hand, its possession in an equal degree by each of the essential forms of association would be not only, to say the least of it, inconvenient, and an invitation to the sort of cat-and-dog fight which went on between church and state in the Middle Ages, but also a denial of the relation of men to associations which is postulated as fundamental in this study. We have seen that a man is a member of an association, not with his whole personality, but with that part of it which he puts into the association in pursuance of the common object which is its function. This being so, the association has at the most no right to coerce the individual in his whole personality, but only in that part of it which he puts into the association. The right to the higher forms of coercion cannot, then, reside either in any one association or in all such associations. It must, however, be in the hands of a single body, if only for reasons of convenience; and this body can therefore only be the co-ordinating body which is a synthesis of the various essential forms of association.

Even so, there is a strict limit to the coercive power to which even the co-ordinating body is entitled. For, as we have seen, the individual puts into society, that is into social organization, not his whole personality, but only those parts of it which can find expression through social organization. The coercive right of society as a whole is therefore limited, and there remains a sphere untouched by social organization in which the individual retains his freedom from coercion. It follows that society has no right to put any many to death; for death involves a total cessation of personality – on this earth, at any rate.

Even with this safeguard, I rather suspect that many readers have been regarding what has been said in this chapter with a good deal of suspicion and dislike. So much talk about coercion, they will say, augurs ill for the sort of society which requires it. What is wanted, they will urge, is to get away from the whole idea of coercion as the basis of society; for it is its coercive character that makes the state such a nasty body.

But it is of no use to refuse to talk about a thing because one does not happen to like it. However much one may dislike coercion and seek to reduce its operation in society to a minimum, it is necessary to provide for its exercise, if only to supply a means for its abolition. For only that body which possesses coercive power is in a position to forgo or prohibit its exercise.

Having discovered where coercive power must reside in a functional society, we are now in a position to give vent to our dislike of it. One of the greatest results which, I believe, would flow from the full recognition of functional organization would be a substantial and immediate reduction in the use of coercion in society. For coercion is the consequence of social disorder, and the need for it largely comes, not of innate human wickedness, but of men's failure under existing social conditions to find their proper spheres of social service and to recognize clearly their rights and obligations in society. If we set our social house in order and make it easier for men to recognize their proper sphere of social service, the need for coercion will, I believe, speedily and progressively disappear.

Moreover, there is another huge advantage of functional society over state sovereignty. The theory of the sovereign state means that the pigmy, man, is confronted by the leviathan, state, which encircles and absorbs him wholly, or at least claims the absolute right to encircle and absorb him. It claims to 'represent' fully all the individuals who are its members, and therefore to be absolutely superior to them and over them, and to come always first. The functional principle destroys any such claim; for its denial that the individual can be 'represented' in any complete sense means that social organization, however vast and complicated it may be, leaves the individual intact and self-subsistent, distributing his loyalties and obligations among a number of functional bodies, but not absorbed in any or all of them, because outside the sphere of functional organization there remains always that most vital sphere of individuality whose self-expression is essentially personal and incapable of being organized. The functional principle is, above all else, the recognition of the absolute and inalienable personal identity of every individual person.[5]

There is one further point with which we must deal before bringing this chapter to an end. In dealing with the nature of the state, we discussed briefly the international aspects of social organization. We saw that international action, or the external actions of a particular society, have their various functional aspects, in which they fall within the sphere of the various forms of functional association. There remain those parts of international or external action which involve more than one function or call for action by society as a whole. Foremost among these there will no doubt leap to the mind of the reader the control of armed forces – the army, navy, and air force. Where, in a functional society, would the control of these reside? Who would declare war or make peace or treaties and covenants affecting society as a whole? Who would represent a functional society in a league of nations?

The answers to all these questions follow logically from what has already been established. The external use of force and coercion raises similar problems to its internal use, and it is even more manifest in external relations that the right to use it must be concentrated in the hands of a single body. One part of society cannot be at peace while another part is at war; for the claims of war upon the individual citizen are not limited to an eight hours' day, or to the act of voting; they involve for him the risk of death by violence or starvation. No less clearly is it impossible to entrust external force to any single functional association, both because external affairs involve and interest all the essential forms of association, and because force intended for use externally is also available for internal use, and sole control of armed forces would make the association which possessed it the master of society. We must, therefore, once more conclude that the external, like the internal, means of coercion, must be in the hands of the body which represents the various social functions, and is entrusted with the task of co-ordination.

Here, again, I am dealing with the problem of external force, not because armies and navies and wars are nice things, but because, whether they are nice or nasty, the problem which they present has to be faced. I hope with all my heart that they will disappear before the growth of international co-operation, not only between states, but between all the various forms of functional association. Moreover I believe that functional association, which has already shown itself far ahead of states in its sense of international solidarity, offers the best hope of a condition of world society which will make external force unnecessary, and will also persuade everybody, except the incorrigible and disappointed militarists, that it is unnecessary.

Here, then, is the answer to our last question – Who would represent a functional society in a league of nations? The answer is that an international society, which in embryo a league of nations is, if it is anything more than a sham, would reproduce in itself the functional structure of the smaller societies composing it. International functional associations would undertake, in the wider sphere, the work undertaken in the narrower sphere by national functional organization, and the central co-ordinating body would reproduce internationally the federal structure of the national co-ordinating bodies. This, no doubt, assumes a certain homogeneity of structure among the societies composing the league; but it is at least doubtful whether, without a considerable element of homogeneity, a league of nations could possibly work. A perception of this perhaps accounts for the desire of the 'sovereign states' which have just formed a league, to impress upon all candidates for entry the particular structure, economic and political which they themselves possess.[6]

NOTES

1. See my introduction to Rousseau's *Social Contract* (Everyman edition), p. xxvi.
2. [Omitted here but satisfactorily summarized below – ed.]
3. For a discussion on this point, see Cole *Self-Government in Industry*, especially the chapter on the state and the introductory chapter prefixed to the edition of 1919.

4. For a fuller discussion of this whole problem of the co-ordinating structure required, see the chapters dealing with the 'Commune' in Cole (1920) *Guild Socialism Re-Stated* [London: Leonard Parsons].

5. For a fuller discussion of this point, see my paper on 'Conflicting social obligations', (*Proceedings of the Aristotelian Society* 1915–16), and the chapter on 'The organization of freedom' in my (1918) *Labour in the Commonwealth*, [London: Swarthmore Press, Headley Bros].

6. This point is further discussed in my *Labour in the Commonwealth* chapter 2.

Part Two

CHURCHES IN THE MODERN STATE

J. N. Figgis

Chapter Seven

THE GREAT LEVIATHAN

The refusal of many lawyers to recognize in churches, as such, any real rights of life and development is widespread and inveterate; it cannot be attributed merely to anti-clerical prejudice, strong though that has always been in the profession, for it is based on principles which must also deny the similar right to other non-religious societies. . . .It is not specially English, but European, and it is of the nature rather of an unconscious presupposition than a mere theory. For those holding the current view seem almost unable to conceive what churchmen mean by claiming any freedom for religious bodies. Thus it would appear that the causes of this antipathy are not new, and that we must seek for the historical origin of this prejudice far back in history. It will be. . . [my] purpose. . . to try and show how it arose, and to urge that it relates originally to a condition long since passed away, and that we ought to demand a view of politics which has more vital relation to the facts, instead of what is little more than an abstract theory deduced from the notion of unity. . . . I cannot overestimate my debt to that great monument, both of erudition and profound thought, the *Das Deutsche Genossenschaftsrecht* of Dr Otto Gierke. . . Another work of Dr Gierke, *Die Genossenschafts Theorie*, is less well known in England, but it is worth studying. There it is attempted to show how under the facts of modern life the civilian theory of corporations is breaking down on all hands, and that even in Germany, in spite of the deliberate adoption of the Romanist doctrine, the courts and sometimes even the laws are being constantly driven to treat corporate societies as though they were real and not fictitious persons, and to regard such personality as the natural consequence of permanent association, not a mere mark to be imposed or withheld by the sovereign power. The value of all these books is the greater for our purpose that they are in no sense ecclesiastical in tone, and that the English introduction was the work of one who described himself as a 'dissenter from all the Churches'. More directly concerned with ecclesiastical liberty, but at the same time universal in application, are some of the essays by Acton in the volume on 'Freedom'.

That the problem is really concerned with the liberty alike of the individual and of the corporate society is best proved by such words as those of M. Emile Combes: 'There are, there can be no rights except the right of the State, and there are, and there can be no other authority than the authority of the Republic'. Nowhere, perhaps, has the creed of materialist politics been expressed with such naked cynicism. Such a doctrine, if accepted, [strikes] at the roots of all higher morality and all religious freedom. It is the denial at once of the fact of conscience, the institutions of religion, and the reality of the family. That this is the direction in which the forces represented by M. Combes would wish to drive Europe is clear from many circumstances. And though for the [moment] this orgy of state absolutism may be restrained by certain surviving institutions of freedom and by the facts of human life, the words here quoted show the danger those are in who surrender themselves blindly to those forces, which from Machiavelli through Hobbes and Bodin have come to be dominant in politics, and are at this moment dangerously ascendant owing to the horror of that very economic and industrial oppression which is the distinctive gift of modern capitalism to history. In this country, however, few are likely to go quite so far as M. Combes. Owing partly to the continuance of ideas that have come down from the Middle Ages, partly to the struggles of the seventeenth century, the notion of individual liberty is very strong. Individual rights of conscience are recognized – even in such matters as public health. And though there are not wanting indications that this sentiment is very much on the wane, it is still the case that, so far as principle goes, few English statesmen could deny the authority of the individual conscience. At the same time, utterances like those of M. Combes and certain movements violent at this moment in England should prevent our being too certain in this matter. Entire capitulation to this prevailing tendency to deify the state, if only in the matter of corporate institutions, will in the long run be no more favourable to individual liberty than the so-called 'free-labour' movement organized by capitalists is likely to be to the economic freedom of the artisan classes. Yet our concern. . . is not with individual, but rather with corporate liberty.

And here I have no doubt that objections will be raised. How, it will be asked, can you say that we need to do battle for the rights of corporations when already the country is groaning under their tyranny, and the law of limited companies is the cover under which is carried out every form of that exploitation which, if conducted by millionaires, is known as 'high finance', and if practised by their clerks is called by a different name? I am not denying that corporate societies exist, or that they exist in large numbers; no complex state of civilization can exist without this phenomenon appearing; and if it appears, the law must somehow or other take account of it. What is wrong is not the fact but the nature of existence allowed to these bodies in legal theory. Any corporate body, in the ordinary and not the technical sense, of a society of men bound together for a permanent interest inevitably acts with that unity and sense of direction which we attribute to personality. The question is, how is this personality to be conceived? Is it a natural fact, the expression of the social union; or is it merely something artificial imposed upon the body for its own convenience by the state? Is it real or fictitious, this legal personality? Under the dominant theory the corporate person is a fiction, a *nomen juris*; in order that societies of men may be able to act, to hold property, to sue and be sued, it is necessary to treat them as what they are not, i.e., as persons; therefore the sovereign power by its own act grants to such bodies as it pleases the name of corporation, and with it endows them with a 'fictitious' personality; since, however, it is a mere matter of convenient imagination on the part of the law, and corresponds to no reality in the collective body, its entire genesis and right are merely a delegation of the sovereign authority. All corporations owe their existence to a grant or concession of the state, tacit if not express, which may be given or withheld. Other societies, if they exist at all, are purely contractual, and have no such power of suing or being sued. They are *collegia* or *societates*, not 'universities'. The Romans approached, though they did not entirely reach, this position. The final word was really said by the great canonist Sinibaldo Fieschi, afterwards Pope Innocent IV. With the large number of cathedral chapters and religious orders in the Church, it became very necessary to arrive at clear views on the matter, and Innocent IV, starting from the doctrine of the civil law as to the nature of sovereign power and the rights of individuals, came quite definitely to the view that it was necessary to call such bodies persons; but that their personality was purely fictitious, *nomen juris*, and therefore entirely within the power of the prince. Under the influences which led to the reception of the Roman civil law in Germany and its dominance throughout western Europe, this view developed into the full doctrine of the concession theory of corporate life. Although Roman law, as such, was never accepted in England, yet through the influence of chancellors trained partly as canonists, and through the general development of absolutism in the sixteenth century, a view substantially the same became prevalent in this country, and is still the official doctrine, although more and more influences are tending in the opposite direction. . . . An instance of the way in which facts are proving too strong for it, was the judgment in the *Taff Vale Case* confirmed by the House of Lords. In order to save their funds from certain dangers, the Acts which enfranchised the trade unions in 1875, and relieved them from the law of conspiracy, had expressly denied to them the character of corporations. Thus the common chest of the union could not be raided for any illegal acts of its agents. In the *Taff Vale Case*, however, it was decided that though they were not corporate bodies legally, yet since their acts were of a nature so closely akin to those of persons, so far as the question of damages was concerned they were to be treated as such, and made responsible for the acts of agents. Outcries were raised against this judgment, which was certainly contrary to what had for nearly a generation been supposed to be the law; and eventually the Trades Disputes Act was passed to relieve the unions in regard to picketing. This, however, is irrelevant. Whatever other influences may have assisted in forming the minds of the judges, the truth is that the judgment bears witness to the fact that corporate personality, this unity of life and action, is a thing which grows up naturally and inevitably in bodies of men united for a permanent end, and that it cannot in the long run be denied merely by the process of saying that it is not there. In other words this personality is inherent in the nature of the society as such, and is not a mere name to be granted or denied at the pleasure of the sovereign authority. That so much was actually declared by the House of Lords, I do not say; but that this was the inner meaning of their decision seems undoubted. On the other hand, in the Osborne judgment the old prejudice must have been largely at the bottom of the decision, which forbade to the unions the power to use their funds as a whole to pay Members of Parliament. In other words, the members of the union are a mere collection of individuals, who are unchanged by their membership of the society, and cannot therefore have the funds subscribed turned to a purpose to which, though even in a minority, they object. A similar view is at the bottom of a recent decision about the power of a club to raise its subscription. A well-known London club attempted to do this; one of the members refused to pay the additional amount, and was expelled in consequence. He brought an action, and the courts decided in his favour, i.e., that it was all a matter of contract, and that the club had no authority, no real inherent life, which could enable it to pass beyond the arrangements made with the individual member at his election, who might thus enjoy every kind of new improvement or addition to the club without paying his share in the extra cost.

So long as this doctrine or anything like it be dominant, it would probably be an evil rather than a benefit if the Church of England were to become, what it now is not, a corporation recognized as such by the law. For that would under existing conditions mean that it was subject to all sorts of restrictions, while at the same time it would still be denied inherent rights of self-development. True, facts are always stronger than abstract theories, and the fact of corporate life might not improbably be too strong for any legal theories which denied it. This was the case in the Scotch instance. But at present this could hardly be guaranteed. On the other hand, it was shown in a very interesting essay of Maitland,[1] that part of the practical difficulty has been solved in this country by the institution of trusts. Under cover of trusteeship, a great deal of action has taken place which is really that of corporate personality, without the society being subject to the disabilities incident to the 'concession theory'. He points out in regard to the Inns of Court, which, being bodies of lawyers, may be supposed to know what is their interest, that they have always refused incorporation, finding that they can under the doctrine of trusteeship do what they want and have most of the safeguards without the disabilities of corporate life. At the same time, it was probably through the lack of a proper corporate recognition that a scandal was possible like that by which the property of Serjeant's Inn could be treated as the individual possession of its existing members and divided up between them. The essay is very interesting and valuable, for it shows how the practical good sense of Englishmen has enabled them to accept an abstract doctrine of the nature of the corporation, not germane to the realities of life, while denuding it of many of its most grievous consequences.

It may seem that these considerations are matters merely of legal theory, and that they do not concern us in the practical problem of securing reasonable liberty for the Church as a self-developing body. I think that this is not the case. For let us consider what is at the back of it all. Since the corporate society is only a *persona ficta*, with the name given it by the law, but no real inward life, we have on this view but two social entities, the state on the one hand and the individual on the other. The rights or actions of the one are private, those of the other are public. The state may be of any kind of structure, monarchic, aristocratic, or purely collectivist; but in all cases there are recognized by the law, no real social entities, no true powers, except the sovereign on the one hand with irresistible authority, and the mass of individuals on the other. Societies, so far as they exist, are mere collections of individuals who remain unchanged by their membership, and whose unity of action is narrowly circumscribed by the state, and where allowed is allowed on grounds quite arbitrary. Under such a view there can be no possible place for the religious body, in the sense of a church living a supernatural life, and the claim is quite just that no church should have any standard of morals different from those of the state.

But is not this woefully to misconceive the actual facts of social life, as they present themselves to our eyes, and to get a wrong notion of the state? Let me give an instance. Throughout the education controversy much has been heard against the iniquity of privately managed schools receiving public money, at least in the form of rates. . . . Now surely (except in the case of the one-man manager) this is a total misconception. As opposed to state management, perhaps the word private may be admitted, but when it implies, at it ought, purely individual management, a false view is suggested. These social bodies other than the state are not only not private, but in their working they are more akin to the state than they are to the individual. I mean that both of them are cases of a society acting as one, to which the individual members are subject. The relations between the member and his society are more akin to those of a citizen to a state than to anything in the individual. It is very easy to say that universities, colleges, trade unions, inns of court, etc., etc., are purely private, and in one sense it is true; they are not delegates of the state or parts of its machinery; but they are in a very real sense public, i.e., they are collective, not individual, in their constitution. . . . The point is that it is the public communal character of all such institutions that is the salient fact; and that we do wrong to adopt a rigid division into public and private, if we mean by the latter any and every institution that is not a delegation from the state. What we actually see in the world is not on the one hand the state, and on the other a mass of unrelated individuals; but a vast complex of gathered unions, in which alone we find individuals, families, clubs, trades unions, colleges, professions, and so forth; and further, that there are exercised functions within these groups which are of the nature of government, including its three aspects, legislative, executive, and judicial; though, of course, only with reference to their own members. So far as the people who actually belong to it are concerned, such a body is every whit as communal in its character as a municipal corporation or a provincial parliament.

[The view that regards the state as the sole sovereign public body is not only (ed.)] false to the true character of the state; it is entirely wrong in its view of the individual citizen. As a matter of fact, personality is a social fact; no individual could ever come to himself except as a member of a society, and the membership of any society does not leave even the adult individual where he was. There is an interpenetration of his life with that of the society, and his personality is constantly being changed by this fellowship. Too often on the part of those who strongly believe in human personality, the necessities of controversy against doctrines which virtually deny it has led to an insistence on the individual to the neglect of the social side. . . . We cannot, however, too often emphasize in regard to politics that not the individual but the family is the real social unit, and that personality as a fact never grows up except within one or more social unions. That, however, will be met by the claim that this is just what citizenship means; that 'the state is prior' to the individual, and that true personality is to grow up in the great collective union of national life. This seems to me to lie at the root of the difficulty.

When Aristotle uttered his famous dictum [that man is a political animal (ed.)], the state meant a small body of persons, not more than could be gathered in one place; and although we may hold that the antique state was too all-embracing, at least it was not unreasonable to maintain that the compact city-state of ancient Greece was the social home of all the individuals comprising it, and no more was needed. In the modern world, however, no such assertion is possible. Whatever the state may attempt, she cannot be the mother of all her citizens in the same sense as the city-state of old; and, as a fact, men will grow to maturity and be moulded in their prejudices, their tastes, their capacities, and their moral ideals not merely by the great main stream of national life, but also, and perhaps more deeply, by their own family connections, their local communal life in village or town, their educational society (for it is of the essence of education to be in a society), and countless other collective organisms. It is these that make up the life of the modern world, and to deny them all real existence or power, whether it be in the interests of legal theory or of an abstract economic collectivism, seems to me to be in principle false to the facts, and in practice to be steering straight for the rocks. . . .

What has really happened is that a conception of sovereignty which more or less expressed the facts in the ancient city-state was extended to the vast world-empire of the Romans, developed, and concentrated in the autocrat at its head. The doctrine of the unity of the sovereign power and the complete non-existence of all other real authorities became the settled presupposition of the lawyers, and crystallized into maxims which are familiar to all, such as *quod principi placuit legis habet vigorem* [the Emperor's will has the force of law (ed.)], that the Emperor was *legibus solutus* [the sole source of legislation (ed.)], and so forth. Moreover, the fact that there remained in the account of the *lex regia* a tradition of the popular origin of the Imperial authority has rendered it more easy to apply the same doctrine to a modern state. Whether or no, as the *lex regia* implies, all power was originally in the people who transferred it by irrevocable act to the prince, it is equally clear that the essential doctrine of a single irresistible authority 'inalienable, indivisible, and incapable of legal limitation' is ready to hand in the Roman system, and may be applied with equal facility to a modern democracy like France or an ancient empire like Rome. In either case it is equally destructive of any real recognition of the rights of social unions other than the state. Except as its own delegations, the Imperial government was extremely suspicious of all such societies; and, as I have said, it treated corporations in a way which differed from the more developed 'concession theory' only in that it had not reached so far even as the notion that they were fictitious persons. But the point is that of all real life in such bodies the government was most suspicious, and . . . it was just in this fact, that the Church claimed a different sanction, a separate life, and a new non-Roman unity, that lay the whole ground of the long persecution. Unfortunately, when the Church triumphed, she for the time virtually abandoned the claim to freedom within the state which had deluged the Coliseum with blood. There was no change in the antique Greco-Roman conception of a single all-absorbing omnicompetent power, the source of every right, and facing with no intermediates the vast masses of individual citizens. The only difference made was that this state from being pagan became Christian, and after the proscription of paganism by Theodosius the Great there was no need for men to worry themselves with forming a totally new doctrine of the structure of civil society. The *De Civitate Dei* of St Augustine provided the framework in which all the political thinking of men was done for more than a thousand years, nor is its influence even yet extinct. The medieval doctrine of the *Holy Roman Empire* crystallized this ideal in a form which, if not very practicable, was at least an object to work for, and did as a fact direct the life and work of many of its greatest leaders. An ideal which Charles the Great, Otho the Great, Pope Sylvester II, Henry of Luxemburg were content even to try to realize cannot be dismissed as of no influence on the lives of men. If it was not realized, it at least caused people to do what they would otherwise have left undone and ruled their imaginations, a fact which is plain from Dante's *De Monarchia* and from many of the most striking passages in the *Divina Commedia*.

On the other hand, the Teutonic polity and habit of mind, if it did not quite produce, approached a view of the relation of the individual to the society and of the smaller societies to the whole, which is that to which we are being driven. The enormous development of corporate life in the Middle Ages, guilds of every kind, and the whole notion of the system of estates in the body politic all testified to the same fact. There was a very definite sense of the individual, not as something separate, but as moulded and interpenetrated by the life of the society. There was, further, the very definite sense that the societies all were organic, that they lived by an inherent spontaneity of life, and that as communal societies they had their own rights and liberty, which did not originate in the grant of the sovereign. As Gierke, however, points out, this was instinctive rather than theoretical; they had not reached the difficult and developed conception of corporate personality. And this, among many other causes, is the explanation of the ease with which the ancient ideas of corporate liberty and real social life went down before the logically developed and erudite system which ruled the minds of the lawyers from the Renaissance onwards.

Nor must it be supposed that the Church was an exception. The theory of the Church came from the Roman empire. Neither churchmen nor statesmen believed in two separate social entities, the Church and the State, each composed of the same persons. Nor indeed was that necessary in the medieval idea of a Christian state. Rather, when conflict is spoken of between Church and State, it is conflict between two bodies of officials, the civil and the ecclesiastical. When Henry IV resisted Hildebrand, he admitted that for the case of heresy he might be deposed; and the whole atmosphere of the medieval mind was such that we cannot picture them as treating the two as really separate societies. When the liberty of the Church is claimed, it almost always denotes the liberty of the hierarchy, not that of the whole body. Alike on the Imperial and the Papal side, the claims raised would have been inconceivable, had it not been admitted that both Popes and Emperors were rulers in one society. I do not say that there was no approximation to the idea of a 'free church in a free state'; but so long as persecution was taken for granted, and a coercive church-state was the ideal, the claims which we put forward were not seriously entertained. That was the root of the difficulty.

With the then existing presuppositions and the argument from abstract unity so strong – strong partly because of the universal lawlessness – the claim to freedom, whether put forward by the civil or the ecclesiastical power, because inevitably a claim to supremacy, and was therefore never really admitted by the others. The

Popes could never allow that matters of religion and conscience were to be at the mercy of politicians; the Emperors could never allow that the state merely existed on sufferance of the spiritual power. This conflict could never be solved so long as both parties maintained the right and duty of persecution, i.e., the necessary connection of membership of the Church with citizenship in the state. Furthermore, inside the polity of the Church, the other system had triumphed and the development of the Papal system meant the transference to the Pope of all the notions of illimitable authority claimed by the Emperor in truth. The great *Leviathan* of Hobbes, the *plenitudo potestatis* of the canonists, the *arcana imperii*, the sovereignty of Austin, are all names of the same thing – the unlimited and illimitable power of the law-giver in the state, deduced from the notion of its unity. It makes no difference whether it is the state or the church that is being considered.

Towards the close of the Middle Ages it might seem as though the way was being paved for a more natural system. So far as the European monarchs were concerned, the Imperial claim remained no more than honorific, and after the conflict between Philippe le Bel and Boniface VIII there seemed no possibility of asserting claims of the papacy against the rising national powers. Within those national powers, institutions had arisen all over Europe, which expressed the fact that the state was a *communitas communitatum*. This is the true meaning of our word Commons; not the mass of the common people, but the community of the communities. However imperfect in theory, there was a practical recognition of merchant and craft guilds, with borough charters, guild liberties, the baronial honours, with courts Christian, courts royal, and courts manor, all functioning, with special laws and customs recognized even for fairs and markets and universities. These facts, together with the traditions of fellowship life coming down from a long past, might well make it seem that a system of universal liberties and balanced powers would result, that at last the lion of the throne would like down with the lamb of spiritual freedom in a semi-federalist polity.

But it was not to be. The lion got outside the lamb. Roman Law became more and more the norm; 1495 is the date of its reception in Germany; national and local customs were decried by the civilians, learned, classical, Romanist to the core. The dangers of anarchy under feudalism made the mass of men blind to the dangers of autocracy. All the learning of the Renaissance was in favour of the power of the prince, save for a few dreamers who looked to a republic. Clerical immunities had been abused; the religious orders were too much of an *imperium in imperio*. With the Lutheran movement, there went on the one hand the destruction of the ancient conception of Christendom as a single polity, under the leadership of Pope and Emperor and the Lordship of Christ; and on the other, the transference to the prince as head of a compact territorial unity of the bulk of the prerogatives of both spiritual and secular power. The doctrine of *cujus regio ejus religio* [the religion of the prince determines the religion of the state (ed.)] of the religious peace of Augsburg was the natural expression of this fact; so that one elector could say quite readily that his people's conscience belonged to him. That was, of course, the notion of Henry VIII. It was formulated into a complete theory of the state by Jean Bodin in France, and afterwards by Thomas Hobbes in England. Hobbes denied every kind of right not derived from the sovereign; and devotes one book of his Leviathan to 'the kingdom of darkness', in other words the Roman Church, which he thus denominates because its claims would break up the unity of the sovereign power. In the seventeenth century, both in England and on the Continent, this notion of a compact omnicompetent sovereign, by whose permission alone existed the right to breathe, was mixed up with the theory of the divine right of kings. But it is not really tied thereto. The eighteenth century saw it asserted of Parliament; and the claim to parliamentary omnipotence was the real cause of the American Revolution. In the other hemisphere was set up a state which, as being federal, was largely a denial of this claim; but the civil war seems to have proved the contrary. Even now, however, the doctrine of state rights is still strong, is said to be gaining rather than losing adherents, and we may learn much from the attitude of the American courts to such problems as those of the free development of religious bodies.

In France, unlike England, the theory of sovereignty had been crystallized in the person of the monarch; but it was not over-thrown by the Revolution. What was overthrown was the surviving remnant of feudalism and the last relics of local and partial liberty. The doctrine of a single uniform all-absorbing power has been carried to a height further than even Louis XIV could have dreamed; and, as we have seen, even religious toleration exists only in name. This doctrine has found in England classical expression in the writings of John Austin, which do little more than formulate the Roman theory of sovereignty, and is imbued with the same notion of the entire distinction between public and private, which forbids any right classification of social institutions. Austin has been subjected to much criticism, but with certain slight qualifications his notions still rule the legal mind – except, of course, those who are definitely working towards a new doctrine of corporate life. And in regard to the church, to morals alike, it is taken as an axiom that the law is morally binding, and by many that what is legally right cannot be morally wrong.

This doctrine is, however, becoming more and more difficult to reconcile with the facts. As a mere verbal theory I do not know that this view of sovereign power is assailable; and by means of the proviso that whatever the sovereign permits he commands, we cannot positively say that any measure of freedom is inconsistent with it. Practically, however, it is clear that we need something different and more profound. We have seen one salient instance of the pitfalls it is apt to lead to. We must bear in mind that Parliament is nominally sovereign, not only in England but in every portion of the Empire, and that no local liberty exists in theory but as a delegated authority for the will of the imperial Parliament. Yet in regard to the immigration law in South Africa, it was admitted that the imperial Parliament dare not override the will of the local bodies even though they were doing a manifest injustice to their fellow-subjects. In other words, the local body had a real independent life, and could not be touched.

The theory of government which is at the root of all the trouble is briefly this. All and every right is the creation of the one and indivisible sovereign; whether the sovereign be a monarch or an assembly is not material. No prescription, no conscience, no corporate life can be pleaded against its authority, which is without legal limitation. In every state there must be some power entirely above the law, because it can alter the law. To talk of rights as against it is to talk nonsense. In so far as every state is a state, this view is held to be not only true but self-evident. In so far as it is not true, it is because the state is in a condition of incipient dissolution and anarchy is already setting in. The doctrine of sovereignty is, in fact, a deduction partly from the universality of law in a stable commonwealth, and partly from the abstract notion of unity. . . .

But the truth is, that this state in a sense of absolute superhuman unity has never really existed, and that it cannot exist. In theory it represents a despot ruling over slaves; in practice even a despot is limited by the fact that slaves are, after all, human; deny their personality as you like, there comes a point at which it asserts itself, and they will kill either the despot or themselves. At bottom the doctrine represents a state which is a super-man ruling individuals who are [sub] men. . . . It is partly symbolized by the title-page of the *Leviathan* of Hobbes. Attempts are made to get out of the difficulty by saying that the sovereign power, though theoretically illimitable, is limited in practice very materially, psychologically by its own nature, and externally by the fact that there are certain things which no government can do without provoking resistance, e.g., Louis XIV could not have established Mohammedanism, even if he had wished. In this way custom on the one hand, local liberties or individual rights on the other, would acquire a place. We are, I admit, brought nearer to the facts.[2] But it seems a weakness in a doctrine that you can only fit the facts into its framework by making such serious qualifications, and it would appear a more reasonable maxim to get a theory of law and government not by laying down an abstract doctrine of unity, but by observing the facts of life as it is lived, and trying to set down the actual features of civil society. What do we find as a fact? Not, surely, a sand-heap of individuals, all equal and undifferentiated, unrelated except to the state, but an ascending hierarchy of groups, family, school, town, county, union, church, etc., etc. All these groups (or many of them) live with a real life; they act towards one another with a unity of will and mind as though they were single persons; they all need to be allowed reasonable freedom, but must be restrained from acts of injustice towards one another or the individual; they are all means by which the individual comes to himself. For in truth the notion of isolated individuality is the shadow of a dream, and would never have come into being but for the vast social structure which allows a few individuals to make play, as though they were independent, when their whole economic position of freedom is symbolic of a long history and complex social organization. In the real world, the isolated individual does not exist; he begins always as a member of something, and, as I said earlier, his personality can develop only in society, and in some way or other he always embodies some social institution. I do not mean to deny the distinctness of individual life, but this distinction can function only inside a society. Membership in a social union means a direction of personality, which interpenetrates it, and, according to your predilection, you may call either an extension or a narrowing; it is in truth both. You cannot be a member of any society and be the same as though you were not a member; it affects your rights and duties, limits at once and increases your opportunities, and makes you a different being, although in many different degrees, according to the nature of the society and the individual member. You are not merely John Doe or Richard Roe, but as John may probably be a member of the Christian church by baptism, a Doe by family, an Englishman by [nationality]; all three are social institutions, which have grown into you. In addition to this you are a member of a school, an alumnus of a college, a sharer in this club, a president of that, and so forth. All these groups and unions have their effect, and limit and develop your life, make you do, or refrain from doing, what otherwise you would not, and in so far prevent you being a free and untrammelled citizen of the state. More than that, they penetrate your imagination and your thought, and alter not only what you do but what you want to do. Between all these groups there will be relations, and not merely between the individuals composing them. *To prevent injustice between them and to secure their rights, a strong power above them is needed. It is largely to regulate such groups and to ensure that they do not outstep the bounds of justice that the coercive force of the state exists* [editors emphasis]. It does not create them; nor is it in many matters in direct and immediate contact with the individual. The claim of the church in matters of education is the claim that she shall be recognized as a group, in which the natural authority over its members extends to the provision of a social atmosphere; and this ought to be admitted, provided the requirements of citizenship in secular culture be provided and controlled.

All this, it will be said, lessens the hold of the state over the individual. But this is needful the moment you reach any large and complex society. In a developed state of civilization many interests must be allowed social expression, which in one sense are a separating influence. Even a member of a musical club is so far separated from those who are excluded; and he is changed by the fact of this club life, which enters into him. . . .

Recent discussions are making men ask once more in matters other than religion, what are the limits of the authority of Parliament. The idolatry of the state is receiving shrewd blows. It is said, however, especially in regard to the church, that to recognize its rights is dangerous. But if it is a fact, it must be more dangerous not to recognize its real life. The same is true of individuals. However you may proclaim with M. Combes that 'there are no rights but the rights of the state', you find individuals who habitually act as if they had them; and even when you go on to say that 'there is no authority but the authority of the republic', you do not in practice prevent all kinds of societies from behaving in a way that implies authority over their members. Nor can you. It is impossible. Society is inherent in human nature, and that means inevitably the growth of a communal life and social ties; nor is it possible to confine this to the single society we call the state, unless it be on a very small scale, and even then there is the family to reckon with. Of course such societies may come into collision with the state; so may individuals. Always there is a possibility of civil war. But you will not escape the possibility by ignoring the facts. The only way to be sure an individual will never become a criminal is to execute him; the only way to secure a state from all danger on the part of its members is to have none. Every state is a synthesis of living wills. Harmony must ever be a matter of balance and adjustment, and this at any moment might be upset, owing to the fact that man is a spiritual being and not a mere automaton. It would seem to be wiser to treat all these great and small corporate entities which make up our national life as real, as living beings, i.e., practically as persons, and then when this is once realized, limit them in their action, than it is to try and treat them as what they are not, i.e., as dead bodies, dry bones, into which nothing but an arbitrary fiat gives a simulacrum of life, which may at any moment be withdrawn. After all, the Roman government did not destroy the living unity of the church by denying its claim to exist; but it nearly destroyed itself in the attempt.

126

NOTES

1. *Collected Papers*, vol. 3, pp. 321–404.
2. This view is most lucidly stated by Professor Dicey in *The Law of the Constitution*, pp. 72–81.

Part Three

THE FOUNDATIONS OF SOVEREIGNTY AND OTHER ESSAYS

H.J. Laski

Chapter Eight

THE PROBLEM OF ADMINISTRATIVE AREAS

I

It has become almost a commonplace that we have reached a critical epoch in the history of representative government. Certainly no man would now claim that the large aspirations of those who, with Bentham and the radicals, fought the great battle of parliamentary reform in the early part of the nineteenth century have been to any adequate degree fulfilled.[1] They are, indeed, different; for the direction taken by political activities in the last fifty years has been almost antithetic to that which he would have approved. The English state has become a positive state; by which is meant that instead of trusting to the interplay of possibly conflicting self-interests for the realization of good, it has embarked upon an effort, for some time at least to come, definitive, to control the national life by governmental regulation. . . .

The truth surely is that we have evolved the great society without any safeguards that our political institutions would keep pace with the changes in social and economic structure. No one who examines the large outlines of the English governmental system can point to any vast discoveries. Differences, of course, there are, and some of them are fundamental. The emergence of a labour party, the transference of the centre of political power from the House of Commons to the Cabinet, the consolidation of that pre-eminence given by Mr Gladstone's long career to the office of Prime Minister, a superb improvement in the quality of the civil service, these, and things like these, have an importance no man may deny. But no small part of these changes has been due to the breakdown of the main hypothesis upon which the democracy of the nineteenth century was founded.

Here, once more, it was the influence of Bentham and his followers that was decisive.[2] They believed that all men were more or less equal in their original endowments, and that differences were the product of environment. The more training was equalized, the more power would be distributed in just proportions throughout the state. Universal suffrage and the breakdown of social privilege thus assumed a very vital significance. Once the factors of depression were removed the natural equalities of men would manifest themselves, and the reason of their enlightened self-interest would effect the improvement desired. Bentham expected the average citizen to take an interest in politics which would be based upon a considered judgement of the questions at issue. That may have been more possible than it is now in the negative period before 1870; but, certainly, since that time it has been purely idle as a valid expectation. Conditions have become so complex that no one can follow any problem in its different bearings without an unremitting attention. The average voter could not afford to give the time to the consideration of affairs that their actual understanding demanded; nor had his education been, on any large scale, adapted to the needs of citizenship. . . .

The fundamental hypothesis of government in a representative system is that it is government by discussion [editor's emphasis]. The private Member of Parliament was supposed, as in Burke's magnificent conception, to use his best judgement upon the bills presented by government, and to vote as the dictates of his instructed mind would seem to warrant. There has never, of course, been a time in which such an ideal could have been even approximately realized; and, certainly, anyone who reads the history of the first forty years of George III's reign will have cause to deny that any degeneration has taken place. But parliamentary government in the twentieth century is still essentially different from parliamentary government in the nineteenth. . . .

No one, in fact, who considers, however superficially, the working of the English parliamentary system can doubt that some of its defects are fundamental. The independence of the private member has, for practical purposes, disappeared. The rigidity of party ties has notably been increased. The reality of debate has been largely impaired by the simple necessity of getting business done. It is a commonplace to note the apathy of those not actively engaged in working the machinery of a party. The unreality of party distinctions is at least as obvious as in the days when George III deliberately aimed at their obliteration. Before such issues as Home Rule and woman suffrage that party government which Bagehot declared the vital principle of representative government was simply bankrupt. . . .

In whatever analysis is made of the conditions of the modern representative system, two facts stand out with striking clarity. On the one hand, it is obvious that there is no deliberative assembly that is not utterly overwhelmed by the multiplicity of its business; on the other hand, it is at least equally clear that the average elector, except in times of crisis or abnormal excitement, is but partially interested in the political process. Nor have the attempts to cure the latter evil, which have mainly, as in Switzerland and the United States, taken the form of experiments in direct government, been at all remarkable for their success. The statistics make it evident that the voter is more interested in persons than in events, and the very size of the modern state makes direct government, at best, but a partial aid. Much more is to be said for the possibilities of an adequate educational system on the one hand, and an increased leisure on the other. Certainly we too little realize how pitifully small is the relation between the problems of modern politics and the curriculum of that elementary school which is alone compulsory for the next decade. Modern studies in the problem of industrial fatigue explain how little of intellectual value can usefully, or even rightly, be expected from a population whose energy is so largely consumed in the simple task of earning its own living. Something, too, might here be said of the relation of work to that energy of the soul which Aristotle proclaimed the secret of happiness.[3] Certainly such evidence as we have tends to suggest that the increasing subordination of the worker to the machine does not improve the intellectual quality of our civilization. Indeed, it is not impossible that, in the future, democracy, if it is to become an effective instrument, will be compelled to transfer the centre of importance for at least a large part of its manual workers from the hours of labour to the hours of leisure. But that day is not yet.

Nearly a century ago, the profoundest French observer of the last age [Alexis de Tocqueville – ed.] analyzed the potentialities of that democracy which, as he predicted, was destined to become the universal type of government. An aristocrat both by birth and by nature, but little capable of that enthusiasm for the multitude with which men so diverse as Gambetta and Gladstone were so signally endowed, de Tocqueville could not regard its advent with unmixed gladness. He found himself depressed by the prospect of certain dangerous contingencies. It was possible, he thought,[4] that a people might barter its responsibility for its own government in exchange for material comfort. Democratic rule might degenerate into simple majority rule without any safeguard that the majority would include the best opinion of which the society was capable. A jealous level of dull uniformity might depress the use by each citizen of his utmost talents for the common good. The richness and variety of the national life might well be drawn into the vortex of a governmental omniscience which would emulate a theological authority. The real object of a state, he thought,[5] was the emancipation of individuality; and he did not believe in the possibility of its attainment where the character of its government was a centralized and mercantile parliamentarism. He feared the influence of money upon its politics. He saw with distress the decline of religious faith without any accompanying compensation in the form of social sanctions. He perceived the novelty of the change effected by the Revolution: 'a new political science', he said,[6] 'is necessary to this new world'.

It is difficult to deny the truth of his general attitude. Certainly the best approach to the defence of democracy is through the analysis of previous social systems. For the real justification of a democratic state is, after all, the fact that under its aegis a larger number of men share in the riches life can offer than under any alternative. Nevertheless the evils predicted by de Tocqueville remain, and it is difficult to see any immediate prospect of their amelioration. Certainly in relation to the actual quality of life, the things for which the interest of men can be obtained, it is only to the slow influence of education that we can look for change. Nothing would be more fatal to the working of democratic government than a permanent divorce between the process of politics and the life that is led by the mass of men. The professional politician is clearly necessary in the task of administration; but it would result in the negation of the democratic hypothesis, if the making of policy were not conducted with the active co-operation of the body of citizens. That does not, indeed, imply that rotation of office in which the Greek states placed so large a confidence and for which the American commonwealth still cherishes so singular and so dangerous an affection. Rather does it imply the perpetual and widespread discussion of men and measures, the ceaseless instruction of the public mind, at which Harrington aimed in the clubs that formed so attractive an element in his Utopia.[7] It means the continuous existence of an urgent public opinion.

That is, as Mr Wallas has recently shown,[8] no easy matter. There are problems... upon which a public cannot, in the nature of things, be formed. There are others in which a public opinion seems possible upon matters of principle but, to say the least, extremely difficult on matters of detail. Thus far, it must be admitted we have done but little to utilize, in any full degree, the material we have. The elements that go to the making of a political decision are rarely considered enough, on the one hand, or widespread enough, on the other, to make an external and detached observer convinced that the process by which that decision is reached is at all satisfactory. We have not, indeed, descended so low as that 'man of superhuman mental activity managing the affairs of a mentally passive people', which Mill thought[9] the 'most pernicious misconception of good government'; but, still, the number of people upon whom a decision depends, the number whose thoughts have to be weighed and consulted, is curiously small. ...

It is an obvious fact that the increase of governmental activity has implied a vast extension of the civil service. In France it is said that, in normal times, one-fortieth of the population is so employed. While in Great Britain the proportion is far less, measures like the Insurance Act have notably extended it; and it remains true, as Mr Graham Wallas has significantly remarked,[10] that every scheme of improvement upon which the state embarks entails an increase in the number of public officials. It may, indeed, be admitted that such increase is not necessarily a defect; but its magnitude, in recent years, raises grave questions of which those connected with the public revenue are only the smallest.[11] What remains vital is the fact that the growth of bureaucracy in every civilized country does not seem, on the evidence, compatible with the maintenance of a liberal spirit. ... However beneficial may be the consequences of social legislation – and that a large part of it does confer benefit is unquestionable – it does not compensate for improvements wrought out with their own minds by those upon whom the benefit is conferred. Social legislation has the incurable habit of tending towards paternalism; and paternalism, however wide be the basis of consent upon which it is erected, is the subtlest form of poison to the democratic state.

It may mitigate, but it does not solve, the essential problem: which is to interest the largest possible number of persons in the study of, and judgement upon, political questions. A far wider political enterprise is needed from the mass of men to make durable the gains of the last fifty years. It may even be urged that only in this fashion can we hope to make possible the emergence of that practical and speculative leadership of which the world has need; for a people of which the alternative interests are either half-whimsical contemplation or mere amusement will never produce a great civilization.

It is possible that, in this regard, we too greatly depreciate the significance of political mechanisms. It is, of course, true that the main questions of democracy are what may be termed moral questions, depending far more upon the possession of mind and character than upon any other factors. But mind and character are everywhere useless without the full opportunity of application. It is here that the mechanisms of modern democracy seem most inadequate. For we have not sufficiently related the areas they traverse to the occupations of the average man. We have generally left unconnected the life he leads with the construction of those rules of conduct by which that life is governed. We are suffering, in fact, from an over-centralization which results from placing too great an emphasis upon the geographical factor in government. We have collected so much power at a single point in the body politic, we have so much emphasized the distribution of functions in terms of that point, that the only system of government of which we can conceive is one which takes its orientation from that direction. Yet it is at least uncertain whether new possibilities do not exist.

II

England is what is termed a unitary state. The King in Parliament is there the sole and final source of existent powers. Every species of local authority derives those powers it can exercise directly or indirectly from some parliamentary enactment. It is generally admitted that the result of this system has been to cast an overwhelming burden of business upon the House of Commons, and schemes for the relief of such pressure have taken. . . the form of some measure of decentralization. . . .

The incoherent anarchy of the period before the Municipal Reform Act led, in the course of the nineteenth century, to a complete and necessary reconstruction of local government. Until that time, and ever since the rigid centralization of the Tudor period, practically no administrative connection had existed between the local authorities and Whitehall. The scandals of municipal corruption, coupled with the obvious limitations of government by county justices confined to a particular class, led the more rigid reformers, such as Chadwick, to attempt a complete administrative centralization; but the traditional opinion in favour of some active and quasi-independent local powers was sufficient to prevent the adoption of the rigorous bureaucratic methods which prevail so largely upon the continent of Europe. As it is, the course of development has led to the emergence of a type of authority at once different from the centralized rigour of France, on the one hand, and the loose dispersion of powers in the United States on the other. . . .

What has been done is, in the first place, to lay down the functions it is the business of the local authority to fulfil and, as a later and growing development, to assist and stimulate their performance either by a grant in aid or the conference of an assigned revenue. It does not seem that the latter method has any other advantage than the simplification of national bookkeeping; but the former, the grant in aid, may well be claimed as a capital discovery in the technique of administration. John Stuart Mill long ago insisted on the necessarily greater width of knowledge and experience that is available in the central depository of government; and it is the unique value of the grant in aid that it enables the central authority to oversee performance without that detailed interference which a jealous localism might well consider excessive. It has thus maintained, at least in part, the virtues of a decentralized administration, without suffering it to fall into the vices of negligent parochialism. . . .

What clearly is needed is something that affords the advantages of a territorial federal system without the destruction of parliamentary sovereignty, at any rate in the sense of final control. It is worth while here to insist that there is really no rigid line between federal and unified governments; the only real difference... is in the degree of power retained by, or conferred upon, the localities. The United States may, in theory, ascribe definite functions to the federal government, and the indefinite residue of powers to the states; but no one who watches the interpretation of the Constitution by the Supreme Court will question the impossibility of a final classification.... Federalism undoubtedly results from the coalescence of what were before separate groups, and it is thus distinct from that decentralization which makes a partial separateness where, before, there was complete unity. Yet either system is, in reality, no more than an attempt at finding the most convenient areas of administration. Federalism, as Professor Dicey has insisted,[12] results in the creation of a national state, and, whatever the original powers, it will ultimately become true, as Mr Justice Holmes has pointed out,[13] 'that the national welfare, as understood by Congress, may require a different attitude within its sphere from that of some self-keeping state'. Certainly the result of that wider need is a degree of local subordination which will change as the needs of the nation change. Yet it is the singular merit of a federal system that the creation of a national allegiance does not destroy the special interest of the citizen in the province to which he belongs. The Bavarian does not the less believe in Munich because of the predominance of Berlin.... Eager citizens of Chicago will explain its manifest superiority to Boston or New York; and the claims of size are resisted by the patriotism which the tiny cities of the Middle West can call into being. It is that internal diversity of allegiance which makes possible the creation of active governmental centres distinct from Washington. There is no evidence to prove... that federal government is either weak or conservative. The weakness is the purely theoretical fact that a division of powers opens up legal contingencies of conflict which are avoided in a unified state.... It is not asserted that the administrative areas or the division of powers in the United States are ideal. On the contrary, it is all too evident that they stand in grave need of change. That only means, however, that the frame of government adapted to the ideas of 1787 is inadequate a century and a half later; which, after all, is no cause for complaint in a period which has seen greater material changes than any previous age. It does not invalidate the underlying assumptions of federalism.

Lord Bryce has pointed out[14] that no argument relative to local government which can be urged in favour of federalism does not also hold for a decentralized system. Either will, if adequate, provide a means of experiment which is difficult, if not impossible, if applied to the area of a whole country. Either relieves the pressure of national business by the entrustment of its final charge, where it is merely local in nature, to local authorities. Either provides a substantial check, in these years a greatly needed benefit, against the fears of bureaucracy. And, within England, fiscal reasons seem to make decentralization the preferable method. Whitechapel, for instance, has a proportionately less rateable value than Hampstead, though its governmental needs are greater. Inevitably, therefore, improvements in Whitechapel must lean more upon central assistance than improvements in Hampstead. So long as the system of grants-in-aid is continued, and its cessation would be a matter for deep regret, every local authority must rely upon the national exchequer for subventions. Anything in the nature of fiscal decentralization would at once deeply injure the prestige of the House of Commons – a more serious matter in its remoter ramifications than is lightly to be supposed – and raise every problem the central departments now confront in several places instead of one. Clearly, again, that subvention ought to be made dependent upon an adequate fulfilment of functions. That ought to involve in the central power – whether there are intermediate authorities or no – the retention of some inspective control. . . .

III

The problem of local government in this aspect is only in smaller perspective the problem of the modern state. It raises exactly the same issues as are raised by the general question of the modern representative system. There mere announcement of a plentitude of power in any authority will solve nothing; the essential business is to get that power to work. We are, in fact, beyond the sphere of law. We are dealing not with the conference of rights, but with their realization, which is a very different matter. It is, of course, important to consider the purpose by which such power is informed. But that purpose can never be, except for law, a mere matter of declaration;[15] the Supreme Court of the United States may well declare a statute constitutional which announces civil war. Purpose, in fact, must be discovered in pragmatic fashion, from the actual processes in their joint operation. It is today a commonplace that the real source of authority in any state is with the holders of economic power. The will that is effective is their will; the commands that are obeyed are their commands. Nor is the less true of local than of central government. The city council of Manchester, for example, will, on the whole, represent the normal purposes of a group of middle-class business men; their decisions will be imbued with that 'intuition more subtle than any articulate major premise', which, as Mr Justice Holmes has observed,[16] is the true origin of the convictions expressed by the Supreme Court of the United States. There is herein no suggestion of sinister motive. It is no more than the simple assertion that we cannot escape our environment. Those who hold power will inevitably feel the definition of good is the maintenance, in some fashion, of the *status quo*; exactly as the landowners could find economic ruin in the repeal of the corn laws and the manufacturers commercial disaster in the factory acts. It is a general rule that we identify our private good with the common good and write the result out large in the election returns.[17]

Legislation, then, reflects the minds that make it, whether its makers be Members of Parliament or of the bench or the civil service; and it is only human that this should be so. Once it is perceived, what becomes of importance in the processes of politics is the character of those minds if that legislation is in any broad sense to represent general needs and general desires. The constituency from which its makers are drawn must cast its limits far; but the makers themselves must be not less representative in character. Here, surely, is a source of many of the difficulties by which modern government is faced. In England, at least, we have avoided that bare-faced travesty of the representative system that is embodied in the Prussian franchise; but property, in more subtle and indirect fashion, still securely finds the emphasis it desires.[18] The business of government has, for the most part, been confined to the middle class; and the results have largely reflected the aptitudes and purposes of that class. In local government, for example, we have a wise insistence on adequate sewage systems, a proper supply of good drinking water, reasonable secondary education for those who can, in a wider sense than simple fees, afford it, technical instruction that the middle ranks of the industrial hierarchy may be adequately filled, proper lighting systems – these are the characteristics by which it has been distinguished. They all of them represent common needs; and the local government has been successful in securing those common needs exactly as parliamentary government has been successful in securing the common freedoms. A sewage service can hardly be confined to a single class, any more than a modern university can be (outside Ireland) confined to a single faith; and the flavour of generality that is implied in such service the present system has been able to secure.

But it has proved inadequate exactly at the point where the larger system has proved inadequate. Once, that is to say, we pass the frontier of middle-class needs, we enter the debatable land. English local and English parliamentary government has proved a satisfactory thing for the man whose income is secure and reasonably comfortable; it has accomplished little for the ranks below him. It was the perception of this truth in national politics which led, after 1906, to the revival of the idea of industrial democracy as the paramount issue; labour in politics had discovered to how large an extent theories of government reflect prevailing economic systems. The local government of England is a government for ratepayers, and that largely, under the present system, must mean a government according to the ideas of those who feel the burden of the rates. But it is exactly the needs of the working class which lie outside the realm of subjects to which the will of the ratepayer can be fruitfully directed. Immense housing extension, a large development of the public library system. . . do not interest those who are already satisfactorily provided for in these regards. The result is that the workers' interest, pale enough in any case in the details of national government, is but the shadow of a shadow in local concerns.

It is doubtless a good rhetorical answer to urge that the larger part of the working class has the franchise and that if it does not choose to exert its power it must take the consequences. But that is to mistake the superficial appearance of a political system for its inner reality; it is no more a real expression of the 'general' will of the state than the election of Tweed to a state senatorship of New York expressed contentment with the vices of Tammany.[19] The

King of England does not rule in practice because he rules in theory. England has developed a system of governmental institutions which provide an admirable opportunity for the workings of democracy; but it is a least equally clear that the institutions only partially work. Surely the real source of this disharmony is to be found in the way in which any political system must necessarily reflect its economic environment. The local institutions of England, for example, do not reflect the mind or desires of the working class because they are in substance adjusted to a situation which, economically, at any rate, is far from democratic. They are representative in theory but not in practice. The problem then becomes the permeation of them with the ideas of the working class. Nor is that a simple matter. It does not merely imply the running of working class candidates at local elections. The question of expense apart, there is not sufficient likelihood of their getting elected to make the experiment worth while on any large scale. It is not a sufficient answer that if they cannot get elected the state does not want them. We know too much and too little about the problems connected with the group will to make warrantable such *ex cathedra* pronouncements. The question is whether things like Whitechapel and Angel Meadow are to remain. They will remain so long as the poor endure them; and the poor will endure them until their economic power is so organized as to secure political expression. It was that kind of public opinion which produced the Trade Union Act of 1875–6; which secured the statutory reversal of the Taff Vale decision; which cut at the root of the fatal clause in the House of Lords' judgment in the Osborne case. The problems of labour are, of course, so vast, that it is in general difficult to do more than focus its attention on national questions. But more than that is needed.

It is in some such fashion that we are driven back to that decentralization which, as has been suggested, is in reality a method of securing the results of federalism without the juristic basis upon which the latter, as classically conceived, rests. Here, it is probable, our thinking has been conceived in terms too narrowly spatial in character. What we have mostly done is to think of the average factor in the formation of opinion as a single individual equipped to understand the arguments on either side; with the corollary belief that one vote is in the process the moral equivalent and influence of another. That is, of course, absurdly untrue.

Much opinion there undoubtedly is; man is not less a solitary than a social creature. But, for the most part, it is as a member of a special fellowship that the average man is accustomed both to think and act. He is, maybe a citizen of Manchester; but his desire, say in 1908, to assist his constituency to be represented by a cabinet minister in the person of Mr Winston Churchill is checked, as a churchman, by the memory of Mr Birrell's Education Bill, and as a holder of brewery shares, by a dim feeling that Mr Asquith's licensing proposals have been condemned by the proper authorities who protect those widows and orphans who, in England, so curiously limit their investments to brewery shares. The average elector, in fact, is instinct with that spirit of the herd which he cannot escape by simple virtue of his humanity.[20] All such relationships create what, for want of better word, we call a personality. That does not necessarily imply that a new physical person has come into being. It simply means that we encounter a unified activity which comes from the coalescence of the thoughts and wills of divers men. That personality, as so defined, gives rise to interests; and, in the modern state, it is largely by the interplay of interests that policy is determined.

No one can watch the evolution of politics without seeing that this is the case. Burke has made the necessity of parties politically axiomatic; but we have to admit that only a small part of us is exhausted by that connection. English education, for instance, has been largely determined by a church 'interest'. Agricultural policy has at every stage been dominantly influenced by the 'interest' of the landowners; and even when, as in 1846, the landowning 'interest' has suffered defeat, it was a victory for the temporarily antagonistic 'interest' of the manufacturers. Every country in the world is honeycombed with associations which represent the activity of those 'interests'. No man, for example, is ignorant of the vital part played in English politics by the Licensed Victuallers' Association. What is perhaps more singular is the indirect way in which the power of these associations has had to be exerted. There has not, indeed, been anything in English politics which avowedly corresponds with the unclean selfishness of an American lobby. The representatives of these associations have at least secured their influence through the open door of the party system. But even Bagehot could admit the existence of a railway 'interest' in the House of Commons, at the same time that he viewed with

suspicious dislike the growth of a labour 'interest'. The organization of political life has been so predominantly geographical in
character that these functions have found no direct place in the
structure of government.

It need not be argued that representation by function is more
real than representation by area to make it evident that it has solid
advantages to offer. Such an argument would be, in any case,
untrue; for the interest of men as neighbours has a very solid and
urgent reality about it. Yet there can be little or no doubt that the
political opinions of men are largely determined by their industrial
situation. Disraeli's theory of Tory Democracy was largely based on
that perception. He hoped that a proper receptiveness to working-
class needs, as in his Trade Union Act of 1875, would bring its votes
to the right party. To give that industrial situation a domicile in
politics is to give permanent expression to much which now
escapes the immediate purview of political structure. Professional
representation is not, at least in idea, a new device; and it has a
particular fascination at a time when it is assuming a new
importance in industrial government. Anyone who has watched
the development, particularly in the last few years, of a labour
theory of politics will have noted the tendency of trade unionism
to connect itself, nationally and locally, with that system of ideas
and needs which has least opportunity for self-expression at the
present time. If it is possible to relate that theory to the problems
of government, a new and valuable stream of thought can be
directed into channels where it is badly needed.

But what is wanted in professional representation is not either
an addition, on that basis, to the House of Commons, or a similar
reconstruction of the House of Lords.[21] The geographical basis has
a real value for certain types of problems, particularly with those in
which the interest of consumers is dominantly concerned; and it
would result in mere confusion to connect it with a producers'
interest which is concerned with different problems. Nor does the
suggested second chamber assist much. Its value as an institution
seems, in any case, rather a foible of the political scientists than an
expression of real need; and it looks as though the second
chamber of the future would be less a deliberative assembly than a
body of administrative experts seeing to it that the bill as passed
really represented the will of the lower chamber, and holding
constant inquiries, not necessarily at London, into the process of

administration. The real way, surely, in which to organize the interests of producers is by working out a delimitation of industry and confiding the care of its problems to those most concerned with them. This is, in fact, a kind of federalism in which the powers represented are not areas, but functions. Anyone can see that the railways are as real as Lancashire; and exactly as the specifically local problems of Lancashire are dealt with by it, so could the specifically functional problems of the railways be dealt with by a governing body of its own. The necessary relation to the state is not a difficult matter of adjustment. It would be necessary, in the first place, to see to it that such a governing body did not pass beyond its powers; that would be in part a matter for the courts and in part, on the permissive side, a matter for some such department as the Board of Trade. Where the interest of the public outside defiantly entered in, as, for instance, in such a matter as railway fares, the Railway Commissioners could render invaluable service by performing the functions today so admirably performed by the Interstate Commerce Commission of the United States. In such a fashion, it should not be necessary to go to Parliament at all; though it would, of course, still be possible to use it as a court of last instance and a depository of grievances. It is worth while noting that the attempt to govern industry by joint representative councils, as recommended in the Whitley Report, is in reality an attempt at such administrative devolution which, while it as yet retains the theory of parliamentary sovereignty, is, in fact, by handing over the making of rules to the trade unions and the employers, creating, within certain functions, what is little less than a federal state. The Whitley Report is based, in the first place, upon a division of powers. It divorces the business of production from the business of consumption and leaves the former the control of the processes upon which it is engaged. It is, or course, true that Parliament remains outside and omnipotent; but no one can for a moment doubt that if such a delegated power proves workable, parliamentary control will, whatever theory may say, be as real in practice as it is over the internal legislation of Canada and Australia, both of which are, in strict juristic fact, simply immense instances of decentralization. It is based, in the second place, upon an attempt to discover separate and national units of industrial government which, while they may at first work in independence, will be compelled later to discover some means of connection. The railways, for example, cannot possibly regard with indifference what is happening in the coal mines, and, sooner or later, they will be compelled to work out a basis of relationship for the hinterland of their mutual interests. Neither will, of course, surrender it to the other; and in the debate over terms they will discover the value of its cession to a body representative of both, exactly as has happened in the general history of political federations.

But to confine our speculation to the case of two industries alone is, of course, to obscure the vista that here reveals itself. For if there is one thing that can be predicted with certainty it is the ultimate interdependence of all forms of industry, and though we may, for purposes of convenience, attempt a system of delimitation, the units so formed are bound to look to federation as the means of settling their common differences and realizing their common aims. In the trade union world, indeed, this movement towards federalism has been the real measure of progress. Trade unions grew up by chance in all times and places; but it has only been in the degree to which they have recognized the unity of interest in the working class that they have been saved from the moral and economic quagmire of particularism. Indeed the real weakness of trade unionism has been an internal competition of units; and the immense accession of strength that such things as the Triple Alliance can bring is known to every observer.[22] Of the larger process of production this is not less the case. If we omit, for the moment, any consideration of internal antagonisms within each industry, it is clear that we are facing an industrial future in which the joint interests of all producers must be matters of joint debate. For no state could permit the anarchy that would result if separate bargains of a particularistic kind could be made with every producer of raw materials by the industrial council of each trade. They involve not less than a federal council of producers in which minimum common standards can be erected, with an executive organization to enforce them. These are questions, for instance, of output, wages, hours, training, in which the old criteria of supply and demand are no longer applicable. The only way in which they can even be approached, much less solved, is by agreement through debate. And the more this ideal is approached the more will it tend to create an economic sovereignty either outside the legal sovereignty of Parliament or using the latter merely as an organ of registration. Nor is it difficult to doubt that the immense decentralization that is implied in such effort will be better managed by the producers themselves. They at any rate know the conditions. Their interest is in the making of real solutions rather than in the acceptance of those partial and unsatisfactory compromises to which governmental interference has in recent years accustomed us. Here it is notable that experience of government intervention on a large scale seems, in those industries most closely related to the business of war, to have produced a healthy desire, both in masters and men, for self-determination of conditions under which work is to be carried on. The reaction against officialism has been everywhere intense; and part, at least, of the welcome accorded to the Whitley Report, may be traced to a desire to free the processes of industry from the direct control of government.

The real significance of that welcome lies, however, much deeper. During the nineteenth century there has been growing around us an inchoate but vital economic federalism to which far too little attention has been paid. The rules and standards of things like the legal and medical professions, the trade unions, and, in a less degree, the teachers, constitute expressions of group solidarity of which the state has been compelled to take account. There have been inherent in them ideals of law and of justice. They have implied a decentralization of industrial control which has grown ever wider in its ramifications. The influence of trade union standards, for example, has been obvious in the way in which government has been compelled to insert them in large regions of its own contractual relations. The power was again seen in the attitude assumed by the medical profession to the Insurance Act of 1911 and the concessions it was able to exact. It is a solidarity which the essentially political conception of democracy, as exemplified in the *Loi le Chapelier* in France,[23] . . . was compelled to deny; but it is a solidarity which the Trade Union Act of 1875 and the *Lois des Associations* of 1884 and 1901 tacitly admitted. They are, in reality, the abolition, for political purposes, of the economic abstraction called man as set up by the individualistic thinkers of the nineteenth century. The object of these groups was to safeguard professional interests. Each profession and industry had questions and standards peculiar to itself, upon which its own determination was the most competent. No real benefit was

147

derived from state intervention, after a certain level had been reached, because the external character of government in relation to these groups clothed its action with a mechanical uniformity and a rigorous permanence unsuited to such questions as arise in so delicate and complex a structure as that of modern industry. No state, for example, could possibly enter into the minute ingenuities by which a modern trade union secures the observance of the standard rate. The process by which an agreement is reached between masters and men is left to the interests concerned. The result is a rule of conduct which, if it lacks the binding force of parliamentary enactment, has yet the force of law to the consenting powers. And it is probable. . . that this removal of the settlement from the province of the state has this especial value that it prevents the use of the public power from being perverted to the use of one or other of the parties in presence. So to do would. . . transform every political conflict into a naked class struggle of the most disastrous kind.

The existence of this accidental decentralization, valuable as it is, should not blind us to its imperfections. It has had little or no force behind it save that of strict compulsion in regard to standards. No one imagines, for instance, that the miners won their right to the checkweighman or the eight-hour day other than by the extent to which they had unionized their trade.[24] Industrially, at least, the existence of standards has been less the result of a realization of right than an acceptance of necessity. That is the consequence of the unreal relation in which the state has stood to industry. It has never pretended, for example, to enforce that national minimum of civilized life which ought, at the very least, to be the price of capitalistic existence. Apart from the few cases, like the labour of women and children, in which a very obvious humanitarianism has intervened, every conquest of a fraction of that minimum has been the work of organized labour. There has been, thus far, nothing that could with truth be called, in Rousseau's sense, a 'general will' of the state. What, rather, we have had has been a series of conflicts between particular wills in which now one and now another has prevailed. The attitude in which labour and capital and the state approach each industrial situation is so different that any ultimate harmony between them seems impossible. The real demand of labour is for the democratization of industrial processes, by which is meant that the truths of popular political government are applicable to industrial government as well. That, obviously enough, cannot be the attitude of capital, since it is at the destruction of capitalism that it is aimed. Nor, broadly, is it the attitude of those who operate the machinery of the modern state; for the latter are dominantly influenced by the prevailing economic system and they cannot, in the nature of things, aim at fundamental disturbance of the economic *status quo*. The concessions they seek to secure are not founded upon any theory of abstract justice but upon the minimum that must be given to maintain social peace. The object of labour is the foundation of a new social order which is incompatible with the fragmentary concessions of the last hundred years.

Here, in reality, is the seat of the modern democratic discontent. The liberty and equality implied in the modern state are purely theoretic in character. The industrial worker has the suffrage; but he is caught in the ramifications of a system which deprives its use of any fundamental meaning. He finds that he cannot secure from the operations of politics either that say in the determination of his life or the opportunity to conquer the riches it can offer, that a democratic civilization is supposed to afford. He sees that democracy in politics does not in the least imply democracy in industry and, since the better portion of his life is spent in earning his daily bread, it is to the latter that he has turned. He has found the state useless for the purpose he has in view, and that is why he must refuse to accept it as in any fundamental sense the representative of the community. The economic federalism that exists largely results from his effort to conquer through industrial action what he has failed to gain from political. The labour movement has been his real training ground in politics. It has, of course, thus far been largely confined to material questions of hours and wages but it has come, in more recent years, to turn its attention more and more to questions of policy, such as discipline and the like. It is refusing, for instance, to allow labour to be extracted from the laborer and to be regarded as a commodity which can be bought and sold at will. . . .

The Whitley Report has emphasized the need for a share in that control on the part of the workers. No less important, it has insisted that this control must receive its expression through the trade unions. The solutions that such joint effort as the councils it establishes may propose will, of course, be merely interim solutions; for, in the fundamental sense, there cannot be better relations between two groups one of which is aiming at the abolition of the other. The very admission, indeed, of joint control may well presage the advent of that transition period from capitalism to industrial democracy which will doubtless be characterized by labour's taking a greater share in industrial government. The experiment, whatever its result, is bound to involve far-reaching change. If it fails, an organized labour will confront an organized capital with the knowledge that the immense sacrifices it has made in the last four years were made for a lie; for it the result of the war is not an improvement in the internal conditions of the western democracies, the unrest of the period before 1914 is bound to go further; for no experiment in democratization that is successful can stop short of completeness.

And the immediate implications of its induction are important. The systematic consideration of industrial questions, locally as well as nationally, is a training in self-government of which the significance is not to be minimized. For it is vital to bear in mind that the consideration of industrial questions cannot stop short at industry. Inevitably they will tend more and more to emphasize the connection between industry and the general background of social life.... The Industrial Council,[25] in fact, will find itself taking up attitudes on social questions in exactly the same way that the trade unionist has been driven to consider the general theory of the state, to have an attitude to life, in addition to his specific, immediate economic demands. Indeed it is permissible to suggest that the Industrial Councils will be successful in proportion as they consider profoundly the ramifications of the immediate issue they confront. That does not, of course, mean that they will pass resolutions on secular education or the disestablishment of the church; though it may well lead them locally to insist on the neglect of things like the provision of technical instruction and nationally to influence profoundly such things as fiscal policy and international relations.

It is obvious, in fact, that immediately production is given the opportunity of organized speech, its utterance must profoundly affect political programmes in nation and locality. The light it throws upon the process of production throws light upon the needs of the consumer as well. It in fact acts in such fashion as to orientate the consumer in the realities of the situation. An industrial council that asked for better education in Manchester, for example, could hardly meet with a light refusal from the municipal council. Nor ought one to minimize the value of giving to the employers the opportunity of systematic meetings with labour. That will not produce the abdication of the capitalist. But it will teach him how essentially human are at once the demands of labour and the labour 'agitator' himself. Nothing, surely, is ever lost by the rational consideration of difficulties. The rate of progress towards the realization of labour's programme itself depends upon the degree in which knowledge of its character and implications is spread abroad. The industrial council is a vehicle towards that end. . . .

IV

It has already been suggested that the Whitley Report accepts the chaotic federalism of the modern industrial system and brings into it something like ordered connection. It does not, indeed, suggest, as yet, any relationship between the national industrial councils. That however, as has been pointed out, must logically result from the very fact of industrial interdependence. Such a hierarchical structure, from works to district, from district to national industry, from the national unit to the whole system of production is, in reality, little less than the creation of a state. It brings the whole process of production face to face with the whole process of consumption; for the latter, dominantly an interest of territorial juxtaposition, is the underlying implication of our parliamentary structure. This division of function necessarily throws its shadow far across our usual concepts of the state. We have, indeed, so naturally regarded the latter as the representative of society as a whole that our own erection of an authority which is in a position to challenge the uniqueness of that claim comes with something of a shock. Yet it is nothing less that is involved in the logical outcome of our present tendencies.

Nothing less, at least, on a single supposition. If it is at all true that the centre of power is passing more and more to the working class then this division of control by function has a peculiar significance that demands a close analysis. No one, indeed, who examined the condition of labour as it is organized in the trade

151

unions today could seriously urge that it was fitted to take charge of the state. But it is at least equally true that so long as the state is built upon a class structure of which capitalism is the main characteristic the interest of the working class is not dominantly regarded. Possibly, of course, the outcome of the next few years may be a new kind of industrial feudalism in which the workers will exchange liberty for comfort. Certainly. . . there have been important ways in which the last fifty years have seen a remarkable transition from contract to status. Were that to be the case it is probable that the industrial councils contemplated by the Whitley Report would either serve no useful purpose at all, or act merely as a means towards lulling the creative tenets of trade unionism into somnolence. It is in any event true that they predicate a trade unionism far more virile and intelligent than in the past. What it secures is going to depend in part upon the ability with which its case is presented and in part upon the way in which it organizes each special industry. A trade union defeated at the council table will get even less than it now gets by an appeal to Parliament. But there is no special occasion for such pessimism. Even when the last fears of a guarantee of capitalist existence by the state [26] have been taken into account, it remains true that the forces of education are on the side of labour. It remains not less true that the appeal it can make is to the name of freedom and, however curiously, that appeal has its roots deep in every human soul. If it can be shown that capitalism is incompatible with freedom and that the modern state must necessarily assume a capitalistic complexion, there is every reason to suppose that the movement of events will be in the direction of more democracy rather than less. In that aspect the future of the state becomes an inquiry of special significance. If there is a necessary permanence about the sovereignty of the King in Parliament what, clearly, we must expect is a gradual replacement of a capitalist state by a form of organization in which a vast series of government departments control modern industries as they now control the telephone and postal services. Parliament would represent producer not less than consumer and the business of production would be carried on by officials in something like the fashion in which local government is now organized relative to central control.

Yet it is surely difficult to believe that a simple nationalization has anything of final value to contribute to the general problem before us. Nationalization might well solve the basic problem of property in the sense that expropriation of the capitalist would leave a surplus of wealth for the increase of wages. But that is in no real sense the root of the matter. What our general experience of nationalization suggests is its invariable tendency to the bureaucratic government of the industries concerned. . . . The same is true, in an even greater degree, of municipal ownership. There is a slightly better average rate of wages, and a slight decrease in the average rate of hours of labour. But no real attempt is anywhere made at the democratization of any industry owned, or operated, by the agencies of the state. It is a fact of the highest import that in France the most revolutionary hypotheses of social reorganization should have come from the employees of the state[27]. . . . Any government which charges itself with industrial control will be bound, first of all, to look to continuity of service. In that aspect the officials will be tempted to keep control in their own hands. That, as they believe, is necessary in the interests of standards of efficiency and of uniformity of regulation. But that is also, in sober fact, to state a final case against any systematic national control in the sense of the control exercised by government over the telephones. It implies a centralization which, while it may improve the material condition of the worker, does nothing to offer him a definite spiritual interest in his work. It is not enough. . . to put up a suggestion box in the office and urge that the worker's experience and inventiveness ought to find adequate satisfaction there. That is not and cannot be the case. The only real satisfaction comes from an actual share in deliberation and in the determination of its results. That has been the value of much of the success of the works committees so recently instituted by the war; the opportunity organically to state a case satisfies the hunger for self-determination which cannot be subverted in any system which accepts the criteria of democracy. We cannot, of course, govern industry by public meeting; but we cannot govern industry well until the thoughts and aspirations of its workers find a full place in its institutions.

That is why the organization of industry must necessarily relate itself to federalism. The worker must be given the opportunity of a real voice in the choosing of industrial management. It must be understood that there is a politics of industry not less real than the politics of the House of Commons. A workshop that elects its own foreman, a clerical staff that chooses its own chief, heads of departments who choose their own manager, have a far more real interest in the firm for which they work than if the bond between them and their employers is the merely nominal bond of wages. Nothing, indeed, would be more fatal than such an industrial organization as led to the state being regarded simply as an employer. Trade unions would then, as Mr Webb has insisted, [28] be necessary; but would be necessary for purposes fatal to the underlying conception of the state. They would be organizations of which the purpose would be simply to drive as hard a bargain as possible with the government department which controlled them; and their success would be in proportion to the size and communal importance of the industry concerned. In such a conception there is nothing of that idealism it is so necessary to introduce into political processes. . . .

It is the main problem of the state as well; and that is why we cannot divorce the problem of industry therefrom. What, in reality, is involved is the meaning of freedom, the way in which we translate our definition of its content into the stuff of which the state is made. We perhaps too little remember that the theory of freedom has a history in the light of which its immediate significance must be read. Lord Morley has somewhere said that the definitions of liberty are innumerable, but they have been, for the most part, conceived in narrowly political terms. What we need is rather such a conception as applies to those impulses of men that are mainly at work in political society. It is herein that the value of T.H. Green's definition of liberty is to be found. For our main business is to get the creative impulses of men to work and it is herein that modern organization has so signally failed. Concentration of power has been, in general, the only known source of efficiency, nor has it been seen that it implies the negation of democracy. For, after all, where power is concentrated in a few hands there is lacking that spirit of responsibility without which no man can attain the full expression of his faculties. There is more than a negative danger in such concentration. It is not only, as Acton scathingly said, that it 'corrodes the conscience, hardens the heart, and confounds the understanding' of those who hold power; it deadens in any state the impulses which make for the greatness of a civilization. That is why any state in which the political office is united to the religious will sooner or later tread the path of despotism. That is why, also, any state in which a single class is predominant sooner or later must disregard the public interest in order to retain their power. That disregard, indeed, will cause the destruction of their government; for the belief of Plato that a state ought not to secure obedience if it fails to secure respect is no more than the summary of historic experience. *The real truth is that the members of a state are powerless against an efficient centralization wielded in the interest of any social fragment, however large. It prevents the balance of associations which is the safeguard of liberty* [editor's emphasis]. It secures uniformity of which, from the very constitution of human nature, liberty is the direct antithesis. For where the creative impulses of men are given full play, there is bound to be diversity, and diversity provokes, in its presence, a decentralized organization to support it. That is why the secret of liberty is the division of power. But that political system in which a division of power is most securely maintained is a federal system; and, indeed, there is a close connection between the idea of federalism and the idea of liberty.

In Europe at least this is too little understood, for the sufficient reason that liberty and equality are understood as separate instead of as different facets of the same ideal. Nor can we preserve equality in any state without a measure of federal structure; for the distribution of power is the real check upon its usurpation. It is more than that. It is the only way in which sufficient centres can be created of deliberation and enterprise to enlist the abilities of men in the public service. It is clear, for example, that the real barrier to creative opinion in the Roman Catholic Church is its excessive centralization. So long as ideas radiate outwards from a single point in the circle they will not adequately radiate inwards from the circumference. The concentration of power in the papal hands will mean that thought is inactive everywhere save at the point of responsibility; or, at least, that thought will strive less to master the facts than to distort them to the service of power. A system that cannot contain Lamennais and Döllinger and Tyrrell stands, governmentally, self-condemned.[29] But what is here true of Rome is also true of the political state. We need to federalize the organization of England simply in order to give play to the mass of creative opinion which remains today untouched by political forces. It is here urged that the secret of its revivification is to associate in the exercise of power those who have thus far been too merely its subjects. The principle of tacit consent upon which we work in government is too theoretical in character. It results in the virtual annihilation of every individuality that is not either at the centre of things, or finding its compensation for exclusion in some such activity as art. We have to provide that political consent be no longer passive, but active in character, that it come from free and instructed minds widespread among the mass of men.

V

What, in fact, does this involve? No system of politics is firmly grounded that is not securely built upon the past. We cannot attempt anything like the revolution in spiritual form of which we have need in a day. We cannot, even in our remotest dreams, give every man some actual share in the business of administration . . . . The size of the modern state makes the hope of anything other than a representative system not merely inadmissable but, in the nature of things, undesirable. We have to work with the materials we are given, and that involves the acceptance of their limited capacity.

We start from the theoretic purpose we admit in the state. It aims at the development of the fullest capacity for good possessed by its members. That implies at once liberty and equality; and it implies a federal structure that they may be given their due expression. It does not matter whether the federalism be a division of the unified purpose from above, rather than from below, whether it take, that is to say, the form of decentralization rather than the type of division with which the government of the United States has made us familiar. What is important is that too great power should at no place be concentrated in a few hands lest the individuality of man be repressed by the very institutions he has created to preserve it.

The problem is not merely one of area. Primarily, it is a problem of functions simply because the institutions of areas are, in England at least, reasonably adequate to their purpose, and because it is in the aspect of function that the possibilities of decentralization are most strikingly manifest. Unless we make power a process of democracy we withdraw energy from the consideration of social questions that could with value be directed into its channels. A single illustration will perhaps throw the process at issue into a clear perspective. It is doubtful whether any civil service in the world has so noble a record as the Civil Service of England. Yet no one can examine its workings without being struck at a certain curious intellectual inertia which suggests a too rigid stratification. The reason is not far to seek. Its system of promotion is determined from above. Little or no attempt is made to associate any personnel save that of heads of departments in the determination of any advance other than that of automatic increase of pay. The result is that the ideal of work chiefly inculcated is that of 'correctness'. Too great an activity outside the department is to be deprecated because it leads the heads to believe that one's full energy is not concentrated upon the labour in hand. It is best simply to follow the lines they lay down and establish a reputation for zeal and punctuality. Inventions should be confined to new filing systems or a better method of keeping accounts. Things like this surely explain the abyss that exists between the divisions of the service. If promotion were, within each office, determined by a council in which each section had elected representatives, the heads of departments would learn much and call forth more. No system ought to be considered satisfactory in which the motives to originality are not emphasized. . . .

If this is true of the civil service, it is far more true of business enterprises; for there the exigencies of a capitalistically-organized industrial system have necessitated the retention of oligarchic institutions. That does not mean to say that ability meets no recognition. It implies rather that the only interest organized by capitalistic industry is the material interest. The spiritual factors which self-government calls into play are too widely ignored. . . .

The same holds true in the industrial sphere; and, so far, we have made no effort of any kind to apply it. Everyone knows that profit-sharing and labour co-partnership are no more than. . . [obscure formulas – ed.]. Inevitably, therefore, we have suffered from political inertia and economic discontent. We have suffered from political inertia because the reaction of economic upon political structure is so profound. We have suffered from economic discontent because the structure of industry does not provide an adequate expression for the impulses of men. That is why it is rather upon industry than upon politics, upon function rather than upon area, that the consideration of a revival of political interest must centre. We are presented with a quasi-federal system: that is to say that large functions are left by the state to settle their own problems. But, on the one hand, no real effort has been made to relate that economic federalism to the categories of the political structure, and, on the other, within each function there is no adequate representative system.

The Whitley Report, in substance, thought not in form, answers the first need. It gives state recognition to those industrial units sufficiently organized to warrant it, and provides the means for unorganized units to pass into the stage of organization and recognition. Sooner or later, it has here been suggested, that recognition of control of productive effort, of functions, will tend to influence the control of geographical areas, and so to fructify the normal life of politics. From the purely internal point of view, far less is done. An intermediate economic sovereignty is recognized in the industrial councils in the sense that the solutions they propose for the problems of industry will, for working purposes, become law. . . .

It may be said that there are men in the business world who realize all this and that they are for nothing more anxious than to work out an amicable basis of relationship with labour. There is undoubtedly some truth in such assertions; but of the business world in general it is not even remotely accurate. Capital shows nowhere, on any large scale, a desire to abdicate from its control; rather is its effort, by the highway of compensated nationalization to escape the tragedy that might result from any widespread industrial disruption. It is still widely true, as Mr and Mrs Webb wrote twenty years ago,[30] that 'to the brain-working captain of industry, maintaining himself on thousands a year, the manual-working wage-earner seems to belong to another species, having mental faculties and bodily needs altogether different from his own'. The familiar plea of the businessman that he will manage his factory in his own way is the expression of that sense. But there has everywhere grown up the belief that the full fruition of the democratic state demands that the conditions of production be determined by the democratic co-operation of its agents. In the long run that is fatal to capitalism in its present form. . . . It is coming to be seen quite clearly that the traditions of capitalism are historic categories like any other. . . . No one denies that, however we construct the state, some form of organizing power will be necessary. What is coming more and more to be denied is the belief that, as in modern industry, that power must be clothed in oligarchic garb. The modern businessman, amid many high qualities, has thought so much in terms of money, that the numerous and interlacing social interests, upon which the equilibrium which supports him so largely depends, have in great part escaped his notice.

What, largely, has escaped his notice is the political significance of trade union structure. In a rudimentary way it is coming more and more to assume all the typical characteristics of a state. It is developing organs of reasoned government. It is becoming expert in the processes of which special knowledge was originally supposed to be the prerogative of the man of business. It has worked out a view of life which achieves an ever-greater political influence. It has passed, as has been pointed out, the stage where its influence was confined to hours and wages and more and more becomes concerned for the spiritual freedom of its constituents. It would, of course, be absurd to claim that there is any widespread consciousness of the details of this process in the trade union world; like every great movement, what we see at work is the leaven of an eager minority. But as it becomes every day more obvious that the hold of the business theory of life upon the state is weakening, so does it also become more clear that the trade unions are becoming the categories into which the structure of capitalism may be absorbed. We do not, of course, know the time such evolution will take. We can, also, be very certain that the prophecies of its character will all, in some degree, be mistaken. What we do know is that a capitalist state has failed to specialize in certain final human impulses, and that the trade unions are organizing a means to their satisfaction. We can see, too, how the effort of a government which is not predominantly trade unionist in sympathy unconsciously hastens that evolution by its attempt, however small in scope, to find a representative government for industry. For that is clearly the admission that the oligarchical control of industry has failed. It is the provision of a mechanism which, wisely used, may well serve as the vehicle of transition to self-government in industry. The whole point seems to be that the complexity of the structure of an industrial state is beyond the grasp of a mind, like the capitalist mind, which mainly is specialized in the direction of money-making. For not only is that direction becoming less important, but, within the framework of capitalism there has developed another type of mind which has specialized in the directions in which its forerunner was most notably a failure.

It is difficult, in such an aspect, not to believe that trade unionism is destined to absorb the directive ability that, undoubtedly, capitalism can furnish, and turn it to its own purposes. That prospect has become the more likely as a result of the experience of the last four years. The democratic forces of civilization have been put to the test of conflict against an autocratic system; and it is now indubitable that they will survive. But they have not withstood the shock without serious and searching confusion. Few things have been more obvious than the inability of the capitalist structure, in its pre-war form, to meet the national need. It has had to receive assistance from the state. It has had to be controlled by the state in the interests of national safety. It has had to ask trade unionism for the surrender of those safeguards by which, in the past, an adequate minimum of civilized life could alone be preserved for the workers. The only institutions which, in the course of war, have worked at all well have been those, at least in industry, of democratic tendency. Governmental control has been an unsatisfactory expedient. The abdication of Parliament has made obvious the utter insufficiency, for human needs, of a bureaucratic system. The restoration of industrial conditions, at the close of war, can only be made upon the basis of returning within their basic trades, a large measure of popular supervision. Everything, in fact, has tended to emphasize the human factor in industry at the expense of the money-making factor. The sole condition of industrial peace was the acceptance of this fact as a starting point. Labour was led, from this, to the formulation of a policy which goes down to the foundations of the state. What, at the moment, has clearly emerged, is a two-fold novelty of outlook. On the one hand it has become evident that the state must dictate to industry certain minimum terms upon which alone it can be conducted. Business, on the other, is to be transformed from a chaotic autocracy into, at least in certain aspects, a federal and representative system.

Such, at least, seems the alternative to revolution, but it is to be noted that it is the minimum alternative. . . . [It] is universally agreed that the last four years have made a return to the economic status [quo] before the war impossible; and that, in itself, will change the political system. Political institutions, indeed, are themselves in grave need of change. . . .

We have learned that there is, in any public service, a point in official staffs beyond which mere increase is incompatible with liberalism. Government may be strong, but if it is to be human it cannot have the tentacles of an octopus. The value, also, of publicity has been demonstrated by the very danger of its opposite. A democracy, as we know by hard experience, cannot hope to prosper unless its fundamental fights are contested in the House of Commons.

So much, at least, is gain even though we have paid a heavy price for it. Yet, as our knowledge and the facts we encounter converge, they bring out the first question of all questions in political life. We have to decide what we mean the state to do before we pronounce that what it does is good. If its object is the preservation of individuality, in so far as its specialism contributes to the public good, our present system stands largely self-condemned by the mere description of it. Nor is there any reason in the world why we should expect it to be otherwise. The path of history is strewn with the wreck of social systems; there is no cause why our own should be the sole exception. There is perhaps cause rather for congratulation than regret in the vision of its disappearance. It passes because it fails to fulfil the more generous aspirations of a new time. We seek today the ways and means whereby we can renew in men their interest in the state which so greatly weaves itself into the stuff of their lives. 'War', said Burke in one of his flashes of incomparable wisdom,[31] 'war is a situation which sets in its full light the value of the hearts of people'. What it has revealed to us is the riches that have gone unused. What it has most strikingly shown is the importance of the people. And with its realization there must be, as he said, the end of that 'interior ministry' of which he skilfully portrayed the danger. That, above all, at which we aim is the representation in the structure of the state of all that makes for its enrichment. But we do not believe in the adequacy of a representation without power. We do not believe that a power can be other than futile which is not directly related to the immediate business of men. We believe, as Burke believed, that the 'heart of the citizen is a perennial spring of energy to the state'. But energy is impossible when it is deprived of liberty and liberty is impossible save where there is a division of power. So long as the offices of men do not make their souls erect and their minds intelligent we cannot assert that they have been given the credit of their humanity. That has been, in the past, our failure; it is to its repair we must bend our effort.

NOTES

1. Cf. the introduction to Wallas (1908) *Human Nature in Politics* [London: Constable].
2. Cf. Mr Wallas's remarks in *Human Nature in Politics, passim,* and especially pp. 199ff.
3. Cf. Wallas (1914) *The Great Society* [London: Methuen], chapter 13, where the whole question is brilliantly analysed.
4. See the vital chapter 5 of the fourth part of Tocqueville (1832) *Democracy in America,* [London: Oxford University Press, 1946].
5. Ibid., Part II, chapter 5.
6. Ibid., preface.
7. Harrington (1656) *Oceana* (ed. Toland), pp. 157-60.
8. Wallas *Human Nature in Politics,* Part I.
9. Mill (1861) *Considerations on Representative Government* [London: Dent], Everyman, p. 202.
10. Wallas *The Great Society,* p. 7.
11. Laski (1919) *Authority in the Modern State* [New Haven, CT: Yale University Press], chapter 5.
12. Dicey (1885) *An Introduction to the Study of the Law of the Constitution,* eighth edition [London: Macmillan, 1920], p. 81.
13. See his dissent in the Child Labor Case, *US v. Degenhart,* decided in 1917-18.
14. Bryce (1888) *American Commonwealth* [London: Macmillan], vol. 1, chapter 30.
15. Cf. Laski *Authority in the Modern State,* chapter 1.
16. 198, US, 45, 76.
17. Cf. Wallas *Human Nature in Politics,* pp. 98ff.
18. [The three-class voting system in Prussia divided voters into three groups by taxable income and gave a third of the votes to each group, thus over-representing the wealthy – ed.]
19. Cf. Bryce *American Commonwealth,* vol 2, p. 379, for Tweed episode.
20. Though I do not accept all its implications, I think that [F.H.] Bradley's famous essay, 'My station and its duties', in his *Ethical Studies,* still best expresses this truth even for political purposes.
21. As Mr Graham Wallas has desired, *The Great Society,* p. 339.
22. Cf. Cole (1913) *The World of Labour* [London: G. Bell], pp. 205-84 [The Triple Alliance combined the Railwaymen, Miners and Transport Workers – ed.]
23. [The *Loi le Chapelier* (14 June 1791), passed by the French Constituent

Assembly, proscribed workers' associations and strikes – ed.]

24. Webb, S., and Webb, B. (1897) *Industrial Democracy* [second edition, London: Longmans, Green & Co., 1920], p. 309.
25. [Joint Industrial Councils were a co-determination machinery in the Whitley Report – ed.]
26. Cole (1917) *Self Government in Industry* [London: G. Bell], appendix B.
27. Cf. Laski *Authority in the Modern State*, chapter 5.
28. Webb *Industrial Democracy*, last chapter.
29. See this worked out in detail in chapter 3 of Laski *Authority in the Modern State*.
30. Webb *Industrial Democracy*, 1902 edition, p. 821.
31. Burke (1770) *Thoughts on the Present Discontents* [Cambridge: Cambridge University Press, 1913].

Chapter Nine

THE PERSONALITY OF
ASSOCIATIONS

I

The state knows certain persons who are not men. What is the nature of their personality? Are they merely fictitious abstractions, collective names that hide from us the mass of individuals beneath? Is the name that gives them unity no more than a convenience, a means of substituting one action in the courts where, otherwise, there might be actions innumerable? Or is that personality real? Is Professor Dicey right when he urges[1] that 'whenever men act in concert for a common purpose, they tend to create a body which, from no fiction of law but from the very nature of things, differs from the individuals of whom it is constituted'? Does our symbolism, in fact, point to some reality at the bottom of appearance? If we assume that reality, what consequences will flow therefrom?

Certainly no lawyer dare neglect the phenomena of group life, even if on occasion he denies a little angrily the need for him to theorize about them. For man is so essentially an associative animal that his nature is largely determined by the relationships thus formed. The churches express his feeling that he has need of religion. His desire for conversation and the newspapers results in the establishment of clubs. The necessity of social organization gave birth to the state. As his commercial enterprise began to annihilate distance, the trading company came into being. It would not, one urges, be over-emphasis to assert that in every sphere of human activity associations of some kind are to be found. They are the very life-breath of the community.[2]

And, somehow, we are compelled to personalize these

164

associations. They demand their possessive pronouns; the church has 'its' bishops. They govern a singular verb; the railway company 'employs' servants. . . . The House of Commons is distinct from 'its' members, and, no less clearly, it is not the chamber in which they meet. We talk of 'its', 'spirit' and 'complexion'; a general election, so we say, changes 'its' 'character'. . . . Clearly, there is compulsion in our personalizing. We do it because we must. We do it because we feel in these things the red blood of a living personality. Here are no mere abstractions of an over-exuberant imagination. The need is so apparent as to make plain the reality beneath.

II

Now lawyers are practical men dealing with the very practical affairs of everyday life, and they do not like, in Lord Lindley's phrase,[3] 'to introduce metaphysical subtleties which are needless and fallacious'. The law, so they will say, knows persons; by Act of Parliament[4] 'persons' may include bodies corporate. Persons are the subjects of rights and duties which the courts will, at need, enforce. If a body corporate is a person, it will also be the subject of rights and duties. If it is a person, it is so because the state has conferred upon it the gift of personality; for only the state can exercise that power. And the terms of such conference are strictly defined. The corporation is given personality for certain purposes to be found in its history, in its charter, its constituting act, its articles of association. The courts will say whether certain acts come within those purposes; whether, to use technical terms, they are *intra* or *ultra vires*. This limitation is in the public interest. 'The public', so the courts have held,[5] 'is entitled to hold a registered company to its registered business'. The company has a personality; but it has a personality capable only of very definitized development.

Why is it so limited? English lawyers, at any rate, have no doubt upon this question. The corporation is the creature of the state. Its will is a delegated will; its purpose exists only because it has secured recognition. And, so the lawyers will tend to imply, it is in truth a fictitious thing. Persons, they know well enough, are human beings; the corporation is invisible and *in abstracto*. It has no human wants. 'It cannot', so an American judge has said,[6] 'eat or drink, or wear clothing, or live in houses'; though hereto a sceptic might retort that a theory of domicile has given some trouble, and ask if there is not a solid reality about the dinners of the Corporation of London. 'It is', said Marshall, C.J.,[7] 'an artificial being, invisible, intangible, and existing only in contemplation of law'. . . 'it is precisely', he says again, 'what the act of incorporation makes it'. 'Persons', said Best, C.J., in 1828,[8] 'who, without the sanction of the legislature, presume to act as a corporation, are guilty of a contempt of the King, by usurping on his prerogative'.

Nor are the textbook writers less definite. 'They are legal persons', says Austin,[9] 'by a figment, and for the sake of brevity in discourse'. . . . 'Ten men', notes Professor Salmond satirically,[10] 'do not become in fact one person because they associate themselves together for one end any more than two horses become one animal when they draw the same cart'. 'The most marked distinction', Mr. T. E. Holland has written in a famous textbook,[11] 'between abnormal persons is that some are natural. . . while others are artificial. . . which are treated by law for certain purposes as if they were individual human beings'.

Here is clear doctrine enough – a vivid picture of an all-absorptive state. But when this supposed limitation has once been admitted, it is evident that the state is compelled to do remarkable things with the bodies it has called into being. It fails to regulate them with the ease that might be desired. The definition of *ultra vires*, for example, has become a formidable problem; there seems not a little of accident in the formulation of its principles. Corporations will have a curious habit of attempting perpetually to escape from the rigid bonds in which they have been encased. May we not say that, like some Frankenstein['s monster], they show ingratitude to their creators? Or, as artificial things, must we deem them incapable of such thought? A corporation will possess itself of an empire, and resent[12] interference with its domain. An American colony will incorporate itself; and when its creator shows signs of wanton interference, will take the lead in rebellion against the state which, in legal theory, at any rate, gave it birth. Truly the supposed sovereignty of the state is not apparent in the relations thus discovered. The orthodox doctrine needs somewhat closer examination before we accept its truth.

III

But even when we have so examined, there are associations which technically at least are not corporations. That trust which Maitland taught us to understand as so typically English will embrace many of them under its all-protecting fold.[13] Contract, as in the club, will account for much, and with the aid of a little fiction we need have no fear of theory. A mighty church will in Scotland be a trust and not a corporation.[14] In America the operations of certain trusts which are not corporations will necessitate a famous Act of Congress. For otherwise they can hardly come into the courts. They have no name by which to be sued. To the law, they are not persons, have no personality; they are bodies unincorporate, bodies – the thought is charmingly English – which are bodiless. Yet, curiously, the technical formulae do not by their absence reveal any essential lack of corporate character. The Stock Exchange has, in any real meaning of the term, a personality as assuredly effective as that of Lloyds. If, to the law, they are essentially distinct, to practical men and women it seems useless to insist on the distinction as other than an empty formalism. The Stock Exchange is simply a property vested in trustees for the benefit of a few proprietors. Is it? Dare those trustees use it as property in that unpublic sense?...

[L]egal practice has improved on legal theory. The judges builded better than they knew; or, [perhaps], they have added yet another to the pile of fictions so characteristic of English law. If corporations can alone come up the front stairs, then they will admit the unincorporate association at the back. For, they know well enough, the life of the state would be intolerable did we recognize only the association which has chosen to accept the forms of law.

Clearly, there is much behind this fiction-making. A sovereignty that is but doubtfully sovereign, an unincorporate body of which the bodiliness may yet equitably be recognized – certainly our fictions have served to conceal much. What, as a fact, is their justification? Why do they still invite, as they receive, a lip-given, if a heart-denied, profession of faith?

167

IV

When the history of associations which have been technically incorporated comes to be written, one clear generalization as to its tenor during the nineteenth century will be admitted: the courts have been in practice increasingly compelled to approximate their position to that of an ordinary individual. The history has not been without its hesitations. . . . The evolution, dating, so far as one can see, from no earlier time than the forties of last century, of the doctrine of *ultra vires*, has in many ways acted as a limiting factor. Certain philosophic difficulties, moreover, as the significance of the *mens rea* in criminal liability, have proved stumbling blocks of a serious kind. Yet, on the whole, the progress is clear. The corporation is an obvious unit. It has rights and duties. It acts and is acted upon. The fact that its actions are of a special kind is not to prevent the courts from getting behind the visible agents to the invisible reality. If it is civilly reprehensible, it must bear the burden of its blameworthiness. Should it be guilty of crime the courts will, indeed, be less confident, but, as we shall see, the thin edge of the wedge has already been inserted. It needs but a little courage, and the reality of corporate crime will pass the current coin of legally accepted doctrine. . . .

We turn to contract. We approach it warily, for here is the head and centre of fictional security. Here, we shall be told, it is finally made evident that the corporation exists nowhere save in legal contemplation. For what do we find? Take first the association incorporate by Act of Parliament. Beyond the four corners of its articles of association no movement is possible. Even the corporation which the common-law prerogative has made will have limitations upon its capacity. It cannot do what it will. It has been created for a specific purpose. It must conform to that purpose, because it is the creature of those who called it into being.

Now this theory of *ultra vires* is fundamental in the law of corporations. What is to be said for it? This, of a certainty, that it is in some wise needful to protect the corporators. A man who gives his money to a railway company does not expect it to engage in fishing; he ought to be protected against such activity. But an act incidental to the purposes of the company is not *ultra vires*. What is so incidental? It is incidental to the business of the South Wales Railway Company to run steamboats from Milford Haven,[15] but that function was seemingly beyond the competence of the Great Eastern.[16] One steamship company may, without hindrance, sell all its vessels;[17] but another company makes the mistake of retaining two of its boats, and its act is without the law.[18] There were two railway companies within recent memory which agreed to pool their profits and divide them with judicial blessing;[19] but two other railway companies speedily discovered their powerlessness when they attempted partnership.[20] It is fitting, so the courts have held, that Wigan and Ashton should supply their citizens with water,[21] but there was, so we may suppose, something unfitting when Southampton and Sheffield attempted that enterprise.[22]. . .

Logic here there certainly is not, though the basis of the distinction is easy to understand. 'Where a corporation', said Coleridge, J.[23]

> has been created for the purpose of carrying on a particular trade, or making a railway from one place to another, and it attempts to substitute another trade, or to make its railway to another place, the objection is to its entire want of power for the new purpose; its life and functions are the creation of the legislature; and they do not exist for any other than the specified purpose; for any other, the members are merely unincorporated individuals.

But the doctrine results in manifest injustice. A company has by its charter the right to borrow not more than a specified sum; it borrows more. It is held that the lenders cannot sue for the surplus.[24] Yet it is obviously unjust that a corporation should thus benefit by an error of which it has been cognizant. It is surely an unwise restriction of business enterprise so closely to restrict the interpretation of powers as to refuse a company the legal benefit of its commercial capacity to build a railway.[25] A corporation can be prevented from contributing to a charity;[26] it may, on the other hand, show gratitude to its servants.[27] It is clear enough that we have no straight rule of construction to guide us. It is held that a corporation 'may' not do certain things. Does that imply that it should not have done so, or that it is legally incapable – 'stricken with impotence' is a distinguished lawyer's forcible phrase[28] – of doing them? Is an *ultra vires* act not a corporate act? The courts would seem to uphold this view. 'The question is not', said Lord

Cairns in the Ashbury case,[29] 'as to the legality of the contract; the question is as to the competency and power of the company to make the contract'. But that is not a very helpful observation when it is borne in mind that *ultra vires* acts are performed every day. And if the courts hold such acts *a priori* illegal, why do they time and again enforce them in order to prevent harshness? Is not that a virtual admission of their corporateness? Such admission can only mean that in the great realm of contract. . . we cannot confine the personality of a corporation within the four walls of a document. We are in fact compelled to abandon the doctrine of special capacity. We have to admit that a person, whether a group person or a human being, acts as his personality warrants. Legal theory may deny the fact of a contract which has obviously taken place; but in that event it is only so much the worse for legal theory.

For it results in the divorce of law and justice. A corporator, for instance, severs his connection with a corporation in a manner that is *ultra vires*; ten years later he is held responsible for its debts.[30] Of a surety, no man will claim justice or sweet reasonableness for such an attitude. The courts, again, in the case of a man who has made a contract and then feels it irksome, will not admit the plea that he was originally incapable of making it. . . .

What are we to say? Only one thing surely, and that is that the doctrine of *ultra vires* breaks down when it is tested. It is not true because it fails to confirm to the cannon of scientific hypothesis: it does not fit the facts. We assume the artificiality of our corporation. We suppose that it is no more than we have made it, with the result that common sense must be thrown to the winds. What, in brief, the theory compels us to urge is this, that a class of acts may be performed by the corporation which are not corporate acts. Is it not better to risk a little for the sake of logic? Our fiction theory may, indeed, break down; but we shall bring the law in closer harmony with the facts of life. We shall then say that the corporation, being a real entity, with a personality that is self-created, must bear the responsibility for its actions. Our state may, in the result, be a little less Hegelian, a little less sovereign in its right of delegation. Therein it will only the more certainly make a direct march upon the real.

V

The corporation has rights and liabilities in tort. Here, again, the tendency has been more and more to make it approximate in situation to the ordinary individual. So long ago as the reign of Henry VII the corporation could bring an action for trespass.[31]. . . It can sue for libel where it can show that its property is affected,[32] though it is not clear that it could sue for words spoken in derogation of its honour or dignity.[33] This is, so we are told, due to the physical limitations to which it is subject. 'It could not sue', said Pollock, C.B.,[34] 'in respect of an imputation of murder, or incest, or adultery, because it could not commit those crimes. Nor could it sue in respect of a charge of corruption, for a corporation cannot be guilty of corruption, although the individuals composing it may'. But is this, in fact, true? No one would think of charging an association with incest or adultery. But it can be sued for malicious libel,[35] for assault and imprisonment,[36] for fraud and deceit,[37] and. . . for malicious prosecution.[38] Now when this formidable list of torts is considered it seems curious to say that the corporation cannot sue for libel that touches its honour or dignity. The reason, so far as one can see, is twofold. It is, in the first place, assumed *ipso facto* that the corporation has no mind to feel. It is no more than a way of dealing with certain rights in property in such a way that they can be conveniently protected by the courts. The doctrine of agency, moreover, is used as a means of avoiding the complex metaphysical problem of what is behind the agent. This was well shown in Lord Lindley's remarkable judgement in *Citizens' Life Assurance Co. v. Brown*. 'If it is once granted', he said, 'that corporations are for civil purposes to be regarded as persons, i.e., as principals acting by agents and servants, it is difficult to see why the ordinary doctrines of agency and of master and servant are not to be applied to corporations as well as to ordinary individuals'. In that case, clearly, the actual tort is the act of the agent and the principal is reduced to a mere fund from which adequate compensation may be obtained. But is that in truth a satisfactory method of procedure? Are the 'metaphysical subtleties' of which Lord Lindley spoke so deprecatingly in truth 'needless and fallacious'? Is it not in fact necessary to have some clear view of their nature if a true decision is to be reached?

In order to see this aspect in a clear light let us turn to the criminal liability of corporations. It is now well established that a corporation may be indicted for misfeasance,[39] for obstruction,[40] under the Lotteries Act[41] (though here the courts refused to admit an indictment of the corporation as a rogue and vagabond), for selling impure food,[42] and for adulterating milk.[43] But in all these cases conviction has been obtained on the basis of a supposed liability for an agent's act. This is well brought out in a remark of Alverstone, C.J., 'I think that we ought to hold that a corporation may be liable . . . unless *mens rea* is necessary in order to constitute the offence'.[44] But that is the exact point. Is a corporation to be held guiltless where the presence of *mens rea* is necessary to the crime? A laundry company fails adequately to protect its machinery in accordance with law, and one of its employees is killed. There was clear criminal negligence; but on an indictment for manslaughter the judge, a little reluctantly, refused to allow the action to proceed.[45] In the next year a railway company caused the death of some of its passengers through not keeping a bridge in proper repair; here again, though with obvious difficulty, the court thought the demurrer must be admitted.[46] Clearly, the problem of whether a corporation can have a *mens rea* has, if sometimes a little doubtfully, been answered in the negative.[47] Taken with the cases in tort, we must collect the opinion that it cannot have a mind at all.

VI

Yet we cannot, in fact, do without that mind. Just as we have been compelled by the stern exigencies of events to recognize that the corporation is distinct from its members, so, too, we have to recognize that its mind is distinct from their minds. A corporation votes an annual pension to a servant; its gratitude is not merely the gratitude of the individual members expressed in a single term, for one of those members will endeavour to restrain its generosity.[48] So it may well be urged in the cases of manslaughter noted above a penalty ought to be exacted in some wise commensurable with the offence. When we talk of a company as a 'bad master', there is surely reality behind that phrase. Individually its members are probably meek and kindly; but the company is differently constituted. Where that 'badness' passes into the region in which it becomes criminally culpable, the company ought to suffer the penalty for its blameworthiness. Certainly it does so suffer when it is morally but not legally at fault. Its men work for it with less zeal. It finds it difficult to retain their services. The quality of its production suffers. It loses ground and is outstripped in the industrial race. Why the courts should refuse to take cognizance of that which is an ordinary matter of daily life it is difficult indeed to understand. Take, for example, the charge of manslaughter. Any student of workmen's compensation cases will not doubt that in a choice between the adoption of a completely protective system and the possibility of an occasional accident, there are not a few corporations anti-social enough to select the latter alternative. Human life, they will argue, is cheap; the fencing, let us say, of machinery is dear. But admit the existence of the corporate mind and that mind can be a guilty mind. It can be punished by way of fine; and if it be mulcted with sufficient heaviness we may be certain that it will not offend again. What is the alternative? To attack some miserable agent who has been acting in the interest of a mindless principal, an agent, as Maitland said[49] who is the 'servant of an unknowable Somewhat'. But if that Somewhat be mindless, how can it have selected an agent? For selection implies the weighing of qualities, and that is a characteristic of mind.

VII

When, therefore, we look at the association which has chosen to incorporate itself, we cannot but feel that less than the admission of a real personality results in illogic and injustice. It is purely arbitrary to urge that personality must be so finite as to be distinctive only of the living, single man.[50] Law, of a certainty, is not the result of one man's will, but of a complex fusion of wills. It distills the quintessence of an infinite number of personalities. It displays the character not of a Many, but of a One – it becomes, in fact, unified and coherent. Ultimately pluralistic, the interactions of its diversities make it essentially, within the sphere of its operations, a single thing. Men obey its commands. It acts. It influences. Surely it is but a limitation of outlook not to extend the conception of personality into this incorporeal sphere.

It is urged that to neglect this is to commit injustice where the corporation is concerned. Even less happy shall we feel when we turn to the association that is, oddly enough, termed voluntary; as if your unincorporate body were any less the result of self-will than its corporate analogue. We shall find no law of associations. What we shall find is rather a series of references to the great divisions, contract, tort, and the like, or ordinary law. For here, in the legal view, we have no bodiliness, nothing more than a number of men who have contracted together to do certain things, who, having no corporate life, can do no more than those things for which the agreement has made stipulation. Legally they are no unit, though to your ordinary man it is a strange notion that a Roman Church, a Society of Jesus, a Standard Oil Trust – the most fundamentally unified persons, so he would say, in existence – should be thus devoid of group will because, forsooth, certain mystic words have not been pronounced over them by the state. Laughable to most of us this may indeed be; yet none the less certainly is it good law.

We take the voluntary society in contract. Its acts are *ultra vires* unless they were clearly implied in the original agreement. You join a club. An unwise draftsman has failed through inadvertence to make binding the right to change the rules. When, therefore, the club falls on evil days and changes its subscription you may refuse to pay on the ground that you have not contracted to do so.[51] It does not matter that the subscription had been already raised several times; it does not matter that you had assented to the previous changes; that there was practical unanimity among the members as to the need for the change; that without it the whole future of the club was jeopardized. Of all this the courts made entire abstraction. The contract is a fundamental agreement which cannot admit of change. A society clearly living a life of its own will be denied the benefits of that life because it has failed to take advantage of a section in an Act of Parliament.

Nor is the full significance of this judgment clear until one places it side by side with the case of *Thellusson v. Valentia*.[52] The Hurlingham Club from its origin indulged in pigeon-shooting. It was decided to do so no longer, and the plaintiff sought to obtain an injunction preventing the change on the ground that he had contracted for this sport on joining the club. Yet it was held that the change came under the clause admitting the alteration of the rules and was not a fundamental change. It surely will not be argued that a change in a subscription rate is any more fundamental than this. As a plain matter of common sense it is surely obvious that if a society can do the one thing the other should be permitted. If the courts will not protect the prejudices of members whose sporting tastes verge on the antiquarian, why should it protect those whose social tastes verge on the sullen disagreeableness of the boor?

Nor are matters improved when the trust conceals the reality of this group life. The trust, says Maitland,[53] 'has served to protect the unincorporated *Genossenschaft* against the attacks of inadequate and individualistic theories. We should all agree that if an *Anstalt* or a *Genossenschaft* is to live and thrive it must be efficiently protected by law against external enemies'. If it is to live *and thrive* – let us repeat the words in the way in which we would wish the emphasis to lie. The association is to thrive. It is not to have its life cramped, its development impeded. It is to be sheltered against the attacks of men willing to take advantage of its corporality. So, at least one would think, the trust came into being. And yet it is in precisely the opposite way that the courts have interpreted their purpose. Men's minds may change. Their purposes may change. Not so the purposes of men bound together in an association. The famous Free Church of Scotland case needs no retelling; the House of Lords chose to regard its life as fixed for it by the terms of a trust – not seeing that the fact that the church has a life must necessarily connote its right to develop the terms on which that life is lived[54]. . . . We must, surely, accept the point of view of Lord Haldane when he argued that 'the test of the personal identity of this Church lies not in doctrine but in its life'. To insist on the strictest adherence to the letter of a trust means that the dead hand shall regulate the living even when they have outgrown that hand's control, sixty or six hundred years after its decease. Is there any answer to the protest of Mill when he urged that no person ought thus to be exercising the rights of property six hundred years after his death?[55] It is more plausible to take one's stand on the spirit of the trust. . . .

It is no light stumbling-block that this cover of trusteeship has proved. It may be that the trustees of a club will incur liabilities on that club's behalf, though the rules have failed to provide for their indemnity. In that event the members will be able to avoid payment on the ground that they have contracted for no more than their subscriptions, even though the club (and they as its members) enjoy the benefit of the trustees' action.[56] Yet it would appear to the man in the street more equitable to make the club pay for that of which it enjoys the benefit. If, for example, the committee of a football club employs an incompetent person to repair a stand which collapses, sanity would appear to require that just as the club would have enjoyed the profits, so, on the collapse of the stand, it is right that it should suffer the penalties. Yet the courts, taking their stand on the principles of the law of contract, held that the members of the committee were responsible and must pay as individuals.[57] This is surely the violation of the ordinary principle of English law that he who holds property must bear its burdens no less than enjoy its advantages; nor should an agency or trusteeship obscure the real relation. A case can be conceived, can easily arise, where, without any knowledge on the part of the trustees, and by sheer misadventure on the part of one of their servants, they become liable for damages and the members go scot free. This is surely the *reductio ad absurdum* of legal formalism. . . .

And the contractual theory of voluntary associations can result in fictions compared to which the supposed fiction of corporate personality has less than the ingenuity of childish invention. . . .

Certain property rights serve to bring out the failure of the contractual attitude with striking clearness. The luckless fate of Serjeants' Inn, of Clements' Inn, and Barnard's Inn shows how disastrous can be the attempt to conceal corporateness to the public interest. No one believes that the distribution of their property among the surviving members fulfilled the pious purpose of their founders. The property of the unincorporate association can now be taxed,[58] (and for income tax at that); but the courts did not tell us whether this was a new method of double taxation or an attempt to recognize the fact of corporateness. . . .

Yet another curiosity deserves some notice. The courts do not regard a volunteer corps as a legal entity, so that it cannot be bound by contract. It can become bound only by particular members pledging their liability on its behalf, not for it as agents but for themselves as principals. So a commanding officer of a volunteer corps will be held responsible for uniforms supplied to the corps,[59] though, anomalous as it may seem, he is not responsible to the bankers of the battalion for its overdraft.[60] If a corps cannot have a liability for uniforms, why can a liability for its overdraft exist? And, further, if 'it' is no legal entity at all, why do we use collective nouns with possessive pronouns and singular verbs?

Now in all conscience these are absurdities enough; yet note what has followed from the denial of a right to sue and be sued. It was the mere accident of his membership of the Middle Temple which made Lord Eldon grant to a body of Free Masons the right to a representative action. It might have been, as he said,[61] 'singular that this court should sit upon the concerns of an association, which in law has no existence', but it was just because it had an existence in life that the law had to take some account of it. 'The society must', as Eldon saw, 'some way or other be permitted to sue'. Why? Because without that permission the gravest injustice would occur and to refuse it is to negate the whole purpose for which the courts exist. It was, again, a great advance when a private Act of Parliament enabled a voluntary society to sue in the name of its chairman.[62] But it does not go far enough. The entities the law must recognize are those which act as such, for to act in unified fashion is – formality apart – to act as a corporation. When the Scottish courts upheld a verdict against the libellers of 'the Roman Catholic authorities of Queenstown', they knew that no corporation had been libelled, but a body of men to be regarded as a unit for practical purposes. That body had suffered in reputation from the libel; it was right and fitting that it should receive compensation.[63] And when a voluntary society in the pursuit of its functions libels a company without justice, it seems rational, even if it is legally an innovation, to make the society pay.[64]

Nothing has brought in to more striking prominence the significance for practical life of this controversy than the questions raised in the last decade and a half by trade union activity. . . . Just as surely as the decision of the House of Lords marked, in the great Taff Vale case,[65] a vital advance, so, no less surely, did its decision in the Osborne case[66] mark a reactionary step. The Taff Vale case decided, as it appears to us, quite simply and reasonably, that a trade union must be responsible for the wrongs it commits – a point of view which so impressed the Royal Commission that they did not recommend the reversal of the judgment.[67] The Osborne case decided that a method of action which a trade union thinks necessary for its welfare and protection may be illegal because it is political and not industrial in its scope – political objects being *eo nomine* beyond the province of a trade society. But that is surely a too narrow interpretation of the facts. Where does a political object end and an industrial object begin? It is obvious to anyone who has eyes to see that at every point modern politics is concerned with the facts of everyday life in its industrial aspect. Therein they clearly touch the worker, and the trade union is an association formed for his protection. On this view the political activity of trade unions means no more than giving emphasis to one particular branch of their industrial policy. It is, then, one would urge, open to the courts to declare the transaction void on grounds of public policy; but it is probable that they would pay dearly for so doing in the loss of the respect in which they are held. It is wiser when dealing with the group person not to interfere with its individual life. The experience of the Privy Council as an ecclesiastical tribunal might herein have given a lesson to the House of Lords. There was it sternly demonstrated that the corporation of the English Church – a corporation in fact if not in law – will not tolerate the definition of its doctrine by an alien body. The sovereignty of theory is reduced by the event to an abstraction that is simply ludicrous. It may well be urged that any similar interference with the life of trade unions will result in a not dissimilar history.

VIII

We have travelled far, but at least there has been direction in our travelling. We have asked a question: is corporate personality a real thing? Is the collective will that is the inevitable accompaniment of that personality but a figment of the imagination? The thesis that has been here maintained is a simple one. It is that when the man in the street calls (let us say) Lloyds and the Stock Exchange corporations he is profoundly right in his perception. He has brushed aside the technicalities of form and penetrated to the reality, which is but a cloud serving not to reveal but to obscure. This, it may be pointed out, Erle, J., perceived nearly sixty years ago.[68] 'According to the plaintiff', he said,

> it is supposed to be a corporation created for the purpose of the navigation, and having the legal incidents of its existence limited for that purpose. But it appears to me that, by common law, the creation of a corporation conferred on it all the rights and liabilities in respect of property, contracts and

litigation which existence confers upon a natural subject, modified only by the formalities required for expressing the will of a numerous body.

Here, at any rate, is the basis of much-needed innovation. A corporation is simply an organized body of men acting as a unit, and with a will that has become unified through the singleness of their purpose. We assume its reality. We act upon that assumption. Are we not justified in the event?

After all, our legal theories will and must be judged by their applicability to the facts they endeavour to resume. It is clear enough that unless we treat the personality of our group persons as real and apply the fact of that reality throughout the whole realm of law, what we call justice will, in truth, be no more than a chaotic and illogical muddle.

English lawyers, it is said, have a dislike of abstractions. Such excursions as this into the world of legal metaphysics have for them the suspect air of dangerous adventure. But life, after all, is a series of precipices, and we have to act upon the assumptions we make. Here we urge a radical thesis; we say that the distinction between incorporate and voluntary association must be abolished. We say that the trust must be made to reveal the life that glows beneath, that we must have the means of penetrating beyond its fictitious protectiveness. No one doubts that the change will be vast. No one doubts that the application will need courage and high resolve. But it is in its very difficulty that we shall find its supreme worth.

IX

A last word remains to be said. If what we have here been urging is true, it reacts most forcibly upon our theory of the state. Thus far, for the most part, we have sought its unification. We have made it intolerant of associations within itself – associations that to Hobbes will appear comparable only to 'worms within the entrails of a natural man'. As a result we have made our state absorptive in a mystic, Hegelian fashion. It is all-sovereign and unchallengeable. It has, if it be the papal state, and the Pope its personification, the *plenitudo potestatis*; be it imperial, its emperor is *legibus solutus*; be it Britannic, its parliament has . . . no limit in power save the laws of nature. . . . Admirable enough this may be in theory; of a certainty it does not fit the facts. We do not proceed from the state to the parts of the state, from the One to the Many, on the ground that the state is more unified than its parts. On the contrary, we are forced to the admission that the parts are as real, as primary, and as self-sufficing as the whole. 'The pluralistic world', said [William] James,[69] 'is ... more like a federal republic than an empire or a kingdom. However much may be collected, however much may report itself as present at any effective centre of consciousness or action, something else is self-governed and absent and unreduced to unity.' But sovereign your state no longer is if the groups within itself are thus self-governing. Nor can we doubt this polyarchism. Everywhere we find groups within the state which challenge its supremacy. They are, it may be, in relations with the state, a part of it; but one with it they are not. They refuse the reduction to unity. We find the state, in James's phrase, to be distributive and not collective. Men belong to it; but, also, they belong to other groups, and a competition for allegiance is continuously possible. ... [E]very great crisis must show its essential plurality. Whether we will or no, we are bundles of hyphens. When the centres of linkage conflict a choice must be made.

Such it is submitted, is the natural consequence of an admission that the personality of associations is real and not conceded thereto by the state. We then give to this latter group no particular merit. We refuse it the title of creator of all else. We make it justify itself by its consequences. We stimulate its activities by making it compete with the work of other groups coextensive with or complementary to itself. As it may not extinguish, so it may not claim pre-eminence. Like any other group, what it is and what it will be, it can be only be virtue of its achievement. So only can it hope to hand down undimmed the torch of its conscious life.

NOTES

1. Dicey (1905) *Lectures on the Relation between Law and Public Opinion in England in the Nineteenth Century* [second edition, London: Macmillan, 1920], p. 165.
2. On the relation between the individual personality and social groups the reader will find much of deep interest in Wilfred Richmond (1900) *Personality as a Philosophical Principle* [London: Arnold]. I personally owe much to this fascinating book.
3. *Citizens' Life Assurance Co. v. Brown* [1904], A.C. 423, 426.

4. 52 & 53 Vict., Ch. 63, para. 19.
5. *Attorney-General v. Great Eastern Ry. Co.*, L. R. II, Ch. D. 449, 503 (1879), per Lord Bramwell.
6. *Darlington v. Mayor, etc., of New York*, 31 N.Y. 164, 197 (1865).
7. *Dartmouth College v. Woodward*, 4 Wheat, (U.S.) 518, 636 (1819).
8. *Duvergier v. Fellows*, 5 Bing, 248, 268.
9. [*The Province of Jurisprudence Determined* – ref. missing in original – ed.]
10. Salmond *Jurisprudence*, edition of 1902, p. 350.
11. Holland (1893) *Jurisprudence*, eleventh edition, p. 385.
12. [A reference to the English East India Company – ed.]
13. [Maitland (1911) *Collected Papers*, Cambridge: Cambridge University Press, vol. 3 – ed.]
14. [Cf. The Free Church of Scotland case – ed.]
15. *South Wales Ry. Co. v. Redmond*, 10, C.B. n.s. 675 (1861).
16. *Colman v. Eastern Counties Ry. Co.* 10 Beav. 1 (1846).
17. *Wilson v. Miers* 10 C.B. n.s. 348 (1861).
18. *Gregory v. Patchett*, 33 Beav. 595 (1864).
19. *Hare v. London & N.W. Ry. Co.*, 2 J. & H. 80 (1861).
20. *Charlton v. Newcastle & Carlisle Ry. Co.*, 5 Jur. n.s. 1096 (1859).
21. *Bateman v. Mayor, etc. of Ashton-under-Lyne*, 3 H. & N. 323 (1858), and *Attorney-General v. Mayor, etc. of Wigan*, 5 DeG. M. & G. 52 (1854).
22. *Attorney-General v. Andrews*, 2 Mac. & G. 225 (1850); *Sheffield Waterworks Co. v. Carter*, 8 Q.B. 632 (1882).
23. *Mayor, etc. of Norwich v. Norwich Ry. Co.*, 4 E. & B. 397, 432 (1855).
24. *Wenlock v. River Dee Co.*, 10 A. C. 354 (1885).
25. As in the great Ashbury case.
26. *Tomkinson v. South Eastern Ry. Co.*, L. R. 35 Ch. D. 675 (1887).
27. *Hampson V. Price's Patent Candle Co.*
28. Mr E. Manson in 12 *Encyclopedia of the Laws of England*, 1 ed., p. 360.
29. *Ashbury Railway Carriage Co. v. Riche*, L. R. 7 H. L. 653, 672 (1875).
30. In *re* Stanhope, 3 DeG. & Sm. 198 (1850).
31. Y. B. 7 Hen. VII, pl. 9.
32. *Metropolitan Saloon Omnibus Co. v. Hawkins*, 4 H. & N. 87 (1859); *South Hetton Coal Co. v. North-Eastern News Ass'n*, L. R. [1894] 1 Q. B. 133.
33. *Mayor, etc., of Manchester v. Williams*, L. R. [1891] 1 Q. B. 94.
34. *Metropolitan Saloon Omnibus Co. v. Hawkins*, 4 H. & N. 87 (1859), at p. 90.
35. *Whitfield v South-Eastern Ry. Co.*, 27 L. J., (Q. B.) 229 (1858).
36. *Eastern Counties Ry. Co. v. Broom*, 6 Exch. 314 (1851).
37. *Barwick v. Eng. Joint Stock Bank*, L. R. 2 Ex. 259 (1867).
38. *Citizen's Life Assurance Co. v. Brown* [1904], A. C. 423, 426.
39. *Queen v. Birmingham & Glouc. Ry. Co.*, 3 Q. B. 223 (1842).
40. *Queen v. Great North of England Ry. Co.*, 9 Q. B. 315 (1846).
41. *Hawke v. Hulton & Co.*, L. R. [1909] 2 K. B. 93.
42. *Pearks, etc. v. Ward*, L. R. [1902] 2 K. B. 1.
43. *Chuter v. Freeth, etc.* L. R. [1911] 2 K. B. 832.
44. Cited in *Pearks, etc. v. Ward*, L. R. [1902] 2 K. B. 1, at p. 8.
45. *Queen v. Great West Laundry Co.*, 13 Manitoba Ref. 66 (1900).

46. *Union Colliery Co. v. H. M. The Queen*, 31 Can. Sup. Ct. 81 (1900).
47. Perhaps Lord Bowen in *Queen v. Tyler & International Commercial Co., Ltd.*, felt some difficulty also. L. R. [1891] 2 Q. B. 588. See especially pp. 592, 594, 596.
48. *Cyclists' Touring Club v. Hopkinson*, L. R. [1910] 1 Ch. 179.
49. Introduction to Gierke (1900) *Political Theories of the Middle Age* [Cambridge: Cambridge University Press], p. 40.
50. Cf. F. H. Bradley (1893) *Appearance and Reality* [London: Swan Sonnershein], p. 532. 'For me a person is finite or is meaningless.'
51. *Harrington v. Sendall*, L. R. [1903] 1 Ch. 921.
52. L. R. [1907] 2 Ch. 1.
53. Maitland *Collected Papers*, vol. 3, p. 367.
54. On all this Dr. J.N. Figgis (1913) *Churches in the Modern State* is of very high value.
55. *Dissertations and Discussions* p. 36.
56. *Wise v. Perpetual Trustee Co.* [1903] A. C. 139.
57. *Brown v. Lewis*, 12 T. L. R. 455 (1896).
58. 48 & 49 Vict. c. 51, and *Curtis v. Old Monkland Conservative Ass'n* [1906] A. C. 86.
59. *Samuel Brothers Ltd. v. Whetherly*, L. R. [1908] 1 K. B. 184.
60. *National Bank of Scotland v. Shaw* [1913], S. C. 133.
61. *Lloyd v. Loaring*, 6 Ves. 773, 778 (1802).
62. *Williams v. Beaumont*, 10 Bing. 260 (1833).
63. *Brown v. Thomson & Co.* [1912] S. C. 359.
64. *Greenlands, Ltd. v. Wilmhurst*, L. R. [1913] 3 K. B. 507.
65. [1901] A. C. 426.
66. [1910] A. C. 87.
67. Report, p. 8.
68. *Bostock v. North Staffordshire Railway Co.*, 4 E. & B. 798, 819 (1855).
69. William James (1909) *A Pluralistic Universe* [London: Longmans, Green & Co.], p. 321. The whole book has vital significance for political theory; see especially the fifth lecture.

Chapter Ten

THE PLURALISTIC STATE

Every student of politics must begin his researches with humble obeisance to the work of Aristotle; and therein, I take it, he makes confession of the inspiration and assistance he has had from the effort of philosophers. Indeed, if one took only the last century of intellectual history, names like Hegel, Green, and Bosanquet must induce him in a certain sense of humility. For the direction of his analysis has been given its perspective by their thought. The end his effort must achieve has been by no other thinkers so clearly or so wisely defined.

Yet the philosophic interpretation of politics has suffered from one serious weakness. It is rather with *staatslehre* than with *politik* that it has concerned itself. Ideals and forms have provided the main substance of its debates. So that even if, as with Hegel and Green, it has had the battles of the market-place most clearly in mind, it has somehow, at least ultimately, withdrawn itself from the arena of hard facts to those remoter heights where what a good Platonist has called[1] the 'pure instance' of the state may be dissected. Nor has it seen political philosophy sufficiently outside the arena of its own problems. Aristotle apart, its weakness has lain exactly in those minutiae of psychology which, collectively, are all-important to the student of administration. Philosophy seems, in politics at least, to take too little thought for the categories of space and time.

The legal attitude has been impaired by a somewhat similar limitation. The lawyer, perhaps of necessity, has concerned himself not with right but with rights, and his consequent preoccupation with the problem of origins, the place of ultimate reference has made him, at least to the interested outsider, unduly eager to confound the legally ancient with the politically justifiable. One might even make out a case for the assertion that the lawyer is the head and centre of our modern trouble; for the monistic theory of the state goes back, in its scientific statement, to Jean Bodin. The latter became the spiritual parent of Hobbes, and thence, through Bentham, the ancestor of Austin. . . .

It is with the lawyers that the problem of the modern state originates as an actual theory; for the lawyers' formulae have been rather amplified than denied by the philosophers. Upon the historic events which surround their effort I would say one word, since it is germane to the argument I have presently to make. We must ceaselessly remember that the monistic theory of the state was born in an age of crisis and that each period of its revivification has synchronized with some momentous event which has signalized a change in the distribution of political power. Bodin, as is well known, was of that party which, in an age of religious warfare, asserted, lest it perish in an alien battle, the supremacy of the state.[2] Hobbes sought the means of order in a period when King and Parliament battled for the balance of power. Bentham published his *Fragment* on the eve of the Declaration of Independence; and Adam Smith, in the same year, was outlining the programme of another and profounder revolution. Hegel's philosophy was the outcome of a vision of German multiplicity destroyed by the unity of France. Austin's book was conceived when the middle classes of France and England had, in their various ways, achieved the conquest of a state hitherto but partly open to their ambition.

It seems of peculiar significance that each assertion of the monistic theory should have this background. I cannot stay here to disentangle the motives through which men so different in character should have embraced a theory as similar in substance. The result, with all of them, is to assert the supremacy of the state over all other institutions. Its primary organs have the first claim upon the allegiance of men; and Hobbe's insistence[3] that corporations other than the state are but the manifestations of disease is perhaps the best example of its ruthless logic. Hobbes and Hegel apart, the men I have noted were lawyers; and they were seeking a means whereby the source of power may have some adequate justification Bentham, of course, at no point beatified the state; though zeal for it is not wanting in the earlier thinkers or in Hegel. What, I would urge, the lawyers did was to provide a foundation for the moral superstructure of the philosophers. It was by the latter that the monistic state was elevated from the plane of logic to the plane of ethics. Its rights then became matter of right. Its sovereignty became spiritualized into moral pre-eminence.

The transition is simple enough. The state is today the one compulsory form of association,[4] and for more than two thousand years we have been taught that its purpose is the perfect life. It thus seems to acquire a flavour of generality which is absent from all other institutions. It becomes instinct with an universal interest to which, as it appears, no other association may without inaccuracy lay claim. Its sovereignty thus seems to represent the protection of the universal aspect of men – what Rousseau called the common good – against the intrusion of more private aspects at the hands of which it might otherwise suffer humiliation. The state is an absorptive animal; and there are few more amazing tracts of history than that which records its triumph over the challenge of competing groups. There seems, at least today, no certain method of escape from its demands. Its conscience is supreme over any private conception of good the individual may hold. It sets the terms upon which the lives of trade unions may be lived. It dictates their doctrine to churches. . . . The area of its enterprise has consistently grown until today there is no field of human activity over which, in some degree, its pervading influence may not be detected.

But it is at this point pertinent to inquire what exact meaning is to be attached to an institution so vital as this. With one definition only I shall trouble you. 'A state', writes Mr Zimmern,[5] 'can be defined, in legal language, as a territory over which there is a government claiming unlimited authority'. The definition, indeed, is not quite correct; for no government in the United States could claim, though it might usurp, unlimited power. But it is a foible of the lawyers to insist upon the absence of legal limit to the authority of the state; and it is, I think, ultimately clear that the monistic theory is bound up with some such assumption. But it is exactly here that our main difficulty begins to emerge. The state, as Mr Zimmern here points out, must act through organs; and, in the analysis of its significance, it is upon government that we must concentrate our main attention.[6]

185

Legally, no one can deny that there exists in every state some organ whose authority is unlimited. But that legality is no more than a fiction of logic. No man has stated more clearly than Professor Dicey[7] the sovereign character of the King in Parliament; no man has been also so quick to point out the practical limits to this supremacy. And if logic is thus out of accord with the facts of life the obvious question to be asked is why unlimited authority may be claimed. The answer, I take it, is reducible to the belief that government expresses the largest aspect of man and is thus entitled to institutional expression of the area covered by its interests. A history, of course, lies [at the] back of that attitude, the main part of which would be concerned with the early struggle of the modern state to be born. Nor do I think the logical character of the doctrine has all the sanction claimed for it. It is only with the decline of theories of natural law that Parliament becomes the complete master of its destinies. And the internal limits which the jurist is driven to admit prove, on examination, to be the main problem for consideration.

There are many different angles from which this claim to unlimited authority may be proved inadequate. That government is the most important of institutions few, except theocrats, could be found to deny; but that its importance warrants the monistic assumption herein implied raises far wider questions. The test, I would urge, is not an *a priori* statement of claim. Nothing has led us farther along the wrong path than the simple teleological terms in which Aristotle stated his conclusions. For when we say that political institutions aim at the good life, we need to know not only the meaning of good, but also those who are to achieve it, and the methods by which it is to be attained. What, in fact, we have to do is to study the way in which this monistic theory has worked; for our judgement upon it must depend upon consequences to the mass of men and women. I would not trouble you unduly with history. But it is worth while to bear in mind that this worship of state unity is almost entirely the offspring of the Reformation and therein, most largely, an adaptation of the practice of the medieval church. The fear of variety was not, in its early days, an altogether unnatural thing. Challenged from within and from without, uniformity seemed the key to self-preservation. But when the industrial history of the state is examined, its supposed unity of purpose and of effort sinks, with acquaintance, into nothingness.

What in fact confronts us is a complex of interests; and between not few of them ultimate reconciliation is impossible. We cannot, for example, harmonize the modern secular state with a Roman Church based upon the principles of the Encyclical of 1864; nor can we find the basis of enduring collaboration between trade unions aiming at the control of industry through the destruction of capitalistic organization and the upholders of capitalism. Historically, we always find that any system of government is dominated by those who at the time wield economic power; and what they mean by 'good' is, for the most part, the preservation of their own interests. Perhaps I put it too crudely; refined analysis would, maybe, suggest that they are limited by the circle of the ideas to which their interests would at the first instance give rise .... There is nowhere and at no time assurance of that consistent generality of motive in the practice of government which theory would suppose it to possess.

We cannot, that is to say, at any point, take for granted the motives of governmental policy, with the natural implication that we must erect safeguards against their abuse. These, I venture to think, the monistic theory of state at no point, in actual practice, supplies. For its insistence on unlimited authority in the governmental organ makes over to it the immense power that comes from the possession of legality. What, in the stress of conflict, this comes to mean is the attribution of inherent rightness to acts of government. These are somehow taken, and that with but feeble regard to their actual substance, to be acts of the community. Something that, for want of a better term, we call the communal conscience is supposed to want certain things. We rarely inquire either how it comes to want them or to need them. We simply know that the government enforces the demand so made and that the individual or group is expected to give way before them. Yet it may well happen, as we have sufficiently seen in our experience, that the individual or the group may be right. And it is difficult to see how a policy which thus penalizes all dissent, at least in active form, from government can claim affinity with freedom. For freedom, as Mr Graham Wallas has finely said,[8] implies the chance of continuous initiative. But the ultimate implication of the monistic state in a society so complex as our own is the transference of that freedom from ordinary men to their rulers.

187

I cannot here dwell upon the more technical results of this doctrine, more particularly on the absence of liability for the faults of government that it has involved. But it is in some such background as this that the pluralistic theory of the state takes its origin. It agrees with Mr Zimmern that a state is a territorial society divided into government and subjects, but it differs, as you will observe, from his definition in that it makes no assumptions as to the authority a government should possess. And the reason for this fact is simply that it is consistently experimentalist in temper. It realizes that the state has a history and it is unwilling to assume that we have today given to it any permanence of form. . . . And if it be deemed necessary to dignify this outlook by antiquity we can, I think, produce great names as its sponsors. At least it could be shown that the germs of our protest are in men like Nicholas of Cusa, like Althusius, Locke, and Royer-Collard.

It thus seems that we have a twofold problem. The monistic state is an hierarchical structure in which power is, for ultimate purposes, collected at a single centre. The advocates of pluralism are convinced that this is both administratively incomplete and ethically inadequate. You will observe that I have made no reference here to the lawyer's problem. Nor do I deem it necessary; for when we are dealing, as the lawyer deals, with sources of ultimate reference, the questions are no more difficult, perhaps I should also add, no easier, than those arising under the conflict of jurisdictions in a federal state.

It is with other questions that we are concerned. Let us note, in the first place, the tendency in the modern state for men to become the mere subjects of administration. It is perhaps as yet too early to insist, reversing a famous generalization of Sir Henry Maine, that the movement of our society is from contract to status; but there is at least one sense in which that remark is significant. Amid much vague enthusiasm for the thing itself, every observer must note a decline in freedom. What we most greatly need is to beware lest we lose that sense of spontaneity which enabled Aristotle to define citizenship as the capacity to rule not less than to be ruled in turn.[9] We believe that this can best be achieved in a state of which the structure is not hierarchical but co-ordinate, in which, that is to say, sovereignty is partitioned upon some basis of function. For the division of power makes men more apt to responsibility than its accumulation. A man, or even a legislature that is overburdened with a multiplicity of business, will not merely neglect that which he ought to do; he will, in actual experience, surrender his powers into the hands of forceful interests which know the way to compel his attention. He will treat the unseen as non-existent and the inarticulate as contented. The result may, indeed, be revolution; but experience suggests that it is more likely to be the parent of a despotism.

Nor is this all. Such a system must needs result in a futile attempt to apply equal and uniform methods to varied and unequal things. Every administrator has told us of the effort to arrive at an intellectual routine; and where the problems of government are as manifold as at present that leads to an assumption of similarity which is rarely borne out by the facts. The person who wishes to govern America must know that he cannot assume identity of conditions in North and South, East and West. He must, that is to say, assume, that his first duty is not to assert a greatest common measure of equality but to prove it. That will, I suggest, lead most critical observers to perceive that the unit with which we are trying to deal is too large for effective administration. . . .

Administratively, therefore, we need decentralization: or, if you like, we need to revivify the conception of federalism which is the great contribution of America to political science. But we must not think of federalism today merely in the old spatial terms. It applies not less to functions than to territories. It applies not less to the government of the cotton industry, or of the civil service, than it does to the government of Kansas and Rhode Island. Indeed, the greatest lesson the student of government has to learn is the need for him to understand the significance for politics of industrial structure and, above all, the structure of the trade union movement. The main factor in political organization that we have to recover is the factor of consent, and here trade union federalism has much to teach us. It has found, whether the unit be a territorial one like the average local, or an industrial one like that envisaged by the shop-steward movement in England, units sufficiently small to make the individual feel significant in them. What, moreover, this development of industrial organization had done is to separate the process of production and consumption in such fashion as to destroy, for practical purposes, the unique sovereignty of a territorial parliament. . . .

The facts, I suggest, are driving us towards an effort at the partition of power. The evidence for that conclusion you can find on all sides. The civil services of England and France are pressing for such a reorganization.[10] It is towards such a conclusion that what we call too vaguely the labour movement has directed its main energies[11]. We are in the midst of a new movement for the conquest of self-government. It finds its main impulse in the attempt to disperse the sovereign power because it is realized that where administrative organization is made responsive to the actual associations of men, there is a greater chance not merely of efficiency but of freedom also. . . . The British House of Commons has debated federalism as the remedy for its manifold ills, and the unused potentialities of German decentralization may lead to the results so long expected now that the deadening pressure of Prussian domination has been withdrawn. We are learning, as John Stuart Mill pointed out in an admirable passage,[12] that 'all the facilities which a government enjoys of access to information, all the means which it possesses of remunerating, and therefore of commanding, the best available talent in the market, are not an equivalent for the one great disadvantage of an inferior interest in the result'. For we now know that the consequence of that inferior interest is the consistent degradation of freedom.

I have spoken of the desire for genuine responsibility and the direction in which it may be found for administrative purposes. To this aspect the ethical side of political pluralism stands in the closest relation. Fundamentally, it is a denial that a law can be explained merely as a command of the sovereign for the simple reason that it denies, ultimately, the sovereignty of anything save right conduct. The philosophers, since, particularly, the time of T.H. Green, have told us insistently that the state is based upon will; though they have too little examined the problem of what will is most likely to receive obedience. With history behind us, we are compelled to conclude that no such will can by definition be a good will; and the individual must therefore, whether by himself or in concert with others, pass judgement upon its validity by examining its substance. That, it is clear enough, makes an end of the sovereignty of the state in its classical conception. It puts the state's acts – practically, as I have pointed out, the acts of its primary organ, government – on a moral parity with the acts of any other association. It gives to the judgements of the state exactly the power they inherently possess by virtue of their moral content, and no other. If the English state should wish, as in 1776, to refuse colonial freedom; if Prussia should choose to embark upon a *Kulturkampf*, if any state, to take the decisive instance, should choose to embark upon war; in each case there is no *a priori* rightness about its policy. You and I are part of the leverage by which that policy is ultimately enacted. It therefore becomes a moral duty on our part to examine the foundations of state action. The last sin in politics is unthinking acquiescence in important decisions.

I have elsewhere dealt with the criticism that this view results in anarchy.[13] What is more profitable here to examine is its results in our scheme of political organization. It is, in the first place, clear that there are no demands upon our allegiance except the demands of what we deem right conduct. Clearly, in such an aspect, we need the means of ensuring that we shall know right when we see it. Here, I would urge,the problem of rights becomes significant. For the duties of citizenship cannot be fulfilled, save under certain conditions; and it is necessary to ensure the attainment of those conditions against the encroachments of authority. I cannot here attempt any sort of detail; but it is obvious enough that freedom of speech, a living wage, an adequate education, a proper amount of leisure, the power to combine for social effort, are all of them integral to citizenship. They are natural rights in the sense that without them the purpose of the state cannot be fulfilled. They are natural also in the sense that they do not depend upon the state for their validity. They are inherent in the eminent worth of human personality. Where they are denied, the state clearly destroys whatever claims it has upon the loyalty of men.

Rights such as these are necessary to freedom because without them man is lost in a world almost beyond the reach of his understanding. We have put them outside the power of the state to traverse; and this again must mean a limit upon its sovereignty. If you ask what guarantee exists against their destruction in a state where power is distributed, the answer, I think, is that only in such a state have the masses of men the opportunity to understand what is meant by their denial. It is surely, for example, significant that the movement for the revival of what we broadly term natural law should derive its main strength from organized trade unionism. It is hardly less important that among those who have perceived the real significance of the attitude of labour in the Taff Vale and

Osborne cases should have been a high churchman most deeply concerned with the restoration of the church.[14] That is what co-ordinate organization will above all imply, and its main value is the fact that what otherwise must strike us most in the modern state is the inert receptiveness of the multitude. Every student of politics knows well enough what this means. Most would, on analysis, admit that its dissipation is mainly dependent upon an understanding of social mechanisms now largely hidden from the multitude. The only hopeful way of breaking down this inertia is by the multiplication of centres of authority. When a man is trained to service in a trade union, he cannot avoid seeing how that activity is related to the world outside. When he gets on a school committee, the general problems of education begin to unfold themselves before him. Paradoxically, indeed, we may say that a consistent decentralization is the only effective cure for an undue localism. That is because institutions with genuine power become ethical ideas and thus organs of genuine citizenship. . . .

Here, indeed, is where the main superiority of the pluralistic state is manifest. For the more profoundly we analyse the psychological characteristics of its opposite, the less adequate does it seem relative to the basic impulses of men. And this, after all, is the primary need to satisfy. It was easy enough for Aristotle to make a fundamental division between masters and men and adapt his technique to the demands of the former; but it was a state less ample than a moderate-sized city that he had in mind. It was simple for Hobbes to assume the inherent badness of men and the consequent need of making government strong, lest their evil nature bring it to ruin; yet even he must have seen, what our own generation has emphasized, that the strength of governments consists only in the ideas of which they dispose. It was even simple for Bentham to insist on the ruling motive of self-interest; but he wrote before it had become clear that altruism was an instinct implied in the existence of the herd. We know at least that the data are more complex. Our main business has become the adaptation of our institutions to a variety of impulses with the knowledge that we must at all costs prevent their inversion. In the absence of such transmutation what must mainly impress us is the wastage upon which our present system is built. The executioner, as [Joseph de] Maistre said, is the corner-stone of our society. But it is because we refuse to release the creative energies of men.

After all, our political systems must be judged not merely by the ends they serve, but also by the way in which they serve those ends. The modern state provides a path whereby a younger Pitt may control the destinies of a people; it even gives men of leisure a field of passionate interest to cultivate. But the humbler man is less fortunate in the avenues we afford; and if we have record of notable achievement after difficult struggle, we are too impressed by the achievement to take due note of the anguish upon which it is too often founded. This, it may be remarked, is the touchstone by which the major portion of our institutions will be tested in the future; and I do not think that we can be unduly certain that they will stand the test. The modern state, at bottom, is too much an historic category not to change its nature with the advent of new needs.

Those new needs, it may be added, are upon us, and the future of our civilization most largely depends upon the temper in which we confront them. Those who take refuge in the irrefutable logic of the sovereign state may sometimes take thought that for many centuries of medieval history the very notion of sovereignty was unknown. I would not seek unduly to magnify those far-off times; but it is worth while to remember that no thoughts were dearer to the heart of medieval thinkers than ideals of right and justice. Shrunken and narrow, it may be, their fulfilment often was; but that was not because they did not know how to dream. Our finely articulated structure is being tested by men who do not know what labour and thought have gone into its building. It is a cruder test they will apply. Yet it is only by seeking to understand their desires that we shall be able worthily to meet it.

NOTES

1. Barker (1915) *Political Thought in England from Herbert Spencer to the Present Day* [London: Home University Library, Williams and Norgate], pp. 68ff.
2. [The 'party' in question is the *Politiques'* – ed.]
3. Hobbes (1651) *Leviathan*, chapter 44.
4. I say today; for it is important to remember that, for the western world, this was true of the Church until the Reformation.
5. Zimmern (1918) *Nationality and Government* [London: Chatto], p. 56.
6. Cf. Laski (1919) *Authority in the Modern State* [New Haven: Yale University Press], pp. 26ff.
7. Cf. Dicey (1885) *An Introduction to the Study of the Law of the Constitution,*

eighth edition [London: Macmillan, 1920], pp. 37ff.

8. Cf. his article in the *New Statesman*, 25 September 1915, I owe my knowledge of this winning definition to Mr. A.E. Zimmern's *Nationality and Government*, p. 57.

9. Aristotle *Politics*, Bk. III, chapter 1, p. 1275a.

10. See Laski *Authority in the Modern State*, chapter 5.

11. Cf. Cole (1917) *Self Government in Industry* [London: G. Bell], *passim*, especially chapter 3.

12. Mill (1848) *Principles of Political Economy*, second edition, vol. 2, p. 181.

13. *Authority in the Modern State*, pp. 93-4.

14. Figgis (1913) *Churches in the Modern State* [London: Longmans, Green & Co.].

Part Four

STUDIES IN LAW AND POLITICS

H.J. Laski

Chapter Eleven

LAW AND THE STATE

I

Every state in the modern world is a territorial community in the name of which some agent or agents exercise sovereignty. By sovereignty is meant the legal competence to issue orders without a need to refer to a higher authority. The orders so issued constitute law, and are binding upon all who come within their jurisdiction.

In some such way as this the modern analytical jurist defines the nature of the state for the purposes of his science. Any explanation of its character is, most usefully, of two kinds. It can be, on the one hand, historical. It is possible to trace the way in which the *Respublica Christiana* [Christian Commonwealth] of the Middle Ages was slowly transformed into the complex of states we know in the modern world, and to show how the demands of unity and order gradually and painfully resulted in the attribution to them of the quality we call sovereignty. Such an explanation has the value of enabling us to see that the modern state is not, either in its form or substance, anything permanent or eternal: it is simply a moment of historical time, obviously born of special needs, and, equally obviously, destined to transformation either when it has ceased to satisfy those needs or when the needs themselves have passed away. The historical study of the state has the great merit of showing us the essentially pragmatic character of all theories about its nature. They are born of the need to satisfy a particular environment, and they die when they cease to render that satisfaction.

Alternatively, the jurist's explanation of the state may dwell in the realm of formal logic. Making entire abstraction of the facts of any given state, it may seek the quintessential form of which all states are more or less imperfect expressions. It may then say that where there is an authority which fixes the norms of all law, and beyond which, in the search for the origin of such norms, we cannot go, there we have a sovereign state. The content of the norms, or of the orders begotten legally of them, is here irrelevant. Neither political nor moral considerations have any bearing upon this aspect of statehood. We have not to consider the goodness or badness, the wisdom or unwisdom, of the norms; no problem arises for the jurist save whether the authority which has fixed them is or is not competent formally to do so, whether it is possible to go beyond that authority to one upon which it depends for its existence. If there is formal competence, if, further, that authority is ultimate in what may be termed the hierarchy of powers, it constitutes a sovereign state.

From a formal point of view, it is clear that the juristic theory of the state explains why commands which are issued in the name of the state are binding upon all who come within its jurisdiction. For it makes the ultimate source of reference from which all legal power to command is derived. But it is important to remember what the theory does not do. It explains how a complex of personalities, both corporate and individual, is geared into unity by subordinating them to a single point in the community. It does not explain whether the method by which this result is attained is good or whether its consequences are beneficial. It defines law as the will of the state without regard to the content of law. It makes that will binding upon the subjects of the state without regard either to what it does or to its power to get itself applied. It does not explain why the state has acted in a particular way, or whether it should have acted in a particular way. It is merely a descriptive technique of competence, independent of the actual world that competence will have to encounter. It is entirely fair, from this angle, to speak of the will of the state as absolute, indivisible, and inalienable. For were it none of these things, it would, in terms of its definitions, cease to be sovereign. Any formal juristic theory of the state conceived in this way must necessarily dwell in a pure world of categories. It is independent of the day-to-day stresses and strains which states have to encounter. The ideal state of formal jurisprudence need not consider public opinion, the wills of other states, the impact upon itself of internal and competing powers, ethical right, or political wisdom. Within the structure of the community of which it is the supreme expression, life is lived in terms of categories which it alone can make or alter. It determines the life of all other wills because it alone makes the principles of behaviour to which they must conform. For their law is conceived in terms of its law, since rules of conduct hostile to its law are illegal in the precise degree in which they depart from it. We are, indeed, entitled to think of them as valid only by reason of state permission, since the possibility that the state may deny them renders their right to be an exercise always in the conditional mood. The state giveth, and the state taketh away; whether we shall add the wonted blessing depends very largely upon our political philosophy.

II

In terms of its axioms, formal jurisprudence is completely justified in the whole of its procedure; in terms of its axioms, neither its method nor its results can be denied. By its own inherent logic, all that it makes law is necessarily legal, all in conflict with it is necessarily illegal; for it could not continue its sovereignty on any other terms. But a philosophy of the state can never rest satisfied with the axioms of formal jurisprudence. It must ask why they have been assumed, and what they do as a consequence of their adoption. It must seek a bridge between the purely logical world of ideal concepts, in which alone the juristic theory of the state dwells, and the actual world about us, in which the states that we know have to perform their function. It needs to know, accordingly, what that function is, and, independently of the juristic theory, to devise an institutional pattern which seems most likely to enable it to be performed to the maximum possible advantage. When the juristic theory is analysed from this angle, its nature and validity begin to assume a much more questionable form.

Let us begin by remembering two things. Every state, from the legal angle, is divisible into a body of persons issuing orders, and a body of persons receiving them and, presumably, acting upon them. The latter encounter the state always through its agents. It cannot act upon them except through its agents. For them, the state itself is an abstraction in the name of which those agents are entitled to speak. They make its will for the subjects of the state, in whom, of course, where the state is a *Rechtsstaat*, they are themselves included. Save through them, the state has no means of declaring its will. It is simply a category of description, a method of attributing formal competence of a specially majestic kind to certain persons and not to other persons. There is nothing about the state, in this context, which enables us to assume that it has special virtues or special wisdom, or an inherent right (apart from a formal legal right) to be obeyed. Its sovereignty is a method of conferring formal power upon men to whom functions of a special kind have been entrusted.

The way in which this kind of power developed is well known. When the western world split up, at the Reformation, into a series of communities no longer recognizing either a single religious head, as in the Pope, or a vague and tenuous overlordship, as in the Emperor, religious conflict made necessary the unification of power within the state if it was to survive the consequences of that conflict. Sometimes the solution took the form of assuming that the decisions for making unity, and, therefore, order, should rest with the prince who became, as with Henry VIII and Elizabeth I, the supreme head of the church; sometimes the unity was made by recognizing papal power as invested with a right to command Roman Catholics, but, also, investing another authority with the right to determine, as in France under the Bourbons, the limits within which that power should be exercised. The Reformation, in fact, transferred to a person, whether individual or institutional, in each of the communities into which Europe was broken up the power to determine the rights of groups and persons in the interests of peace and order. Continuous warfare made men feel that peace was the supreme good; uncertainty whether the claim of a group or person was valid or not seemed to involve the risk of further conflict. To set the monarch, or, as in England, the King in Parliament, above all other persons in the community was a simple way of resolving what rights those persons should possess. None of them, legally, could appeal to a will beyond that of the King, or his analogue. They had, therefore, in the legal realm no alternative but obedience to his decision. The supremacy of the state was, internally, the necessary consequence of the breakdown of religious unity. Its right to determine the boundaries of power in

200

any association or person within the community over which it presided followed directly from that supremacy. Once there was no appeal to Rome, there was no power which could compete with the authority of the state. But it must be remembered, once more, that in all these relationships, the state acted always through agents: it was, for its subjects, Philip in Spain, Louis in France, Cromwell and his major-generals, or William and his Parliaments in England. Their right to issue orders was the expression of a relational context between them and other persons so placed as to be unable, by legal means, to go beyond them. What is termed the personality of the state was, in point of fact, always the personality of the government of the state. The distinction between state and government was nothing more than the means of obtaining a sanction for the norms imposed by the government upon the community.

The international situation greatly helped this development. The growth of commerce meant that, internally, the interests of peace were paramount; and the government of the state, as the authority charged with the preservation of order, enormously increased its authority as a consequence. Once commerce passed, in fact, from the local to the national sphere, the government was able, in the name of the state, to make regulations which, in the interest of the whole community, could be regarded as superseding merely local advantage. And where war was deemed necessary for commercial advantage, obviously it was to the economic benefit of the interests affected to strengthen the authority of the state, therefore, also, of government, for their own sake. By the middle of the seventeenth century, government and state had become so identified that even dynastic wars contributed to the interest of the state's authority. Its power grew by leaps and bounds simply because the purposes it represented were attained by its increasing assumption of authority.

That this is the history of its development is brought out clearly by the history of political philosophy since the Reformation. The classical theory of the state, as it passes from Luther to Bodin, thence to Hobbes and Rousseau, and ultimately to Hegel and his disciples, is essentially the history of an axiom and its justification. Luther vindicated the right of the secular power to be, independently of ecclesiastical trammels. Bodin and Hobbes, writing, each of them, in an age when the power of the

201

government to speak in the name of the state was challenged, insisted that anything less than a sovereign state meant anarchy, because there was then no final source of certain reference for the norms by which men's behaviour is regulated. Both Bodin and Hobbes wrote in an age when the monarchical principle seemed to most thinkers by all odds the most satisfactory. It was a principle Rousseau could not accept. But the real upshot of his work was, by making the state the repository of the general will, to give to its agents a moral sanction they could hardly have otherwise claimed. For his denial that representative government is valid was omitted from the synthesis built in his name; and once it could be stated that the people could act only through its elected representatives, a penumbra of prestige was added to their activity which could in no other manner have been obtained. The inference, in fact, was drawn by Hegel who made the state, and, inferentially, the agents who act in its name, not only the culmination of the social process, but the embodiment of the highest purpose humanity could know. Thenceforward, to challenge the state was not merely to challenge the source of peace and order, but to challenge, also, that in which the highest end of man was incarnate; and since the state could be challenged effectively only by a challenge to its government – since the latter only disposed of the state's sovereignty – the moral beatification of government seemed to follow from the function it performed as the supreme agent of the state purpose.

III

The problem of the juristic philosopher, in short, is the difficult one of validating his purely formal analysis of categories for the actual world about us. Institutions justify themselves, not by their position in a logical hierarchy, and the claims that position formally entities them to make, but by their power to satisfy effective demand. Once they fail in this, new institutions become necessary, and a new hierarchy is developed to make the logical hierarchy more adequate to our needs. And this, in fact, is what is happening today. Social changes, on the one hand, and scientific development, on the other, have operated to revolutionize the position of government both in the national state and in the international community. An adequate legal philosophy, that is to say, must not only explain the legal right of a government to obedience, but its ethical right as well. It must not only do this. It must explain, also, how the sovereignty of the state can be reconciled with a world in which the hinterland between states is organized, must show, therefore, how a state which is the subject of a vast range of determinate obligations can remain subject to no will save its own, and yet remain under compulsion to fulfil its obligations. Increasingly, the inadequacy of the classical theory of the state to express the needs of our time is evident to the new generation. Duguit in France, Kelsen in Vienna, Krabbe in Holland are only the most eminent of those who, in various ways, have admitted its bankruptcy by seeking to built it anew on different foundations. None of the new answers may be adequate; but all of them represent a recognition that a purely formal jurisprudence which seeks to explain the state as justified to its members simply as the highest unity-making factor we know is without meaning for the problems of our time.

This can, I think, be demonstrated by an examination of the axioms on which formal jurisprudence has been constructed. Those axioms arose out of a supreme need for order which had to be established in a way which satisfied a set of given social conditions. The supremacy of the state was achieved because it enabled those who actually held power, those, also, whose tenure of power was accepted, to exert authority in a formal way. Their exercise of authority satisfied their subjects at any rate to the degree that, broadly speaking, was necessary to secure obedience. But power can only be retained upon the saving condition that its exercise continues to satisfy its subjects. Men who are conscious of wants ask themselves whether attention is paid to their wants. They scrutinize the forms of the state in order to see whether those forms are such as to offer them the maximum possible certainty that their wants will be satisfied by them. And, in the long run, the forms are judged by the opinion built out of their actual operation.

Law apart, every community is a congeries of men and associations seeking the satisfaction of wants. Not all of them are attainable; some, at least, are incompatible with each other. Some, by their nature, demand the imposition of uniform rules of behaviour either upon all members of the community or upon all members who fall within a particular category. The desire, for instance, for security of the person means the imposition upon all members of the community of the rule that murder is forbidden and will be punished. A group within the community is charged with the application of that rule. Men generally obey the orders issued for the prevention of murder because they are satisfied by the consequences of that prevention. It is clear that if the group entrusted with the application of the rule were unable to secure its observance, other men would be entrusted with the task so long a men continued to regard security of the person as a desirable object of attainment.

It is in these terms that we must approach the position of the state in society. It is entrusted with power in order that it may satisfy, or organize the satisfaction of, the wants of men on the largest possible scale. It acts through a body of agents, the government, to that end and no other end. It does not possess power for the sake of power; it does not even possess power for the order which power enables it to enforce, since order is not the highest good, but merely a means to the attainment of goods regarded as higher than itself. For, clearly, a savage despot might establish a *régime* in which order prevailed, but from which freedom and justice and honourable dealings between men were all absent. Order, in that event, would be akin to the annihilation of personality and could hardly be regarded as an end. Power, there- fore, is not good in itself; a government which exercises power is not, either, good in itself. Its goodness, or badness, is a function of what it does. Its nature is dependent upon the results it secures by its operations.

Results for whom? I see no answer to this question capable, at least, of ethical justification, except the answer that it must be results for every member of the community. For the community is a body of individuals, and goodness for the community must mean goodness for those individuals or it means nothing; since, if those individuals are abstracted, no community is left. And since the humanity of men is dependent upon their recognition as ends in themselves, goodness for the community must mean goodness for me as well as for another; for, otherwise, I cease to be an end in myself and become merely a means to the ends of others, which, being the definition of slavery, is a denial of my humanity and a refusal to recognize my status as a member of the community. The state, therefore, as it operates, must treat my claim to good as equal to that of another unless it shows that differentiation in its treatment of me involves some good in which my good is involved.

The norms of law, therefore, that are established by the state – that is, established or maintained by the government which is exercising sovereignty in its name – are norms the substance of which is of the first importance for the validation of its claim to my obedience. For its demand that I should obey any given norm clearly depends, at least in part, on my recognition that my good is involved in that obedience. Mostly, without doubt, I shall obey its demand whatever its substance, since the comparison between its power and my own leaves me little alternative. But the norms it establishes may arouse dissent not only in me but also, it may be, in a considerable number of persons like-minded with myself. I may dissent, for instance, as a member of the Roman Catholic Church in the *Kulturkampf*; or I may dissent as a member of the South Wales Miners' Federation in the munitions strike of 1915; or I may dissent as a citizen who, in Russia during 1917, accepts the principles of Revolutionary Communism. In these cases the formal capacity of government to make law is challenged by a refusal to accept the law it seeks to make. In crucial instances, that formal capacity remains purely formal; an attempt by the government to validate it in the event is met by a resistance which changes the government of the state. The unity of the state, of, that is, the legal system summarized in its power, may remain; but it remains on the condition that it is used for different purposes.

From this I draw two inferences. In the first place I infer that the validation of law is not a matter of the source from which it emanates, but of the acceptance which it secures; and, in the second place, I infer that it is the part of wisdom so to organize the ultimate law-making body of the state – that is, the government – that a maximum consent to its operations is assured before it embarks upon them. Consent to law is not merely a function of the source of law. It is doubtless true that innumerable men obey the state simply because the government which issues an order is entitled in law to speak in its name. But analysis would, I think, show that most of such obedience is the product of habit or inertia, and that it is never creative. The obedience that counts is the obedience of an actively consenting mind; and such a mind is concerned less with the source of law than with what the law proposes to do. This is always evident when the will of government is opposed by some powerful will which dissents from its conclusions. Governments, at the margin, are rarely able to get their way if a considerable body of persons announce their refusal to accept their proposals. They can then only exercise their sovereignty at the risk of losing it. The fact is that no government represents the whole community in a way that ensures automatic acceptance of its will. What it represents is an outlook which, because it temporarily possesses effective power, is legally entitled to use the machinery of the state for purposes it deems good. If that outlook conflicts with the outlook of other members of the community, an attempt at its application may meet an attitude which varies from secret evasion, thought passive resistance, to active rebellion. Law is made effective, that is to say, through the fact of consent in those to whom it applies. There are limits to effective legal action. This is another way of saying that the unity the state is legally entitled to make, it cannot practically make except upon conditions. There is thus a serious disparity between the requirements of formal law and the necessities which actual law encounters.

It is easy to see why this is the case. Every community has groups of citizens to whom certain things are fundamental. They will fight for the preservation of those things, and any attempt to invade them by the sovereign power will result in a challenge to the sovereign power. There are English men, I think, who would resist an attempt to abolish the enfranchisement of the working class, or the right to industrial combination, or the re-establishment of limitations upon freedom of religious belief. Legally, the King in Parliament could do any of these things; politically, by doing so, it would probably cease to be the King in Parliament. Legally, I think, the King in Parliament has the formal right to resume an active control of the affairs of the Dominions; politically it must, as in the Declaration of 1926, treat them as equal and independent states individually entitled to make up their own minds about their own problems, capable, of course, of being especially influenced by the opinion of the British government, but never subject to its legal control. Citizens, in a word, expect from government certain standards of conduct; and it lives by its ability to satisfy those standards. Its legal capacity is always set in the perspective of the limitations those standards impose. They determine its will since, when they are set at nought, it ceases to have a will because it is driven to dissolution by refusal of allegiance.

Formal law makes this allegiance single; the facts make it

multiple. Allegiance goes, not with the legal claim of the state, but with the conduct of the organization which demands it. A man may be with his church and against the state, with his trade union, or his party, if the facts seem to him to warrant that answer to the call. He does not recognize an *a priori* hierarchy of claims, which receive their ultimate expression in the state. Law as form is psychologically neutral to him; what gives it the validity of right is its content upon a particular occasion where conflict has arisen. He does not assume in actual life that the state is entitled to his loyalty because, as the state, it is acting in his interest. He examines what is done in its name and makes a judgement upon the moral quality of the order he is asked to obey. He knows, that is, that legal power, as such, is at every instant subject to perversion. No government is, for him, entitled to permanent credit merely because it is a government. It is liable to error, to perversion, to deliberate misuse of power. It may, consciously or unconsciously, identify the interest of a class or a group or a party with the interest of the community, and legislate upon the basis of that supposed identity. It may do this in good faith; it may do this, also, in bad faith. No government can be known from the simple fact that it is a government. It can be known only from the character of its acts. Nothing is more clear historically than the fact that men judge that character as the acts impinge upon them, as they respond or fail to respond, to the expectations they have formed. Allegiance as a psychological and historic fact is always contingent. It becomes actual and effective in terms of the quality of law rather than of its source.

It is because of this that men have sought in every age institutional means of limiting the power of their governors. They have wished to define what law shall be used for, to what purposes alone its coercive authority shall be devoted. Constitutions, Bills of Rights, and the rest, are, after all, nothing more than ways of declaring that the ends of law make law valid, and not the mere source from which it emanates. It is because of this, also, that every age has seen a revival of the idea of natural law. That revival is nothing so much as an effort on the part of thinkers to recall the state to the purposes by which alone the exercise of authority can be justified. It is an announcement that positive law must run in the leading-strings of principle, that it is the thing it is seeking to establish which makes it binding upon those whose behaviour it is to control. Men struggle, in fact, against being imprisoned in the categories of formal law because they realize that unfettered authority as such cannot give rise to an obligation which, *a priori,* is entitled to claim allegiance. The very ideal of a *Rechtsstaat* is an effort to make the legal sovereign the subject of purposes outside itself. It is a denial that it can will what it pleases. It is an insistence that it is justified in willing only what satisfies the demands of those over whom it rules.

IV

At this point, those who defend the classic theory of sovereignty, even in one or other of its contemporary attenuated forms, fall back upon a new line of defence.[1] They admit that the supreme power of the state is merely a description of capacity within the realm of formal law. They agree that such a view of sovereignty as formal law demands is politically inadequate and sociologically unsatisfactory. But they argue that its retention as a concept is necessary because society needs an organ formally entitled to resolve conflict between individuals and groups within itself. Unless there is to be anarchy in society, they say, there must be a highest power somewhere to which reference can be made where disagreement arises. 'A political system', said Madison in the Philadelphia Convention,[2] ' which does not contain an effective provision for the peaceable solution of all controversies arising within itself, would be a Government in name only'. There must, therefore, be some body within the community which, when controversy comes, can say the last word. Or there may even be more than one body, each of which, as in a federal system, is final in the particular sphere in which it presides. Only so can we safeguard ourselves against the danger of particularism.

I am unable to see that the argument is a valid one, and I do not believe that is exponents have adequately examined the presuppositions upon which it rests. In so far as it is an insistence that the state must necessarily perform the chief part in co-ordinating social activities, and that it cannot accept dictation from any other authority in performing that function, it merely repeats the argument of formal jurisprudence; and, as I have here sought to show, so long as it remains within that sphere, it is impossible to controvert the position it assumes from the very nature of the axioms upon which it is founded.

But its exponents go further than this: they claim that its solutions have a validity other than purely formal because, somehow, the state is a safeguard against particularistic interests. It is acting in the name of the whole community. It makes peace possible. It is free from the partial views which permeate – inevitably – the attitude of groups and individuals lesser than itself. The whole of this argument seems to me fallacious in so far as it seeks to make these qualities necessary and *a priori* attributes of the state. It omits certain relevant facts of the highest importance from the view it seeks to establish. It forgets, first, that the state of which it speaks is an abstraction; that what we have to examine are the acts of the government which speaks in its name. We cannot *a priori* say that the decision of this government, in any given instance, is in the interest of the whole community until we know what the content of the decision is. That judgement, obviously, must be pronounced by those who are to be affected by it. To say that they must accept it because its rejection imperils peace is to argue that order is, and always must be, the highest good. I do not see that it is possible to take this view on any scrutiny of historical facts. I do not find it possible to blame, for example, those who resisted Charles I in 1642, or the men who revolted in France in 1789, or in Russia in March of 1917. No government acts in the name of the community save in a formal sense until the opinion of the community upon its action is known. Governments have exercised the sovereign power for particularistic ends in the past, and they will, doubtless, do so again in the future. When Louis XIV revoked the Edict of Nantes [in 1685 and drove out the Huguenots – ed.] his action was dictated by the view that the interest of France demanded a single pattern of religious outlook; his action, we need not doubt, was both sincere and built upon high motives. But I do not see why the Huguenots were not, equally sincerely and from high motives, entitled to resist his decision. The order he sought to establish was, for them, the abrogation of all they held most dear; and their judgement, as with [the Calvinist theologian] Jurieu, that this was a case where acquiesence in the will of the state merely because it was the will of the state was impossible, seems to me a justified one.

I entirely agree with the view that the cases where men or

associations oppose the will of the state should always be cases of last instance; I do not need to be convinced that peace is almost always better than conflict. But it is not so always. Because it is not so always legal claims are merely legal, and, as such, have no necessary connection with justice. Every sovereign act of the state is always, equally with the judgement of every other element in society, someone's act, whether of individual or group. It may be made with good will; it may be made with bad will. It has no inherent virtue as a sovereign act. It draws its quality from its consequences. Both morally and politically, it is neutral save in the context of those consequences. Any theory of sovereignty which would make it more than this suffers from the fallacy which identifies a maintenance of the power of the state with the preservation of general social well-being. There is no way of knowing whether that correspondence is justified until we know what the state actually does.

Now the state, as I have pointed out, exists to satisfy the largest possible volume of demand in the community. It co-ordinates the bewildering mass of activities there to secure the greatest measure of common satisfaction. That is the justification of its legal authority, the sole ground upon which coercive powers are entrusted to it, and to no other group of persons within the community. The question of whether it fulfils its function adequately is obviously incapable of an *a priori* answer. Some of those who have sought to give the juristic theory of sovereignty a place beyond its formal sphere have seen this. They have therefore wished to transfer the argument to the way in which the sovereign power is organized. Obviously, if it is to fulfil its task adequately, it must be organized to that end. Let us so organize it, and it can then claim an authority to which, otherwise, it could not pretend.

The argument is an important one, and it must be developed in some little detail if we are properly to appreciate its significance. Every community is so complex in its nature that, except for the formal purposes of law, it cannot be reduced to the unity of a single common good. There are interests in it which are permanently antithetic, those, for instance, of a Roman Catholic to whom the propositions of the Syllabus of 1864 are ultimate truth, and those of a Marxian Communist who discovers ultimate truth in the pronouncements of the Third International. If there is never a unity of common good, no organ in the society can do more than partially express the common goods upon which men agree. We make unities; we can never make unity itself. What we attain, at best, is never total satisfaction of demands, but partial satisfaction, sufficient, at best, to preserve a working compromise which men accept as less inadequate than any other to which they can lay their hand. Now the state which has power to co-ordinate the demands that are made needs, if it is to be successful, the fullest possible knowledge of those demands. It must not, so to say, either ignore them or legislate for them. It must legislate through them. The organ which exercises its sovereignty must be so constituted as to represent not some part, or aspect, of the demands to be satisfied, but the largest possible area of those demands. Society, if I may so phrase it, is federal in its nature; and the authority, accordingly, that is to co-ordinate its activities, must correspond in structure to that federal nature.

We have, therefore, to take steps to see that the decisions made by the state take full account of the interests that will be affected by those decisions. Whether the interest affected is individual, association, or territorial unit, it must be adequately and effectively represented in the making of the sovereign will. Wherever there is a real interest in the community, means must be found for eliciting the will of that interest before it is presented with a decision about itself by which the contours of its life will be changed. The organization of the sovereign power, that is to say, must, if it is to be adequate, be immensely more complex than in the past. It cannot legislate about trade unions or churches being compelled so to consult trade unions or churches that their will is fully known to it before it makes its solution of the problem before it. The sovereign power must be compelled, *a priori*, to make a comprehensive effort to embody the wills of those over whom it rules in its will before it is entitled to act upon them. Anything less than this is not truly a *Rechtsstaat*; for anything less than this has not truly sought that amplitude of knowledge without which, in any real way, demand cannot be satisfied at its maximum. Anything less than this means a failure to take into account the conditions of that successful co-ordination by which alone the authority of the state can hope for justification. Only in the degree that this is attempted can the state be called true to the law of its being.

I have elsewhere attempted to describe the kind of institutional pattern to which such a sovereign power must conform.[3] Here I can only say that, as a pattern, it seeks to build into the form of the state that reality outside by which the success of law-making is determined. Those who seek to retain the classic theory of sovereignty in new form are ready, it appears, to accept the view that the organization of its instruments stands in need of thoroughgoing revision.[4] They realize that a legal claim cannot hope for the validation of fact except by genuinely meeting the needs it encounters. They see that the historic formulae of representative government – whether in its parliamentary or congressional form – are no longer adequate to the kind of society in which we live. But they make, I think, the mistake of assuming that the problem is solved when a reconstruction of the pattern has taken place, however adequate that reconstruction may be. They believe that there is some mechanism for making sovereignty an expression of what Rousseau termed the general will of the community.

That belief, I suggest, is profoundly mistaken for the simple reason that there is no general will in the community at all. We never encounter any will that can be denominated good by definition. We do not, indeed, ever encounter in the community a will the unity of which is effectively comparable to the unity of will in a human being. A number of minds does not become one mind any more than a wood is a tree or a hive a bee. The will of the state is the will of certain persons exercising certain powers. This will cannot be termed 'general' in the sense that Rousseau gave it, until we know what it is seeking to do and the motives which underlie its effort. Its value becomes attached to it as we meet its nature and declare its character: it is not simply *a priori* there. The will of the state may be made to approach 'generality' the better it is organized for that end. But organization as such can never assure it of generality until we know the purpose to which it proposes to devote its powers. It is not even decisive that a state should announce its will in full conformity with the terms of the constitution. For before we could declare that it was entitled to obedience, we should need to know both the character of the constitution, on the one hand, and the purpose to which, on the particular occasion, it was being devoted upon the other.

No theory, in fact, which seeks to make the transference from state to government can fail to admit the possible perversion of power. And no theory which scrutinizes the historical process to discover the conditions under which power is usually perverted can be satisfied to declare the inherent primacy of the state will in any other than a formal sense until steps have been taken to erect safeguards against those condition of perversion. If, as I have argued, for instance, each member of the state has an equal claim with others to well-being, conditions which are historically incompatible with the realization of that equal claim must be removed simply because their presence alters the evidence of state action to the advantage of some special section of the community. The state becomes an instrument of that section. It has been, in the past, the instrument of the aristocracy, whether of race or birth, of a particular religion, of a special class. When the state undertakes to enforce its interpretation of social need, the validity of that interpretation depends very largely upon the influences to which those who make it are interpreted. In a state, for example, divided, like the modern capitalist state, into a small number of rich and a large number of poor, that unequal distribution of wealth inevitably introduces bias into the character of state action. *Mutatis mutandis*, the same is true of a community like Russia. There, the demands the state proposes to satisfy are the demands which the Bolshevik Party believe it is desirable to satisfy. That Party has identified its conception of good with the total well-being of the community. Its interpretation may be made from the highest motives; but it is a biased interpretation, which ignores the factor of consent and assumes that power as such creates right. I cannot accept that view. I should agree that when a constitution is built upon the wants of men and operates so as continuously to satisfy those wants, it is entitled to obedience. But this raises the questions: (a) What is a good constitution? (b) who decides whether it is good? (c) and who decides whether it is good in operation?

My own view is clear that these questions can only be answered in terms of the judgement of individual citizens. They are the persons who feel the results of state action in their lives; they, therefore, are the only persons who are entitled to pronounce upon its quality. They make the law valid by consenting to it. They consent to it as it satisfies their desires. A good law, therefore, is a law which has, as its result, the maximum possible satisfaction of desire; and no law save a good law is, except in a formal sense, entitled to obedience as such. This view, of course, involves an empirico-historical theory of politics. It means that a constitution is not likely to be good unless men equally co-operate in making it, and working it, for the simple reason that, historically, classes and persons excluded from a share in power are always excluded from a share in benefit. Because, therefore, each citizen is an end in himself, each citizen must know that his desires are so counted that, equally with other persons, he has a chance of self-realization. He is entitled to the conditions which assure him that his desires will be counted; and these conditions must be inherent in the fabric of any state which seeks to present itself as worthy of obedience. Where, alternatively, those conditions are absent, those for whom they are absent are entitled to deny that the state is the guardian of their interests; and that denial carries with it a title to disobey.

I have termed this view the pluralistic theory of the state because it is rooted in a denial that any association of men in the community is inherently entitled to primacy over any other association. Neither legal authority nor width of declared purpose can give that primacy; title to it depends always upon performance, and of that performance individuals are always the judge, because it is in the quality of their lives only that it is in fact measurable. It is objected that this is a doctrine of contingent anarchy, that no state worthy of the name can be satisfied with a view which leaves open the possibility of dissent from its will. Such a state, it is said, will be, in Madison's phrase, 'a Government in name only'. But the objection, after all, is purely formal. Ever since Hume showed that even the most despotic of governments is ultimately dependent upon public opinion, theories have been illegitimate which sought to confuse legal unity with moral unity. Pluralism is simply an explicit protest against that confusion. It is an attempt to recover the individual conscience as the only true source of a law which claims obedience from its subjects. It is a recognition that no jurisprudence can hope for adequacy which separates the idea of law from the idea of justice. It seeks the content of the latter conception in terms of the initial postulate that man is an end in himself and, therefore, entitled to the conditions which enable him to realize himself as an end; those conditions, where equally maintained for all, it equates with the idea of justice. It does not deny the need in society either for rules or for organizations to maintain those rules; but it does deny that such a need involves the concept of a sovereign state, or the attribution to that state of an inherent supremacy which enables it to dominate all other associations in the community. It insists that the right to make rules is always conditioned by the quality of the rules that are made.

To the critic who points out that someone must define the limits of authority in the individual and the group, that the sovereign state is merely a convenient hieroglyphic for this purpose, the pluralist has, I conceive, at least two answers. He can argue, first, that as a matter of history the function of definition is never wisely performed unless certain conditions are fulfilled, and, second, that once sovereignty is possessed by a state, those who exercise it in the name of the state always effect the transition from legal formality to moral right. Every government claims that it is wrong to break the law. To the pluralist that judgement can only be made when it is known what law is broken and under what circumstances. There are realms of conduct, both individual and collective, into which, under circumstances, he would deny that the state has a right to enter. He would not merely question the wisdom of its entry; he would go even farther and argue that the organization of the power under which government operates ought formally to deny the existence of such a right. Seeking, also, the realization of the individual as an end, he would postulate the conditions upon which that realization depends as principles which the ultimate authority, however organized, must respect, which, also, under all circumstances it must be powerless to change. The state, for him, is an organization, like any other, charged with the performance of certain functions. He cannot see that the character of those functions entails the right to sovereignty. For realism compels him to admit that this is the entrustment of unlimited authority to ordinary and fallible men. There are no guarantees possible that such authority will be justly used. The need, consequently, is paramount to deny title to its possession.

A right to sovereignty, moreover, does not exist for the sake of sovereignty; it exists for the ends sovereignty is to serve. A right to sovereignty must be correlative with the duty of fulfilling those ends. These, as I have said, are in their sum the maximum possible fulfilment of desires. The logical inference, therefore, from a right to sovereignty would be a duty so to organize and exercise the

sovereign power as to secure the ends for which it exists. To argue
. . . .that the theory of auto-limitation [by the sovereign] fulfils this
condition is to miss the point that a will bound only by itself cannot
be conceived as objectively bound; for an obligation of a form of
conduct which the body obliged can alter at will, and yet never
chooses to alter, either suggests a power outside that body and
controlling it (in which case it ceases to be sovereign), or suggests
the subordination of the body to principles inherent in human
personality of which the state will is then the subject.

These dialectical tangles are unsatisfactory. It is better to say
quite simply that the idea of a sovereign state is at variance with the
idea of law once that idea is conceived as related to a moral end.
For any other conception of law makes it unconnected with reason
or good except by its own choice; and would leave unexplained
why that choice should be made. The action of a sovereign state
binds as such without regard to whether that action fulfils the
obligation to which the state is bound by its inherent character.
The character of such a state proclaims not only in its inability to
discriminate between right and wrong, but even a positive
indifference between them. The sovereign state makes positive
law; it does not make a law in which there is any inherent relation
to justice. Such a positive law is merely an expression of power;
power is morally neutral until its substance is examined. Since no
state automatically wills that by which men ought to be bound, it is
neither necessary nor desirable to accept is sovereign character.
The state must derive its law from principles beyond itself, if the
character of its policy is to have a morally valid claim upon the
allegiance of men. In any other context, law is empty of all title to
consent save the naked assertion of its power to enforce
obedience.

V

Nor must we omit the international aspect of the problem. The
doctrine of the sovereign state becomes a theory of international
law in two ways. On the one hand, by the rigorous logic of its
primary assumptions, since law is the will of the state, it is
compelled to insist that no rules of international relations have the
force of law save as the state consents to them; on the other, most
largely through the influence of Hegel, by its argument that the

state is the ultimate embodiment of moral values, it assumes that international rules are valid only in so far as the state chooses to accept them for its purposes. Since the state is the ultimate and highest form that allegiance can take, it either denies altogether the existence of an international community which is above, or beyond, states; or it argues that while the mutual life of states may make such a community, its rules cannot be binding upon them since the interests each state protects in that international community are the highest it can know. To bind the will of the state, therefore, to an objective international law outside its own will is both mischievous and undesirable.

It is difficult to put in moderate terms the degree to which either aspect of this doctrine is undesirable. By making the self-preservation of the state the highest duty it can know, it insists that the state is bound by no rules which it does not regard as serviceable to that end. International law merely becomes a body of convenient doctrines which a state is free to reject or accept as it pleases. It is not bound by any agreements or treaties; it is not responsible for any wrong; there are no moral obligations governing its relations with other states. As an eminent exponent of this view has pointed out,[5] its logic demands that right and wrong be the outcome of the exercise of successful force, and victory in war is made the true judge of international controversy. I reject this view of the state claim in the international field upon exactly the same grounds as in the municipal. The sovereign state in international relations is a body of persons making decisions. They have the legal right to make those decisions; but nothing is, or can be, *a priori* known of the moral quality of the decisions made until we know their content. That a state refuses to fulfil a treaty it has signed makes it no more valid that it should refuse to accept its obligation than that a merchant should refuse to fulfil a contract he has freely made. That a state should make war without provocation no more makes that war just than that a man should commit an unprovoked murder. A treaty forced upon a defeated state against its will is no more right than a contract forced upon one of the parties to it under consent. The goodness or badness of law is independent of the parties to it, or of their power. It is a function of the substance of law, a judgement upon what some decision actually proposes to do. It is no more logical to allow a state both to make its own law and then judge its validity than it is

217

to allow the private citizen to be judge of his own actions. Law must be objective to the state in the international, as it is objective to the individual in the municipal, field. Adequate international relationships are impossible if, on conflict, law is merely to mean the rule of the stronger. For that is exactly the divorce of law from justice which defeats the whole purpose law is intended to serve.

Nor is it true to say that international law finds its sanction in the sovereign will of states.[6] The recognition of a new state is not followed by an announcement from that state that it accepts the rules of international law; nor is it possible for the new state to pick and choose between them. To argue, as Oppenheim does, that a demand for recognition, by Communist Russia, for instance, is to be taken as an implicit acceptance of the binding force of international law is to introduce fiction of a peculiarly unedifying kind. The facts have to be explained very differently. What we are presented with is a system of states equal in the sense that each has an identical right to the protection of the law. That is a position inherent in the notion of states as sovereign; for, logically, once sovereignty is in question there can be no discussion of superior and inferior. But this right to equal protection of the law is obviously incompatible with the idea of law as merely a subjective state right which each state imposes on others if it will or can. Law here must mean an objective body of principles above all states, laying obligations upon them they have no legal alternative but to accept. The very fact, indeed, of a need for recognition means that states cannot, in the international sphere, make or unmake law as they please. But the power to make or unmake law is what the formal theory of jurisprudence means by sovereignty, and if this power be absent in states it cannot be claimed that they are sovereign.

Or let us take a doctrine like the famous maxim *pacta sunt servanda*. The classic theory of sovereignty says that this rule is binding because states will to observe it, and they are equally free to refuse to will its observance if they so please. If we ask why states so will it as law we are told that it is because of the difficulties to which any other attitude would give rise. But that is an explanation which formal jurisprudence is not entitled to adopt. It can only say that the rule is binding independently of the will which accepts it, or the causes which make for acceptance. The will is in fact binding from its inherent nature. It is an objective norm of a legal order which must be postulated as underlying all states and providing them with the principles by which their life is lived. To say that states break the rule no more deprives it of its validity than the law against murder is rendered invalid because a man commits murder. Any other hypothesis, as Bluntschli saw long ago, would make international law not merely an inferior kind of contract, but one in which no agreement was ever binding when a state changed its mind, and in which, as he said, a change in the state's will produced a change in the law. Such an outlook results in impossible contradictions. Jurisprudence must be subject, not less than other sciences, to the maxim that no more causes are to be predicted than are necessary to explain the phenomena. To make international law the creature of the sovereign state's will is to pile the Pelion of fiction upon the Ossa of undemonstrable assumption to a degree that is intolerable.

The difficulties of the lawyer who insists that international law is merely the will of the state in the external field are by no means over even at this point. The whole history of the practice of international arbitration is the history of the adoption by tribunals of rules of international law the source of which cannot, even by the wildest use of fiction, be found in the will of the state. Phrases that desire a decision to be made in accordance with 'principles of justice', or 'considerations of equity', or, again, 'on the basis of respect for law', all clearly indicate that the idea of law is, for international purposes, outside and not inside the state's will. Nor, moreover, can one read the Statute of the Permanent Court of International Justice without seeing that its underlying assumption is the notion that the absence of a fixed rule must not mean a refusal to judge. The business of the Court is not to pronounce itself without jurisdiction, where the will of states is undiscoverable, but to make a suitable rule in terms of alternative sources which can only be explained as valid on the hypothesis of objective norms sanctioning inferences of the widest character in terms of the needs of an international legal order above individual states.[7]

Nor need we accept the view that only states can be the subjects of international law. The post-war world is littered with organizations which are certainly not subject states, but, equally certainly, are the subjects of international law. This is an antiquated view which flows from the assumptions of formal jurisprudence and not from the facts of international life. International law has to concern itself with the rights and duties of the League of Nations, of international unions, of the members of the British Commonwealth of Nations, of pirates, of rebels who are recognized as belligerents, none of whom possess the formal indicia of statehood. It is by no means inconceivable that, in the future, we shall see individuals recognized as possessing an international status, able, for instance, to sue a state that has done them wrong in an international court. International law is theoretically capable of laying rights and duties upon men as well as upon states; the present conception arises only from the way in which its foundations have been formulated and not from its inherent nature. For it is equally as valid to postulate the existence of an international community the character of whose law requires that every person who acts internationally shall be a subject of the law of that community as to postulate a society of states in which no persons save states shall be recognized as the subjects of rights and duties. The present system is a deposit of historic categories invented to explain a given body of facts. It is no more valid for all the facts we encounter, or all the needs we have to meet, than Euclidean geometry is valid for the total universe of geometry.

At this point, indeed, we can go farther. International law has been built upon the idea of the state as a legal personality the will of which embodies a will compounded from the separate wills of all its subjects. Now this view of the state is metaphorical only, since the state itself can act only through persons. When we take a community politically organized into a state the will of that state is the will of the person or persons entitled to act in its name. There is not a single will in any other sense than that of a legal capacity attaching to some persons and not to other persons. From the angle of an international community concerned to maintain law as the inherent expression of its ultimate nature the will of the state must be a will for that law; a will against it cannot be legal in any sense which is valid. For that would mean a right in the state to will the absence of law, to overthrow the system of jural relations in which it is necessarily involved by the fact of being a state. From this angle it must follow that legal supremacy belongs to the body of rules which make up international law, and that the rules of any other society are of lesser significance than these. The state, that is to say, is bound in the rules it makes by the superior rules of the international community to which it belongs. It cannot make and unmake them any more than the individual can make or unmake the law of the state of which he is a subject. The personality of the state is, so to say, an inference from the fact that it is a part of the international community. It is a way of conferring legal capacity upon certain persons within a juridical community to enable them to formulate rules which have no validity if they conflict with the fundamental rules of the society in and through which its capacity arises. A state, therefore, cannot legally will what it pleases; it can only will what is consistent with the superior will of the international community. Its personality is a capacity in its rulers to act for that end, but for no other end.

From this, I infer the supremacy of international law over the law of any given individual state. I assume that a jurisprudence which seeks to be scientific has no alternative but to regard the community of states as what has been termed a *civitas maxima*, the law of which is primary over all other law.[8] States, in this conception, appear to me as provinces of this *civitas maxima* whose authority is derived from the rules discovered to be necessary for the maintenance of the common international life. Apart from this conception, I see no way of arriving at a body of axioms capable of explaining the relationship between states assumed to be equal in international intercourse. No state can have a legal right to enforce its will upon another state if both are sovereign; force in the international sphere can only be valid upon the assumption that there is a body of legal rules over and above both to which each equally conforms. A state is then entitled to force in order that the legal rules may be maintained. Any other view must assume ultimately that force makes law; that what is alone valid in the international sphere is the rule of the strongest which is in fact law. I have already rejected this view as incompatible with the facts, especially with the doctrine of recognition, in international relations. International law cannot be, as Hegel argued, merely an external municipal law, since it would then be changeable, as it is not, at the will of each individual state. It is not merely, as Austin suggested, a 'positive morality', since it is the rules of a society which, even if more loosely and feebly organized than the state, is, in Westlake's phrase, 'as necessary to human existence as the state itself'.[9] Right and wrong are notions relevant to the relationship between states, and such notions predicate the existence of a society of which those states are a part. But a society without law is inconceivable. The norms, therefore, of that society are the necessary rules of its intercourse for the realization of right and the avoidance of wrong. The universality of this international society presupposes the primacy of its norms over those of its parts. The state, therefore, is a subject of law which presides over its being and limits the nature of the objects it can seek to attain.

VI

In the light of this conception let us return to the formal theory of law on its internal side. Law, it is maintained, is the will of the sovereign state; and the will of the sovereign state is law because it knows no superior. For jurisprudence, therefore, the content of law, the nature of the norms made by the state, is irrelevant. What it is concerned with is capacity to act, not what that capacity actually does. Any attempt to go beyond this view belongs not to the field of jurisprudence, but to politics, or morals, or psychology. No questions in these realms can, it is held, affect the validity of the formal conceptions of law. It is, indeed, even claimed that this methodology will have the desirable result of removing confusion from political theory.

I suggest that this is an entirely mistaken point of view. Were the categories of formal law axiomatic in the sense of being inescapably necessary to the structure of a scientific jurisprudence the problems they involve might assume a different character. But, in fact, they have an origin which is meaningless apart from a system of special historic conditions in Western Europe, and they only partially summarize those conditions. They make the construction of a philosophy of law impossible because they refuse to consider the relation of law to the totality of circumstances under which it must operate; they omit from their equations all the problems to answer which it is in fact necessary to construct a science of law. They refuse to consider the problems of conflict and valuation. They see no meaning in the grave issues which arise from the choice of a point of departure, and the application to life of its results. The validity of their results, therefore, holds only of a static world in which there are no stresses and strains with consequences which exist and alter life. If ethical conceptions have altered the law, if economic change has meant its adjustment, law cannot neglect either ethics or economic change. It is the static character of the formal theory of sovereignty which explains its helplessness before the phenomena of international law; these it can only resume by the invocation of fictions utterly unconnected with reality. The formal theory, indeed, is like the relation between the ceremonial and the operative parts of the British Constitution. The King may ride in the carriage, but it is the Prime Minister on the pavement who effectively makes the decision. A theory of the state which emphasizes formality at the expense of substance is not likely to possess final value. It abstracts the legal system from the context in which alone its meaning can be found.

Formal jurisprudence, therefore, is an answer to the problems of power existing at any given time; and even to that it is only a partial answer. The categories it employs are those which enabled effective demand to be satisfied roughly since the Reformation; but there is no sort of certainty that they will continue to provide that satisfaction. The new facts of a world order both in the legal and in the economic sphere are making our political conceptions rapidly obsolete for the purposes they have to fulfil; and formal jurisprudence has been built by its makers in terms of those conceptions. Men live to satisfy demands, and they recognize as valid only the institutions capable of their effective satisfaction. Our system was constructed, by men like Bodin and Hobbes, and Hegel, at a period when the hinterland between states was not only not organized but was not unnaturally deemed incapable of organization. Our whole theory of the state has accordingly been conceived upon the assumption that it was the final form of institutional pattern, and even a body like the League of Nations was constructed by men faithful, in the main, to that ideal.

The facts, I suggest, have outgrown this view, and the developments require the construction of a new juristic edifice. The institutional pattern we need for an adequate theory of politics must take regard to the demands which require satisfaction and the way in which that satisfaction is to be attained. Here, surely, the unity we have to consider can only be properly understood in terms of the universe of facts to which it is relevant. If miners in England demand an adequate wage, it is the international coal problem and not the national that we must seek to compass. Stable financial conditions in London are a function of Chicago and Calcutta, of Berlin and Tokyo. These interrelations have to be organized in order that we may render satisfaction to those who live by their results; and the inference that must be drawn herefrom is the need for a political philosophy, not in terms of the nation-state as the final source of unity but of a cosmopolitan order in which the nation state is being rapidly reduced by the facts to the position of an uneasy and unsatisfactory province. The solutions made by the law-making body in any given state will only work in even the national sphere if they fit the facts of this cosmopolitan order. They have no assurance of adequacy save as they are built upon the working consent of at least its major part.

The inference from this is, I think, of supreme importance for a working theory of law. The epoch of Grotius, so to say, is drawing to a close. Instead of building up the conceptions of international law from the relation of states one to another, we shall, in the future, have to built up national law as a system of inferences from the rules of an international law far wider in its incidence than national law can claim to be. It is not likely, in this new world, that any state will have, even formally, ultimate powers: it will be much more akin to the province of a federation, having authority over a defined sphere, but finding that its powers beyond that sphere are strictly limited. England, for instance, may well discover that while it may prescribe the penalties for murder, it cannot control the hours of work for miners; that while it may make its own traffic regulations, it cannot settle the scale of its tariffs. The process of government, in a word, has escaped from the categories in which the nation-state sought to imprison it. Some part of its functions, at least, is obviously destined to transference to a new authority by whose commands the nation-state will be bound. It will lack, from the very nature of the cosmopolitan order, the power to make final decisions in any sphere save that allotted to it by the needs of that order. It will fail to correspond to the formulae of classical jurisprudence, and new formulae will be developed more adequate to the needs jurisprudence must meet.

This indicates, I venture to think, that the approach to law cannot usefully be made in any terms which postulate the state as its ultimate source. Law is the operative satisfaction of effective demand, and its sources are as varied as life itself. The state is the organ through which the government registers the fact that some given demand has secured a factual title to satisfaction: it is an announcement that behind this given demand there lies, prospectively, the coercive power of society. But, clearly, the state is no more than the form such registration now assumes. There is no *a priori* necessity that it should assume this particular form and no other form. That depends upon the character of social organization at the time when some effective demand searches for satisfaction. And the value of approaching the problem from this angle is that we are not compelled by our definition to put the orders of the government into a category different from the orders of other organizations. We learn to see them, as we ought to see them, as species of a wider genus. Any association which issues orders to its members makes law for them which differs in degree rather than kind from the laws made in the name of the state. The power, also, of other associations is a power it is difficult to differentiate, again except in degree, from that of the state. It may be granted that the authority of the state is utilized to make its orders binding upon all within its jurisdiction: it seeks, within that jurisdiction, universality. But we must be careful not to mistake the character of that universality. It is a universality simply of formal reference. It makes unity upon the ground that unity in some given realm of conduct is held by those who operate the machinery of state to be desirable. It does not tell us why it is so held; it does not tell us whether its recipients will so regard it; and it does not, finally, tell us whether it ought so to be regarded. Yet a true philosophy of law ought to explain all these things if it is to satisfy those over whom its sanctions operate.

A theory of law, in fact, which does not start by postulating an end for law, can never explain why law ought to be obeyed; and there is, surely, no point in making rules except upon the assumption that they are entitled to obedience. If we assume that law is made in order to satisfy human demands at that maximum which is socially possible we have at least a criterion by which to create an effective system of values. Therefrom we can infer a pattern of institutions which, at any given moment of historic time, enables us to explain the character of their operation. Such a theory of law has the merit of escaping subordination to the state. It attaches values to the institutions which satisfy its purpose, and to no other institutions. It explains why associations live and die, for it shows that their life is set by their ability to satisfy effective demand. It does not perish in the formalism of that categorical hierarchy which makes the state ultimate either on legal or on moral grounds. It makes the state ultimate only when its activity enables maximum demand to be satisfied. But it insists, as the facts insist, that maximum demand may be satisfied only by refusing obedience to the state, or, conceivably, by going beyond it to a cosmopolitan order which must make the rules if demand is to hope for satisfaction.

This is, of course, a pluralistic theory of law. It is so because the facts before us are anarchical. We reduce them ourselves to order by being able to convince men that some unity we make means added richness to their lives. We encounter everywhere not allegiance, but allegiances in men. We are not warranted in seeking their reduction to a Procrustes-like unity which is formal only in character. An institution cannot seriously expect to be obeyed merely because it is an ultimate point in a series where that series itself is a merely logical construction. Institutions can only secure obedience in terms of the values that obedience creates; and if the values are denied by those in whose lives they are to be effective in the long run, obedience will be denied also. From this angle, in short, we can make the necessary bridge between the formal demands of law, and those other contexts, ethical, economic, political, psychological, which give the abstract legal claim its validation in the event. Above all, such a view as this puts the source of law where it most truly belongs, in the individual consenting mind. For we each of us judge the commands we receive by their relation to our experience of life; and the success of the institutions which formulate commands is a function of their ability to convince us that their response to that experience is continuously and deliberately creative.

NOTES

1. McIlwain (1939) 'Sovereignty', in *Constitutionalism in a Changing World* [Cambridge: Cambridge University Press]; Coker (1921) *American Political Science Review* 15 (2): 86-213; Elliott (1928) *The Pragmatic Revolt in Politics* [New York: Macmillan], *passim*.
2. Farrand *Records of the Federal Convention*, iii, 537.
3. Cf. Laski (1925) *A Grammar of Politics* [London: Allen & Unwin], chapter 7, *passim*.
4. Cf. Elliott op. cit., especially the last chapters.
5. Kaufmann (1911) *Das Wesen des Völkerrechts* [Tübingen: J.C.B. Mohr].
6. See all this put admirably in Lauterpact (1927) *Private Law Analogies in International Law* [London: Longmans, Green & Co.], chapter 2. I

cannot overemphasize my debt to this brilliant monograph – the most significant British contribution to post-war international law.
7. Cf. Lauterpacht, op. cit., pp. 215ff.
8. Cf. Kelsen's famous monograph *Das Problem der Souveränität,* second edition (1923) [Tübingen: J.C.B. Mohr].
9. Westlake (1914) *Collected Papers in Public International Law* [Cambridge: Cambridge University Press], p. 13.

BIBLIOGRAPHY

Anderson, P. (1968) 'The components of the national culture', *New Left Review* 50 (July/August).

Aristotle (1958) *The Politics of Aristotle*, translated and introduced by E. Barker, London: Oxford University Press.

Augustine, Saint (1945) *City of God*, introduced by E. Barker, London: Dent, Everyman edition, 2 vols.

Austin, J. (1832) *The Province of Jurisprudence Determined*, introduced by H.L.A. Hart, London: Weidenfeld & Nicolson, 1954.

Barker, E. (1915a) *Political Thought in England from Herbert Spencer to the Present Day*, London: Williams & Norgate, Home University Library.

Barker. E. (1915b) 'The discredited state', *Political Quarterly* 5 (February): 101–21.

Barker, E. (1918) 'The superstition of the state', *Times Literary Supplement*, July.

Barker, E. (1930) *Church, State and Study*, London: Methuen.

Barker, E. (1951) *Principles of Social and Political Theory*, Oxford: Oxford University Press.

Barker, E. (1953) *Age and Youth*, London: Oxford University Press.

Belloc, H. (1913) *The Servile State*, London: T.N. Foulis; Indianapolis: Liberty Classics, 1977.

Belloc, H. and Chesterton, C. (1913) *The Party System*, London: H. Latimer; London: S. Swift, 1911.

Black, A. (1984) *Guilds and Civil Society in European Political Thought from the Twelfth Century to the Present*, London: Methuen.

Bobbio, N. (1987) *The Future of Democracy*, Cambridge: Polity Press.

Bobbio, N. (1988) *Which Socialism?*, Cambridge: Polity Press.

Bodin, J. (1955) *Six Books of the Commonwealth*, abridged and translated by M.J. Tooley, Oxford: Blackwell.

Bowles, S. and Gintis, H. (1986) *Democracy and Capitalism*, London: Routledge.

Bradley, F.H., (1876) *Ethical Studies*, London: King; London: Oxford University Press, 1962.

Bradley, F. H. (1893) *Appearance and Reality*, London: Swan

Sonnenshein; second edition, Oxford: Clarendon Press, 1930.

Briggs, A., and Saville, J. (eds) (1971) *Essays in Labour History*, London: Macmillan.

Brittan, S. (1983) *The Role and Limits of Government*, London: Temple Smith.

Bryce, J. (1888) *American Commonwealth*, 3 vols, London: Macmillan.

Buckland, W.W. (1921) *A Textbook of Roman Law*, edited by Peter Stein, Cambridge: Cambridge University Press; third edition, 1975.

Burke, E. (1770) *Thoughts on the Present Discontents*, edited by W. Murison, Cambridge: Cambridge University Press, Pitt Press series, 1913.

Burnheim, J. (1985) *Is Democracy Possible?*, Cambridge: Polity Press.

Carpenter, L.P. (1973) *G.D.H. Cole: An Intellectual Biography*, Cambridge: Cambridge University Press.

Carpenter, N. (1922) *Guild Socialism: An Historical and Critical Analysis*, New York: D. Appleton & Co.

Cohen, M. (1919) 'Communal ghosts and other perils in social philosophy', *The Journal of Philosophy* 16: 673–90.

Coker, F.W. (1921) 'The technique of the pluralist state', *American Political Science Review* 15 (2): 86–213.

Cole, G.D.H. (1913) *The World of Labour*, London: G. Bell.

Cole, G.D.H. (1914–15) 'Conflicting social obligations', *Proceedings of the Aristotelian Society*, NS 15: 140–59.

Cole, G.D.H. (1915–16) 'The nature of the state in view of its external relations', *Proceedings of the Aristotelian Society*, NS 16: 310–25.

Cole, G.D.H. (1917) *Self-Government in Industry*, London: G. Bell; revised edition, London: Hutchinson, 1972.

Cole, G.D.H. (1918) *Labour in the Commonwealth*, London: Swarthmore Press, Headley Bros.

Cole, G.D.H. (1920a) *Guild Socialism Re-Stated*, London: Leonard Parsons.

Cole, G.D.H. (1920b) *The Social Theory*, London: Methuen & Co.

Cole, G.D.H. (1920c) 'Guild Socialism', *Fabian Tract* 192, London: Fabian Society.

Cole, G.D.H. and Mellor, W. (1919) *The Meaning of Industrial Democracy*, London: Allen & Unwin.

Cole, M. (1971a) *The Life of G.D.H. Cole*, London: Macmillan.

Cole, M. (1971b) 'Guild Socialism and the Labour Research Dept', in A. Briggs and J. Saville (eds) (1971) *Essays in Labour History*, London: Macmillan.

Dahl, R.A. (1956) *A Preface to Democratic Theory*, New Haven, CT: Yale University Press.

Dahl, R.A. (1982) *Dilemmas of Liberal Democracies*, New Haven, CT: Yale University Press.

Dahl, R.A. (1985) *A Preface to Economic Democracy*, New Haven, CT: Yale University Press.

Dangerfield, G. (1962) *The Strange Death of Liberal England*, London: Constable.

Dante, A. (1954) *De Monarchia (Monarchy)*, translated and introduced by D. Nicholl, London: Weidenfeld & Nicolson.

Deane, H.A. (1955) *The Political Ideas of Harold J. Laski*, New York: Columbia University Press.

Delisle Burns, C. (1915–16) 'The nature of the state in view of its external relations', *Proceedings of the Aristotelian Society*, NS 16: 290–301.

Dicey, A.V. (1885) *An Introduction to the Study of the Law of the Constitution*, eighth edition, London: Macmillan, 1920.

Dicey, A.V. (1905) *Lectures on the Relation between Law and Public Opinion in England in the Nineteenth Century*, second edition, London: Macmillan, 1920.

Dorrien, G.L. (1986) *The Democratic Socialist Vision* New Jersey: Rowman & Littlefield.

Duguit, L. (1913) *Transformation du Droit Public*, translated by H.J. and S.F. Laski as *Law in the Modern State*, introduced by H.J. Laski, London: Allen & Unwin, 1921.

Duguit, L. (1917) 'The law and the state', *Harvard Law Review* 31 (1): 1–185.

Durkheim, E. (1957) *Professional Ethics and Civic Morals*, London: Routledge.

Elliott, W.Y. (1928) *The Pragmatic Revolt in Politics*, New York: Macmillan.

Ellis, E.D. (1920) 'The pluralistic State', *American Political Science Review* 14 (3): 393–407.

Figgis, J.N. (1913) *Churches in the Modern State*, London: Longmans, Green & Co.

Figgis, J.N. (1914) *The Divine Right of Kings*, second edition, Cambridge: Cambridge University Press, 1922.

Figgis, J.N. (1915) *The Fellowship of the Mystery*, London: Longmans, Green & Co.

Figgis, J.N. (1916) *Studies of Political Thought from Gerson to Grotius*, second edition, Cambridge: Cambridge University Press.

Figgis, J.N. (1917) *The Will to Freedom: or the Gospel of Nietzsche and the Gospel of Christ*, London: Longmans, Green & Co.

Figgis, J.N. (1921) *The Political Aspects of St Augustine's 'City of God'*, London: Longmans, Green & Co.

Fine, B. (1984) *Democracy and the Rule of Law*, London: Pluto Press.

Follet, M.P. (1918) *The New State*, London: Longmans, Green & Co.

Gierke, O. von (1868–1913) *Das Deutsche Genossenschaftsrecht*, 3 vols, Berlin: Weidmann.

Gierke, O. von (1887) *Die Genossenschafts Theorie. . .*, Berlin: Weidmann,

Gierke, O. von (1900) *Political Theories of the Middle Age*, translated and introduced by F.W. Maitland, Cambridge: Cambridge University Press; paperback edition, 1988.

Gierke, O. von (1934) *Natural Law and the Theory of Society*, Cambridge: Cambridge University Press.

Gierke, O. von (1939) *The Development of Political Theory*, London: Allen & Unwin.

Glass, S.T. (1966) *The Responsible Society*, London: Longmans, Green & Co.

Green, T.H. (1882) *Lectures on the Principles of Political Obligation*, London: Longmans, Green & Co., 1963.

Hadden, T. (1977) *Company Law and Capitalism*, second edition, London: Weidenfeld & Nicolson.

Hailsham, Lord (1978) *The Dilemma of Democracy*, London: Collins.

Harden, I., and Lewis, N. (1987) *The Noble Lie*, London: Hutchinson.

Harrington, J. (1656) *Oceana*, in J.G.A. Pocock (ed.) (1977) *The Political Works of James Harrington*, Cambridge: Cambridge University Press.

Hayward, J.E.S. (1960) 'Solidarist Syndicalism: Durkheim and Duguit', *Sociological Review* 8 (1): 17–36; 8 (2): 185–202.

Hearn, F. (1985) 'Durkheim's political sociology: corporatism, state autonomy and democracy', *Social Research* 52 (1): 151–77.

Held, D. (1987) *Models of Democracy*, Cambridge: Polity Press.

Hirst, P. (1979) 'The law of property and Marxism', chapter five in *On Law and Ideology*, London: Macmillan.

Hirst, P. (1986) *Law, Socialism and Democracy*, London: Allen & Unwin.

Hirst, P. (1987a) 'Retrieving pluralism', in W. Outhwaite and M. Mulkay (eds) *Social Theory and Social Criticism*, Oxford: Blackwell.

Hirst, P. (1987b) 'Carl Schmitt's decisionism', *Telos* 72 (Summer): 15–26.

Hobbes, T. (1651) *Leviathan*, edited by M. Oakeshott, Oxford: Blackwell, 1960.

Hobhouse, L.T. (1918) *The Metaphysical Theory of the State*, London: Allen & Unwin.

Hobson, S.G. (1914) *National Guilds: An Inquiry into the Wage System and the Way Out*, edited by A.R. Orage, London: G. Bell.

Hobson, S.G. (1920) *National Guilds and the State*, London: G. Bell.

Hobson, S.G. (1936) *Functional Socialism*, London: Stanley Nott.

Hobson, S.G. (1938) *Pilgrim to the Left. . . .*, London: Arnold.

Holland, T.E. (1893) *The Elements of Jurisprudence*, sixth edition, Oxford: Clarendon Press.

Holme, R. (1987) *The Peoples' Kingdom*, London: The Bodley Head.

Holmes–Laski Letters (1953) *The Correspondence of Mr Justice Holmes and Harold J. Laski, 1916–1935*, 2 vols, Cambridge, Mass.: Harvard University Press.

Hsiao, K.C. (1927) *Political Pluralism*, London: Kegan Paul, Trench, Tubner & Co.

James, W. (1909) *A Pluralistic Universe*, Hibbert Lectures, London: Longmans, Green & Co.

Katzenstein, P.J. (1985) *Small States in World Markets*, Ithaca, NY: Cornell University Press.

Kaufmann, E. (1911) *Das Wesen des Völkerrechts*, Tübingen: J.C.B. Mohr.

Keane, J. (1988) *Democracy and Civil Society*, London: Verso.

Kelsen, H. (1920) *Das Problem der Souveränität. . . .*, Tübingen: J.C.B. Mohr.

Korf, Baron S.A. (1923) 'The problem of sovereignty', *American Political*

Science Review 17 (3): 404–14.

Kosselleck, R. (1988) *Critique and Crisis*, Oxford: Berg.

Krabbe, H. (1922) *The Modern Idea of the State*, English translation of *Die Moderne Staats-Idee* (1919), New York & London: D. Appleton.

Laski, H.J. (1917) *Studies in the Problem of Sovereignty*, New Haven, CT: Yale University Press.

Laski, H.J. (1919) *Authority in the Modern State*, New Haven, CT: Yale University Press.

Laski, H.J. (1921) *The Foundations of Sovereignty and Other Essays*, London: Allen & Unwin.

Haski, H.J. (1925) *A Grammar of Politics*, London: Allen& Unwin, fifth edition, 1967, seventh impression 1982.

Laski, H.J. (1932) *Studies in Law and Politics*, London: Allen & Unwin.

Lauterpacht, H. (1927) *Private Law Sources and Analogies of International Law*, London: Longmans, Green & Co.

Lewis, J.D. (1935) *The Genossenschaft Theory of Otto von Gierke*, Madison, Wis.: University of Wisconsin Press.

Lindsay, A.D. (1914) 'The state in recent political theory', *Political Quarterly* 1 (February): 128–45.

Locke, J. (1690) *Two Treaties of Civil Government*, edited by P. Laslett, Cambridge: Cambridge University Press, 1963.

McIlwain, C.H. (1939) *Constitutionalism in a Changing World*, Cambridge: Cambridge University Press.

Maeztu, R. de (1916) *Authority, Liberty and Function*, London: Allen & Unwin.

Magid, H.M. (1941) *English Political Pluralism*, New York: Columbia University Press.

Mairet, P. (1936) *A.R. Orage: A Memoir*, London: Dent.

Maitland, F.W. (1900) 'Introduction' to Otto von Gierke *Political Theories of the Middle Age*, op. cit., pp. vii–xlv.

Maitland, F.W. (1911) *Collected Papers*, 3 vols, edited by H.A.L. Fisher, Cambridge: Cambridge University Press.

Marquand, D. (1988) *The Unprincipled Society*, London: Cape.

Martin, W. (1967) *The New Age under Orage*, Manchester: Manchester University Press.

Matthews, F. (1979) 'The ladder of becoming: A.R. Orage, A.J. Penty and the origins of Guild Socialism in England', in D.E. Martin and D. Rubinstein (eds) *Ideology and the Labour Movement*, London: Croom Helm.

Michels, R. (1911) *Political Parties*, English translation, New York: Free Press, 1962.

Mill, J.S (1848) *Principles of Political Economy, Collected Works*, vols 2 & 3, Toronto: Toronto University Press, 1965.

Mill, J.S. (1861) *Considerations on Representative Government*, introduced by A.D. Lindsay, London: Dent, Everyman edition, 1910.

Mill J.S. (1905) *Dissertations and Discussions*, London: Routledge.

Mogi, S. (1932) *Otto von Gierke*, London: King.

Neumann, F. (1986) *The Rule of Law*, Leamington Spa: Berg.

Nicholls, D. (1975) *The Pluralist State*, London: Macmillan.

Peirson, S (1979) *British Socialism: The Journey from Fantasy to Politics*, Cambridge, Mass.: Harvard University Press.

Polan, A.J. (1984) *Lenin and the End of Politics*, London: Methuen.

Pribicevic, B. (1959) *The Shop Stewards' Movement and Workers' Control*, Oxford: Blackwell.

Reckitt, M.B., and Bechofer, C.E. (1920) *The Meaning of National Guilds*, second edition, London: Cecil Palmer.

Renner, K. (1921) 'Democracy and the council system', in T.B. Bottomore and P. Goode (eds) *Austro-Marxism*, Oxford: Oxford University Press.

Richmond, W. (1900) *Personality as a Philosophical Principle*, London: Arnold.

Richter, M. (1964) *The Politics of Conscience: T.H. Green and His Age*, London: Weidenfeld & Nicolson.

Rousseau, J.-J. (1762) *The Social Contract-Discourses*, translated and introduced by G.D.H. Cole, London: Dent, Everyman edition, 1913.

Russell, B. (1916) *Principles of Social Reconstruction*, London: Allen & Unwin.

Russell, B. (1956) 'The nature of the state in view of its external relations', *Proceedings of the Aristotelian Society*, NS, 16: 301–10.

Russell, B. (1967–9) *Autobiography*, 3 vols, London: Allen & Unwin, one-volume edition 1978.

Rustin, M. (1985) *For a Pluralist Socialism*, London: Verso.

Sabine, G.H. (1923) 'Pluralism: a point of view', *American Political Science Review* 17 (1): 34–50.

Salmond, J.W. (1966) *Jurisprudence*, twelfth edition, P.J. Fitzgerald, London: Sweet & Maxwell.

Schmitt, C. (1930) 'Staatsethik und pluralistischer Staat' in *Positionen und Begriffe in Kampf mit Weimar-Genf. Versailles 1923–39*, Hamburg: Hanseatische Verlaganstalt, 1939.

Schmitt, C. (1976) *The Concept of the Political*, translated and introduced by G. Schwab, New Brunswick: Rutgers University Press.

Schmitt, C. (1985) *Political Theology* translated and introduced by G. Schwab, Cambridge, Mass.: MIT Press.

Selver, P. (1959) *Orage and the New Age Circle*, London: Allen & Unwin.

Smith, M.G (1974) 'Institutional and political conditions of pluralism', in *Corporations and Society*, London: Duckworth.

Tocqueville, A. de (1835) *Democracy in America*, translated by H. Reeve, abridged by, H.S. Commager, London: Oxford University Press, World's Classics, 1946.

Wallas, G. (1908) *Human Nature in Politics*, London: Constable.

Wallas, G. (1914) *The Great Society*, London: Methuen.

Walzer, M. (1983) *Spheres of Justice*, Oxford: Basil Blackwell.

Webb, S., and Webb, B. (1897) *Industrial Democracy*, second edition, London: Longmans, Green & Co., 1919.

Webb, S., and Webb, B. (1920) *A Constitution for a Socialist Commonwealth of Great Britain*, Cambridge: LSE/Cambridge University Press, 1975.

Westlake, J. (1914) *Collected Papers on International Law*, Cambridge: Cambridge University Press.

Wollheim, R. (1959) *F.H. Bradley*, Harmondsworth, Middx.: Penguin.

Wright, A. (1979) *G.D.H. Cole and Socialist Democracy*, Oxford: Clarendon Press.

Zimmern, A.E. (1918) *Nationality and Government*, London: Chatto & Windus.

Zylstra, B. (1970) *From Pluralism to Collectivism: The Development of Harold Laski's Political Thought*, Assen: Van Gorcum.

INDEX

235